Maria Montessori

Titles in the *Bloomsbury Library of Educational Thought* Series:

St Thomas Aquinas, *Vivian Boland OP*
Aristotle, *Alexander Moseley*
St Augustine, *Ryan N. S. Topping*
Pierre Bourdieu, *Michael James Grenfell*
Jerome Bruner, *David R. Olson*
Confucius, *Charlene Tan*
John Dewey, *Richard Pring*
Michel Foucault, *Lynn Fendler*
Paulo Freire, *Daniel Schugurensky*
John Holt, *Roland Meighan*
John Locke, *Alexander Moseley*
Loris Malaguzzi and the Reggio Emilia
Experience, *Kathy Hall, Mary Horgan,
Anna Ridgway, Rosaleen Murphy, Maura
Cunneen and Denice Cunningham*

Maria Montessori, *Marion O'Donnell*
A. S. Neill, *Richard Bailey*
John Henry Newman, *James Arthur and
Guy Nicholls*
Robert Owen, *Robert A. Davis and Frank
O'Hagan*
R. S. Peters, *Stefaan E. Cuypers and
Christopher Martin*
Jean Piaget, *Richard Kohler*
Plato, *Robin Barrow*
Jean-Jacques Rousseau, *Jürgen Oelkers*
Rudolf Steiner, *Heiner Ullrich*
Leo Tolstoy, *Daniel Moulin*
Lev Vygotsky, *René van der Veer*
E. G. West, *James Tooley*
Mary Wollstonecraft, *Susan Laird*

Series Editor: Richard Bailey is a writer and researcher in education and sport. A former teacher in both primary and secondary schools and a teacher trainer, he has been Professor at a number of leading Universities in the UK. He now lives and works in Germany.

Members of the Advisory Board

Robin Barrow, Professor of Philosophy, Simon Fraser University, Canada.

Peter Gronn, Professor of Education, Head of Faculty, University of Cambridge, UK.

Kathy Hall, Professor of Education and Head of the School of Education at University College Cork, Ireland.

Stephen Heyneman, Professor of International Educational Policy at the College of Education and Human Development, Vanderbilt University, USA.

Yung-Shi Lin, President Emeritus and Professor, Department of Education and Institute of Graduate Studies, Taipei Municipal University of Education, Republic of China, Taiwan.

Gary McCulloch, Head of Department of Humanities and Social Sciences at the Institute of Education, University of London, UK.

Jürgen Oelkers, Professor of Education at the University of Zurich, Switzerland.

Richard Pring, Emeritus Professor at the Department of Education, and Emeritus Fellow of Green Templeton College, University of Oxford, UK.

Harvey Siegel, Professor and Chair of the Department of Philosophy, University of Miami, USA.

Richard Smith, Professor of Education, University of Durham, UK.

Zhou Zuoyu, Professor, Faculty of Education, Beijing Normal University, People's Republic of China.

Maria Montessori

MARION O'DONNELL

Bloomsbury Library of Educational Thought
Series Editor: Richard Bailey

B L O O M S B U R Y
LONDON • NEW DELHI • NEW YORK • SYDNEY

Bloomsbury Academic
An imprint of Bloomsbury Publishing Plc

50 Bedford Square	1385 Broadway
London	New York
WC1B 3DP	NY 10018
UK	USA

www.bloomsbury.com

First published 2007 by Continuum International Publishing Group
Paperback edition first published 2014 by Bloomsbury Academic

British Library Cataloguing-in-Publication Data
A catalogue record for this book is available from the British Library.

ISBN: PB: 978-1-4725-1901-6
ePub: 978-1-4411-0066-5

Library of Congress Cataloguing-in-Publication Data
O'Donnell, Marion.
Maria Montessori/Marion O'Donnell.
p. cm.
Includes bibliographical references and index.
ISBN-13: 978-0-8264-8406-2 (hardcover)
ISBN-10: 0-8264-8406-9 (hardcover)
1. Montessori, Maria, 1870–1952. 2. Montessori, Maria, 1870–1952–Criticism
and interpretation. 3. Educators–Italy–Biography. I. Title.

LB775.M8O36 2007
370.92–dc22
[B]

2007018520

Typeset by Aptara Books Ltd
Printed and bound in Great Britain

Contents

Series Editor's Preface

Education is sometimes presented as an essentially practical activity. It is, it seems, about teaching and learning, curriculum and what goes on in schools. It is about achieving certain ends, using certain methods, and these ends and methods are often prescribed for teachers, whose duty it is to deliver them with vigor and fidelity. With such a clear purpose, what is the value of theory?

Recent years have seen politicians and policymakers in different countries explicitly denying *any* value or need for educational theory. A clue to why this might be is offered by a remarkable comment by a British Secretary of State for Education in the 1990s: 'having any ideas about how children learn, or develop, or feel, should be seen as subversive activity.' This pithy phrase captures the problem with theory: it subverts, challenges, and undermines the very assumptions on which the practice of education is based.

Educational theorists, then, are troublemakers in the realm of ideas. They pose a threat to the status quo and lead us to question the common-sense presumptions of educational practices. But this is precisely what they should do because the seemingly simple language of schools and schooling hides numerous contestable concepts that in their different usages reflect fundamental disagreements about the aims, values, and activities of education.

Implicit within the *Bloomsbury Library of Educational Thought* is an assertion that theories and theorizing are vitally important for education. By gathering together the ideas of some of the most influential, important, and interesting educational thinkers, from the Ancient Greeks to contemporary scholars, the series has the ambitious task of providing an accessible yet authoritative resource for a generation of students and practitioners. Volumes within the series are written by acknowledged leaders in the field, who were selected for both their scholarship and their ability to make often complex ideas accessible to a diverse audience.

It will always be possible to question the list of key thinkers that are represented in this series. Some may question the inclusion of certain thinkers; some may disagree with the exclusion of others. That is inevitably going to be the case. There is no suggestion that the list of thinkers represented within the *Bloomsbury Library of Educational Thought* is in any way definitive. What is incontestable is that these thinkers have fascinating ideas about education and that, taken together, the *Library* can act as a powerful source of information and inspiration for those committed to the study of education.

Richard Bailey
Roehampton University, London

Foreword

This volume is a very valuable contribution to the *Continuum Library of Educational Thought*. In what is both a scholarly and an affectionate account of the life, work, and influence of Maria Montessori, Marion O'Donnell clearly sets out the theoretical and practical insights that are the unique legacy of Montessori to current educational thinking and practice. The author portrays Montessori as one of the key pioneers of child-centered education in the first half of the twentieth century. Having distilled her own ideas from a fascinating range of philosophical and psychological sources, Montessori herself became an internationally influential figure as both a theoretician and a practitioner.

This volume not only provides an authoritative and comprehensive synopsis of Maria Montessori's writings and the didactic materials and methods of Montessori Education, but also gives a fascinating insight into the personality of this extraordinary woman and a glimpse into her somewhat turbulent private and public life as a citizen of the world. She dedicated her life to her work on behalf of children, traveling widely and giving lectures and influential addresses in many different countries. She met or corresponded with many other influential figures of the early twentieth century – John Dewey, Jean Piaget, and Bertrand Russell, to name but three.

Throughout her lifetime, Montessori was a passionate advocate on behalf of children as active agents not only in their own education but also in society in general. In taking this stance, she was quite prepared to speak out against the prevailing orthodoxies of the time. She advocated freedom rather than control, self-discipline rather than compliance, and spontaneity rather than formality. She favored careful observation of children's behavior in the learning environment, but opposed behaviorist views on extrinsic

reinforcement. She strongly rejected ideas of fixed, measurable intelligence and showed that children rejected by the system as uned-
ucable could achieve at a high level, if provided with a conducive
environment. In all of these respects, Montessori was clearly ahead of
her time and one hundred years after the opening of the first of her
'Children's Houses' in 1907, her ideas have a unique freshness and
relevance to current educational thinking.

While Montessori's views on child development and her practical
guidance for the education of children sit comfortably within the
mainstream of current pedagogical thinking and practice, there are
undoubtedly elements of her approach which might seem to a contemporary professional audience as somewhat quirky. For example,
the role of 'directress', which is her preferred term for the teacher, is
to assist the child's natural development by unobtrusively providing a
rich environment equipped with carefully prepared and meticulously
ordered practical materials, with which the child should be free to
engage. This view of the teacher, or directress, as a facilitator of learning may not seem too controversial, but Montessori's recommendations regarding the conduct and demeanor of the directress might
raise some contemporary eyebrows: the directress should, as stated
in, *To Educate the Human Potential*, first published in India in 1948,
be 'attractive, preferably young and beautiful, charmingly dressed,
scented with cleanliness, happy and graciously dignified' (p. 87).

It is a pleasure and a privilege to have been asked to provide this
foreword, writing from Scotland at a time when the school curriculum
for children aged 3 to 18 is being radically reviewed under the aegis
of the Scottish Executive's program, 'A Curriculum for Excellence,'
which challenges long-standing assumptions about the content of the
curriculum and adopts an approach which places the child as learner
at the center and sets expectations that the main purpose of education should be to create 'successful learners,' 'confident individuals,'
'effective contributors,' and 'responsible citizens'. These aims would
have been close to the heart of Maria Montessori and it is interesting
to speculate how her ideas, given due consideration, might influence
the educational community of practitioners who have the responsibility to develop and implement the revised curriculum framework.
In Scotland, as in countries throughout the world, many of the

currently espoused features of teacher professionalism bear traces of the ideas of Montessori, for example, respecting children's voice, focusing on the needs of individual learners, fostering independence and interdependence, and seeing the teacher as researcher and clinical practitioner engaging in action research in the classroom. All of these were heralded by Montessori more than one hundred years ago in her scientific approach to pedagogy.

Marion O'Donnell argues convincingly that while the evidence of the influence of Montessori on twenty-first-century education is abundant, the degree to which her legacy has been properly acknowledged falls far short. This splendid book makes a significant contribution toward rectifying the injustice this represents.

Donald Christie
Professor of Childhood and Primary Studies
University of Strathclyde
Scotland

Part 1

Intellectual Biography

1 Montessori and the Origins of Montessori Education

Before the appearance of child psychology as an empirical science toward the end of the nineteenth century, perceptions of childhood in Western societies were radically different from those of today. From the sixteenth century, the treatment of children was often cruel and inhumane, both at home and at school. Many children were abandoned at birth and left to die, while many died in infancy from illness and disease. Unwanted children in foundling homes faced near-certain death (Piers, 1978). Those who did survive infancy were expected to behave like adults and were frequently beaten for any infraction. As soon as possible, children were sent to work, some as young as six, and many were, like animals, expected to obey instant orders and, like fractious colts in need of breaking in, have their wills broken. No consideration or provision was made for childhood itself and documentary evidence of children's lives until the twentieth century reveals a grim picture (Clarke-Stewart et al., 1985). It is arguable that the roots of Montessori education date back to the sixteenth century when the beginnings of modern science began to appear. According to Butts (1955), the beliefs and assumptions of modern scientific pedagogy included three particular elements. First, there was a certainty that the secrets of nature could be revealed. Second, it was increasingly accepted that 'science' was what could be learned from nature itself rather than a body of knowledge from the past. Third, new knowledge was from the actual observation of nature, and after objective, clinical verification, the data were formally collated. It was a rationale that appears to mirror Montessori's own scientific methodology. For Maria Montessori, childhood was a special period of life and the education we associate with her name began with practice rather than theory. A century after her work first attracted the attention of the world, her novel ideas of child development, the learning process, the role of the teacher, and curriculum content, all continue to excite a lively interest.

Maria Montessori was born on 31 August 1870 at Chiaraville, Ancona, Italy, the only child of Renilde Stoppani and Alessandro Montessori. She died at Noordwijk ann Zee, Holland, on 6 May 1952. Valuable insights into her life and work, which spanned the most horrific wars ever waged by mankind, have been documented by Montessori herself but there are also important biographies, notably by E. M. Standing (1957) and Rita Kramer (1976), that have helped to bring attention to her experiments in education. As a child she was educated at home where she showed a keen interest in mathematics and then was enrolled in a boys' technical school to further her studies in mathematics and science. When her interest turned to medicine, there were many obstacles to overcome before she was allowed to enrol at the University of Rome as the very first Italian female to study medicine. Her first practical ventures in medicine were in nervous disorders and by 1895, while still a student, she was working in the psychiatric department of the pediatric clinic attached to the University of Rome where she came in contact with children of the inmates. Montessori observed them closely, noting particularly how they played with food dropped on the floor during mealtime. That behavior she interpreted as deriving from an inner urge to be active (Schulz-Benesch, 1997: 189). Graduating in 1896 with Doctor of Medicine and Doctor of Surgery degrees, both with honours, Montessori went into private practice, at the same time acquiring an appointment as surgical assistant at the hospital run by Rome University, along with a post in the university's psychiatric clinic. It was in the latter that she met Dr. Giuseppe Montesano who fathered her love-child Mario (born 1898). Montessori's interests swiftly turned in the direction of children's mental diseases, becoming more and more convinced that a key to solving the contemporary problems regarding these children was that mental deficiency presented chiefly a 'pedagogical rather than a medical problem' (Montessori, 1964: 31). Here she differed from her colleagues who treated mental diseases through gymnastics (motor education). When she sought ways to ease the plight of these hapless children, she became intimately acquainted with the pioneering work of two French doctors, Itard and Séguin, later acknowledging that she 'followed Séguin's book and also derived much help from the remarkable experiments of Itard' (ibid.: 36). Another whose work she paid tribute to was Giuseppe Sergi, the Italian anthropologist who ardently promoted 'the principles of a new civilization based upon education' (ibid.: 2).

Jean-Marc Gaspard Itard (1775–1838) ranks as the first to exert a seminal influence on Montessori's philosophy of education. A French physician and student of philosophy, he was the founder of a branch of medical science known as Otiatria, concerned with diseases of the ear. From 1800, he worked as physician at the Paris Institute for Deaf Mutes where he developed a methodical education for the sense of hearing. In his first year at the Institute, a boy about twelve years of age, described as possessing animal behavior, was discovered by the villagers of Aveyron. Itard was invited to examine and treat the boy who had been abandoned in the forest at birth and left to die. This wild boy of Aveyron, named Victor, stripped of all human social life and culture, had no language, walked on all fours, and acted like the wolves with whom he had lived in the forest – a true child of nature (Montessori, 1964). Although the boy was seen by the most eminent medical authorities as ineducable, Itard accepted the challenge to civilize him and worked with him for the following eight years. In 1801, he chronicled his observations of Victor in his classic book *Des Premiers Développements physiques et moraux du Jeune Sauvage de l'Aveyron*, which was translated into English as *The Wild Boy of Aveyron* in 1802. His method was an extension of the successful program he had been following with students with hearing impairment, using the sensorial materials he had designed specifically for them. Itard was 'the first educator to practice observation of his pupil in the way the sick are observed in hospitals, especially those suffering from diseases of the nervous system' (ibid.: 34). His minute descriptions of a child's behavior were formally documented in a diary which Montessori called 'practically the first attempt at educational psychology.' For Itard, Victor's education had a twofold aim: to lead him from a natural life to a social life; and to provide him with an intellectual education. Itard noted that the boy loved and immersed himself in nature – the sun, the moon, the stars, and the weather all providing a source of natural joy. He laughed with delight at flashes of lightning, danced with joy in the rain, and howled in empathy at the full moon. He began very slowly to take pleasure from new social experiences (Cole, 1950). He learned to dress, feed, and attend to personal needs. The work required great patience since Victor had no experience of human relationships. He invariably ran since walking was unknown to him and Itard ran behind him to keep up. It was a telling case of the teacher adapting to the pupil and modifying his own behavior to suit his student. Discarding long-held philosophical theories, Itard began experimental psychology through observation, developing a bond with his pupil while following his pupil's lead and building up a repertoire of teaching methods for the development of the boy's senses (Montessori, 1964). In his book, Itard had described 'the moral work which led the savage to civilisation as he was surrounded with loving care' (ibid.: 150). The wild boy of Aveyron experiment still evokes keen debate today but Itard's rationale was simplicity itself: he studiously observed Victor. There are elements of Itard's scientific methodology found in Montessori education. Like Itard, she did not start with a theory but followed children's natural tendencies. Each child was closely observed as an individual case study, with detailed notes and records kept of each child's progress. Children found themselves in a stable, supportive environment which helped to nurture the human spirit. The Montessori teacher was to adapt to each pupil in a deliberate reversal of traditional roles in order to create happy learning experiences.

Edouard Séguin (1812–80), a teacher and then physician of deaf-mutes in Paris, was the second major influence on Montessori. As an adolescent, he had come under the spell of the Comte Claude de Saint-Simon (1760–1825) who advocated a social reconstruction based on 'love one another' and whose social theory 'developed into socialism' (Cole, 1950: 542). William Boyd has also noted that Séguin applied to education Comte's belief that 'the aim of education was not individualistic but a preparation for an ideal society,' a community in which love would be the dominant motive of life and 'moral education the crown of education' (Boyd, 1921: 363–5). Séguin agreed with Rousseau and Itard that individual sensory-motor training was essential in early education. For Séguin, education depended on two things: first, the individual acting on the environment (nature), and second, harmonious social relationships (nurture). He became a doctor specifically to treat diseases of deafness, paralysis, and idiocy. Mentally retarded children at that time were categorized as 'morons,' 'imbeciles,' and the lowest group as 'idiots' who were considered to be unteachable. In 1846, Séguin founded the first school for feeble-minded children in Paris where he modified Itard's experiments over a period of ten years while working with children taken from asylums (Kramer, 1976: 60). Everything he did was recorded in his *Traitement moral, Hygiène et Education des Idiots et des autres Enfants arrières* (1846). Most of his pupils were inert and helpless, spending much of the day in bed and requiring full-time care (Hans, 1994: 191). The curriculum used by Séguin included practical things to help their development. Muscular education involved lessons to help the children in feeding and clothing themselves, learning to walk unassisted, maintaining equilibrium, and walking upstairs and downstairs. In so doing, they felt muscular sensations and began to grow independent of adults. Muscular sensations fostered through touching and feeling led his students from simple perceptions to a more sophisticated sensory appreciation using the mind and the senses. The students learned to care for themselves, which helped reduce the costs of their care at the school (Cole, 1950: 545–7). Séguin's lessons, given individually, were designed to be joyful, spiritual, practical hands-on experiences. He made a close individual study of his pupils, recognizing each as an individual and designing and constructing didactic (self-correcting) materials for each one. With his methods, 'the education of idiots was actually possible' (Montessori, 1964: 37). Everything Séguin did was described in detail in his book *Traitement moral*, the English translation of which *Treatise on Idiocy* (1866) still remains a standard work for teachers of hearing-impaired children. Montessori education incorporates a number of Séguin-related exercises including 'walking the line' designed for good posture, and exercises in practical life to help children become completely independent of adults (Montessori, 1964). Other identifiable elements of his philosophy and practice found in Montessori classrooms were democracy and harmony, all children being encouraged to take an active part in their own education as their rightful due and to live and work together amicably. The immediate goal was a school society at peace with itself, the long-term goal being global peace in perpetuity.

The third great influence on Montessori's emerging philosophy of education was Giuseppe Sergi, founder of the Institute of Experimental Psychology at the University of Rome in 1876, and Professor of Anthropology at the University of Rome from 1884 to 1916. Sergi's long-term goal was to see all men living together in harmony and to this end, he sought to establish natural, comprehensible methods by which teachers took 'numerous, exact and rational observations of man as an individual, principally during infancy, which is the age at which the foundations of education and culture must be laid' (ibid.: 3). He was convinced that educational methods urgently needed to be reconstructed to bring about a desirable human regeneration, and in his lectures, collated in *Educazione ed Instruczione*, he encouraged teachers to join the new movement. Sergi also advocated a 'methodical study of the one to be educated under the guidance of pedagogical anthropology and experimental psychology' (ibid.: 2, 3). Such a methodology was clearly pivotal in Montessori's own method.

There were also other notable influences on Montessori's work. Because of her interest in childhood mental diseases, Montessori enrolled in courses in pedagogy and educational theory during 1897 and 1898, becoming familiar with the theories and writings of Locke, Rousseau, Froebel, Pestalozzi, and Owen. These educators visualized education as a means of creating a new, ideal society, particularly Robert Owen who set out in practical ways to help his poor factory workers improve their education, their lifestyles, and their general happiness in life. In his model village infant school and school at his cotton mill in Scotland's New Lanark, these dramatic changes in the human condition became a reality (Conservation Trust, Scotland, 1997). In 1897, while still on the threshold of a career as an educator, Montessori attended the National Medical Congress in Turin, which discussed the causes of delinquency in retarded and disturbed children. The following year, she returned for the National Pedagogy Congress (1898) on reforming school policy by segregating 'degenerate' children from normal pupils. Studies in penology had convinced her that punishment did not provide a deterrent to criminality and that criminals behaved destructively because of the nature of their feelings and their flawed reasoning (Kramer, 1976: 74). She expressed her opinions in a paper on 'Moral Education', the result of which was an invitation from the Minister of Education, Guido Baccelli, to present to the teachers of Rome a course of lectures on the education of feeble-minded children. These lectures aroused so much interest that a Medical Pedagogical Institute was established and Montessori was put in charge of classes made up of children from Rome's elementary schools considered to be seriously or hopelessly deficient. Also enrolled were 'idiot' children selected from the asylums (Montessori, 1964: 32). During 1898–99, Montessori taught these abnormal children in Rome from eight in the morning to seven in the evening, making a thorough study of what she called 'remedial pedagogy.' Her plan was to help the deficient children's mental condition by 'elevating their minds to a higher level through curative pedagogy' (ibid.: 31). At that time, she designed and constructed a great variety of new didactic materials and through their application obtained the most surprising results. She found the work with deficient (abnormal) children exhausting but pointed out that the more encouragement, comfort, love, and respect she gave 'the more we renew and reinvigorate the life about us' (ibid.: 36, 37). At the end of those two years, she presented some of the children for the Italian Open Examination. All passed the rigorous tests in reading and writing, whereas some children from the state schools failed. With the conspicuous success of her children in the open examination, in 1900, Montessori was appointed as director of a Demonstration School in Rome and invited to train teachers for children suffering mental diseases. In attendance were twenty-two pupils, hitherto unsuccessful learners at schools, with whom Montessori used the opportunity to trial the materials of Itard and Séguin. The results were impressive and sixty-four teacher-trainees of abnormal children were inducted into the profession using these methods (Kramer, 1976: 85, 86). The quality of work she was obtaining with subnormal children led Montessori to suspect that serious deficiencies existed in the established and accepted practices in government schools (Montessori, 1964: 31, 32). She became increasingly convinced that the methods she used were more rational and more beneficial than those in current use in state schools and had potential for helping normal children as well. She determined to undertake the teaching of normal children based on her own findings and withdrew from active teaching of deficient children *per se* in order to re-study the works of Itard and Séguin, and also to find time for what she called 'meditation' (ibid.: 41).

In 1899, Montessori traveled to London where she was presented to Queen Victoria, then she went on to Paris to study practical ways 'of educating deficients' and visit schools where new methods were being utilized. Some were using Séguin's didactic materials, most of them faithfully following his rules to the letter, but not one attained the spectacular results he had documented in his writings. For Montessori, the reason was simple: the materials were being used in a cold, mechanical way without the human, spiritual ingredient Séguin had injected, and lacking the warmth of involvement that he had evoked from his young charges. In 1901, Montessori returned to the University of Rome where her studies included philosophy, experimental psychology, and research into pedagogical anthropology in elementary schools. During that research period she carried out her own empirical studies (Müller and Schneider, 2002), taking particular notice of children sitting motionless and silent all day listening to the teacher talking. What they were undergoing, she concluded, was impersonal rote learning in which they were coerced into doing what the teacher chose for them to do. Miscreants were punished severely for any errors (Montessori, 1964: 21, 33, 42). She soon saw that such schools were not happy places and determined to devise better methods for students of all ages. It was during this time that she translated by hand Séguin's *Traitement moral* (1846) from the original French, a monumental task which filled her with awareness 'of the immensity and importance of a work which should be able to reform the school and education' (ibid.: 42). On completion of those university studies begun in 1901, Montessori was offered the Chair in Anthropology at the University of Rome in 1904. Concurrently she continued her private medical practice and maintained her interests in the feminist and socialist movements (Standing, 1957). By this time, education had become her consuming passion, and it could not but benefit from her wide-ranging and eclectic outside interests, including scientific pedagogy and her own private practice. Later she was to put in words the essence of her evolving philosophy. She wrote in 1909 about what she perceived as a crisis in education, more convinced than ever that 'pedagogy must join with medicine' (Montessori, 1964: 20). Her words articulated what was a prevalent notion at the time. Hers was not a voice in the wilderness. At the end of the nineteenth century, those pioneers in education who were experimenting with ways of making education more relevant used scientific terms that were not clearly defined. Lawson and Silver identify among those pioneers Matthew Davenport (1822) who concluded 'education was of the nature of science' because 'it involved the study of phrenology, psychology and philosophy' and Alexander Bain (1870) who defined 'education as science, and teaching as an art form from a scientific point of view which could lead to the formulation of general psychology and physiological rules' (Lawson and Silver, 1973: 353). For Montessori, scientific pedagogy, like medicine, had to prove itself, through clinical, scientific experimentation, and with her specialized medical expertise as a pediatrician with a particular interest in mental health, she determined at the first opportunity to 'make a study of normal pedagogy and the methods used for the education of normal children' (Montessori, 1964: 33).

Toward the end of 1906, Montessori was invited by Eduardo Tamalo, Director General of the Association for Good Building in Rome, to open an infants' school in one of his model tenement buildings in the San Lorenzo district of Rome. Signor Tamalo wanted the children aged two and a half to seven years to attend school in order to reduce the rampant vandalism caused by unsupervised children while their parents were at work in the nearby factories and he planned to open sixteen infant schools in the surrounding area. He offered Montessori one entire ground-floor apartment which opened onto an enclosed courtyard for the school along with another apartment within the building for a teacher. Here was Montessori's golden opportunity to study non-deficient children in a scientific manner, even if they were socially disadvantaged. She swiftly accepted, intending from the outset 'to make this school a field for scientific experimental psychology' (ibid.: 72). It was, as she explained later, her own 'laboratory of psychology' (ibid.: 49) where she could observe free children within a classroom environment, just as anthropologists and scientists observed free, natural groups of people. Her method was to be a close and detailed observation of each child's development 'without clinging to any dogma about the activity of the child according to age' (ibid.: 72).

2 The *Case dei Bambini* (or Children's Houses)

The first *Casa dei Bambini* opened in 6 January 1907, at 58 Via dei Marsi, Rome (Montessori, 1964: 42, 43). Forty children aged between two years and seven years were enrolled under the care of an inexperienced directress, Candida Nuccitelli, a caretaker's daughter who had completed elementary studies. She was helped by one assistant. Montessori's instructions to them were simple and clear. Children were to be free but within prescribed parameters. First, the two carers were responsible for 'checking whatever offended or annoyed others or whatever tended toward rough or ill-bred acts' because 'we cannot know the consequences of stifling a spontaneous action ... perhaps we stifle life itself' (ibid.: 87). Second, the liberty of each child was strictly limited or curbed by an awareness of the rights of others. In a nutshell, children were encouraged from the earliest years to be conscious of the collective interest of all. The role of the directress was a passive one, her most important function being to observe the children without interrupting their learning or social experiences. The directress, Montessori noted, required a 'capacity and desire to observe natural phenomena (children)' (ibid.: 87), along with the innate skills of a researcher who worshipped nature, possessed the self-sacrificing spirit of a scientist, and the warmth of a generous-hearted human being with a reverent love for children. Another requirement was that she should learn 'how to perfect herself as an educator' which could be achieved by observing and working with children (ibid.: 8–13). One guiding principle alone drove Montessori and that was 'to aid the development of young children adapted to their entire personality' (ibid.: 45). There had been no formal guidelines to follow since 'anthropology and psychology had never before devoted themselves to the question of educating children in schools' (ibid.: 4). From the amorphous movement known as Scientific

Pedagogy, Montessori derived the ingredient she wished to introduce into education: the fundamental freedom of the pupil. In her words, 'If Scientific Pedagogy is to be born ... then schools must permit natural manifestations of the children' (ibid.: 15, 28). It was natural manifestations of children that she wished to study.

On 7 April 1907, a second *Casa dei Bambini* opened its doors with 'an untrained, unspoiled young woman as directress' (Kramer, 1976: 123). It too was in what Montessori described as the ill-favored quarter of San Lorenzo. 'This quarter is notorious,' she told her audience on the day of its opening, explaining how the tenements for Rome's wretched and down-and-out were never envisaged for San Lorenzo, the cemetery district of the Italian capital. It had simply exploded into life between 1884 and 1888 when buildings mushroomed all over the locality without regard to sanitation or building standards in general. Of the children born there in 1907, Montessori spoke with deep compassion: 'They do not first see the light of day; they come into a life of gloom.' She described the overcrowded, filthy conditions within the tenements where each apartment housed twenty or thirty persons originally built for three or four tenants. The water supply was enough for drinking only and as a result children could not 'be other than filthy of body.'

The streets, she wrote, were 'the scene of bloodshed, of quarrel, of sights so vile as to be almost inconceivable ... spectacles of extreme brutality are possible here ... because of a new fact which was unknown to past centuries, namely, the isolation of the masses of the poor' (Montessori, 1964: 52, 53). Yet in all this wretchedness of the human spirit, there was much that was uplifting about that second Children's House. 'The parents know that the Children's House is their property, and is maintained by a portion of the rent they pay,' Montessori told the world in 1907 (ibid.: 63).

On 18 October 1908, a third *Casa dei Bambini* was opened in Milan in a section of the city occupied by working men, with Montessori's close friend Anna Maccheroni as directress and one untrained assistant. It had the financial backing of the Milan Humanitarian Society, founded by Jewish socialists (Kramer, 1976: 134), which also undertook the manufacture of all the materials required (Montessori, 1964: 44). Benito Mussolini, a young journalist at that time, was a member of the Humanitarian Society staff (Kramer, 1976: 135) and he took a great interest in the new classroom. On 4 November 1908, a fourth *Casa dei Bambini* was opened in Rome in the middle-class suburb of Prati di Castello, Via Famagosta. Unlike the first two established in slums of San Lorenzo, this was opened in a modern building. The Montessori Movement was underway. In January 1909, Italian Switzerland 'began to transform its orphan asylums and children's homes in which the Froebel system had been used into Children's Houses adopting [Montessori] methods and materials' (Montessori, 1964: 44).

3 Special Features of Montessori Education

It was in these first four *Case dei Bambini* that Montessori refined what was to become known as her 'method.' Each Children's House was a carefully prepared environment in which active, exuberant learners were to experience physical, psychological, and spiritual freedom. A basic principle of Montessori education was 'the liberty of the pupils in their spontaneous manifestations' (Montessori, 1964: 80). Physical freedom was not entirely new. Montessori acknowledged that Rousseau and others had suggested 'vague notions of liberty of children' but she felt their main interest lay in 'social liberty which did not inform education' (ibid.: 15). A responsible sense of freedom was encouraged in which children learned to respect everyone as well as respecting every piece of material within the environment. It was a socially controlled freedom which had as its limit the group itself. A child was not free to do as he pleased, simply free to become master of himself and to be able to work independently. The essential point about this innovation of freedom was the eradication of what Montessori called 'depression of the child's spirit.' She inaugurated a radical reform to rid classrooms of what she perceived as slavery, proof of which was 'to be seen in stationary desks and benches' in other schools (ibid.: 21) with children condemned to a state of immobility and silence. She claimed that children attending state schools were worse off than criminals in gaol, who at least had a voice to make a protest. The physical health of children was also at risk because lack of movement all day meant muscles became deformed. Such radical thoughts, especially the liberation of children, were not in vogue in 1907 and Montessori promoted physical freedom for all children but especially in infants' classes.

There were practical life materials which Montessori had used within the asylum to help children care for their environment and their personal needs. Every piece was introduced to each child individually through demonstration, without words, just as Séguin had done with deaf-mute children. The purpose of the practical life activities, using specially made child-sized household items in the Children's Houses, was to help co-ordinate muscular movements as the children swept or mopped the floor, cared for pets and plants, prepared food, set the table, or served lunch. They learned to become conscious of the presence of others and to treat them with unfailing courtesy. Socially acceptable behavior was to become an obligatory way of life in the Children's House. One of the most important features of the Children's Houses was the sensorial materials. Two millennia before Montessori, Aristotle had informed us that 'everything we know is first in the senses,' but it was Montessori who made clear to educators that it was the senses that were most neglected in the learning process. She modified Itard's sensory materials to use with deficient children, certain that rewards lay in waiting for them. It was experimental psychology at work and from the results she hoped that psychology would 'be able to draw conclusions from pedagogy and not vice versa' (ibid.: 167). The aim of the experiment was to cause each child to exercise his senses because children 'must proceed to the making of trials and must select the didactic material in which they show themselves to be interested' (ibid.: 168). Another observation made by Montessori was that once normal children were introduced to sensorial materials they 'taught themselves' (ibid.: 171). Each child was free to choose his own materials and work with them for as long as he wished but out of respect for other children he was obliged to return them to the exact place from which they had been taken, in perfect condition and with no missing pieces.

Social relationships between the teacher and the child were also radically different in 1907. Until Montessori education, the traditional relationship between teacher and child was one of superiority of the one over the other. It had been a teacher's right to dominate the child and control all classroom activities and Montessori called for reform. Since children taught themselves using the didactic materials, the role of the new Montessori directress was to help each child become independent and self-reliant. She was to relinquish power by not forcing her will on children, and by not selecting every task they performed each day. In Montessori's words, the directress had to be 'inspired by a deep worship of life while she observes with human interest, the development of child life' (Montessori, 1964: 104) at the same time promoting the 'keys of life' which were the simple pleasures of joy and happiness derived from harmonious and pleasurable experiences within the prepared environment. Children could move about freely, talk to each other, and were, in a sense, suddenly emancipated by the unprecedented freedom. As a teacher, Montessori saw this as an issue of simple justice, but as a pediatrician, she also saw even more helpful benefits in the improved mental health for children brought about by anxiety-free learning conditions which fostered 'spontaneous psychic development' (ibid.: 230). Children learned how to co-operate and live together in harmony. Clearly defined boundaries inculcated a keen awareness of responsibility and those as young as three years old swiftly realized their obligations to others within the group.

At the bottom of all Montessori's theory and practice was the simple notion that understanding the way children developed was the key to successful education. Observation of child development was not new. Plato had observed stages of development centuries before Montessori, and the Romans too had observed '*mens sana in corpore sano*' – 'a healthy mind, a healthy body.' Through observation she did discover ways of helping the development of children from the moment of birth to eighteen years. Montessori 'succeeded in opening a field to further developments of others' and because of this 'she could be considered a pioneer in the field of child development' (Ornstein, 1977: 117). The aim of her first experiments in the first Children's House had been 'to discover ways of aiding child development, that is, child life' (Montessori, 1964: 45). Never before had observations been made of free, active children, each working with a different piece of didactic material of their own choice, with no time limits.

It was a new phenomenon in infant education. Observation of each child as an individual became the main tool for Montessori directresses. In Montessori's view, it was impossible to make observations in public schools because children were like 'dead butterflies pinned to place,' sitting immobile and listening passively to the teacher yet all were expected to learn by rote 'barren meaningless knowledge' in the same time, and to obey every command made by the teacher. These children were 'repressed in spontaneous expression of personality, like dead things' (ibid.: 14), always seen as a whole group and always referred to generically as 'the class.' When the first Children's House opened, she was struck with 'how clearly individual differences show themselves' (ibid.: 95). One very special feature of the four Children's Houses of 1907–08 was the close link between family and school. Parents were deeply involved in Montessori education. At that first-ever, long-day care center opened on 6 January 1907, Montessori explained to the mothers that their children were 'to be clean and co-operative with the directress so they could take advantage of their good opportunities.' There were no fees, with collective ownership of the school. It was new, very beautiful, and profoundly educational (ibid.: 63). Mothers could 'leave their little ones in a place, not only safe, but where they had every advantage' and they could go to work with easy minds just like rich mothers who were the only other privileged group in Rome's society who had that advantage (ibid.: 64). They were invited 'to go at any hour of the day to watch, to admire or to meditate upon the life in the Children's House' (ibid.: 64, 65), but each one was required 'to go at least once a week to confer with the directress, giving an account of her child and accepting any advice the directress may be able to give in regard the child's health and education' (ibid.: 61). A physician had been assigned to the Children's House as well as a directress. Parents were helped to understand child development, and instructed on how to help rather than hinder development from birth. They were assured that they could help each child from birth by providing a safe, calm, loving environment ensuring the child was free of swaddling clothes to be able to exercise all muscles. Unconditional love given by the family was the greatest aid in development. As Montessori made new discoveries, she informed the parents about how they could contribute to their children's well-being, and these too became part of her unfolding method. They were asked to slow down and take their lead from the child and encouraged to see matters from the child's point of view. Montessori drew attention to the advantages of a close union between family and school in the matter of education, contrasting her institutions with state schools where the family was 'always something far away from the school' and regarded as often 'rebelling against its ideals' (ibid.: 63). Parents and directresses were to collaborate by finding ways to provide for the inner needs of each developing child.

By the middle of 1907, the children who attended the first Children's House were demanding 'to be taught to read and write' (ibid.: 267). Initially Montessori refused, because of the long-entrenched thinking that it was necessary to begin such formal teaching at seven years when they started school. But she relented when the illiterate mothers pleaded with her to do so. 'If you teach them to read and write, they soon will learn and spare them the great fatigue in the elementary school,' the mothers begged (ibid.: 268). They made an enduring impression on her, and this became another seminal incident of her evolving method. As early as 1898, Montessori had concluded that Itard and Séguin had not found a rational method by which writing could be learned (ibid.: 246) and decided that a logical method was needed 'based essentially on articulate language' (ibid.: 310). She first visited mainstream classrooms where she discovered that written language was 'taught without any consideration of its relation to articulate language' (ibid.: 310) and she saw clearly a link between spoken language and handwriting. She observed children, focusing on the writer not the writing, 'the subject not the object' (ibid.: 260). It was to mark a stark break with the past. From her direct observations of infants, Montessori maintained that the natural function of speaking began at birth through the child's unconscious absorbent mind. The whole process engaged physical and psychological processes. Every infant created his mother tongue for himself through his own efforts, beginning with an isolated sound which his hearing apprehended. By six months he was able to articulate syllables. Intentional words appeared at about one year of age and syntax at about two years when the average child showed that he could use every part of speech correctly. Montessori's detailed notes show the gradual development of the mechanics of language, 'a necessary antecedent of the higher psychic activities which are to utilise it' (ibid.: 312). At the same time she noted that there was also a link between thought and language. 'Spoken language,' she declared, 'begins with the child when the word pronounced by him signifies an idea' (ibid.: 314).

Unable to find someone to make a replica of a wooden alphabet Montessori had used with deficient children in 1898, she began to cut out letters from sandpaper and discovered that these were better because they would act as a guide for children to control movement as they traced letter shapes. The accidental discovery of sandpaper letters involved major modifications to Montessori's original method. As she worked cutting out sandpaper letters 'there unfolded before my mind, a clear vision of a method, in all its completeness, so simple that it made me smile' (ibid.: 269). She decided on three pieces of material for children learning to write and read. First there were metal insets. Her observations had shown that writers made two movements – manipulating the instrument for writing and reproducing the form of letters. Working with a pencil and the insets would provide each child with an opportunity to perfect both pencil grip and pencil control. Second, the sandpaper letters utilized the sense of touch to begin to learn letter forms. And third, there was a movable alphabet of loose single letters which would allow each child to compose words for himself. Montessori trialed these materials, her aim being to increase the child's receptive and expressive language abilities through auditory, visual, and cognitive experiences and activities. The processes were recorded minutely in 1909 so that any directress could implement the correct procedures and so gain the same results. So too were details of Montessori's unique sandpaper letters and 'moving alphabet.' The autodidactic sandpaper letters (all lower-case letter shapes) were used to introduce the alphabet. Each sandpaper letter represented a vocal sound, not the alphabetic name of the letter and it became a direct link with spoken language. Next, children were introduced to two letters (lower case), as different in shape and sound as possible, using Séguin's brief three-period lesson. The child heard and pronounced sounds clearly and knew how to trace the sandpaper letter shapes using his first two fingers. From this, he was able to make a connection between sounds in language and graphic writing. When a child knew three or four sandpaper letters, he was introduced to the appropriately named movable alphabet comprising ten copies of each alphabet letter, all in lower case. He was asked to select letters from the movable alphabet to match the sounds the directress said. If successful, he was encouraged to compose words by selecting letters after a word was said by the directress and placing them in order. The time to introduce a child to composing words was 'left to the judgement of the teacher' (ibid.: 278), the best judge of his level of development. Children were free to compose words by sounding each word phonetically. Generally it took about six weeks for four-year-olds to compose words using the movable alphabet from the time they were first introduced to the sandpaper letters and Montessori confidently claimed that any Italian child who could compose any word pronounced clearly by the directress 'goes forward by himself composing his own words with signs corresponding to sounds, placing them one after the other' (ibid.: 283).

4 The 'Explosion' into Writing and Reading

Montessori has recounted the incident of a boy discovering how to write in her first Children's House in 1907. He had been prepared with the basic knowledge of sounds by way of the sandpaper letters and then with the help of the moving alphabet was poised to take the next step. Montessori gave him chalk and asked him first to draw a picture of a chimney then write the word 'chimney.' On completion, the child called out excitedly, 'I can write! I can write! I know how to write!' Others crowded round to see, took up chalk and also began to write. It was the first time they had ever written and they wrote whole words correctly (Montessori, 1964: 288). On that memorable day, the children wrote all day, filling notebooks with words once they had experienced their first 'indescribable emotion of joy' at creating a written word (ibid.: 288). The incident illustrates yet another of the 'mental explosions' described by Montessori, with plausible proof of her thesis that 'written language develops not gradually, but in an explosive way' (ibid.: 289). In 1907, that achievement of four-year-old children writing spontaneously became headline news, worldwide.

Children, whose hands were prepared in writing, wrote 'entire words without lifting the pen' (ibid.: 295) while maintaining perfect slant, shape of letter, and distance between each letter. A visitor once commented after observing a child at work: 'If I had not seen it I would not have believed it' (ibid.: 295).

In written language, Montessori had followed exactly the natural stages of development for spoken language – sounds, syllables, words, and syntax. The emphasis she laid on children comprehending the direct link between speech and the written word was to help them become successful at composing and writing spoken words at four years. She had provided time for children to prepare their hands through sensorial materials, to use insets to learn pencil grip and control, and to have sandpaper letters introduced by individual three-period lessons. Throughout, children traced and perfected letter shapes through their stereognostic sense, they met and mastered the movable alphabet for composing words, phrases, and sentences, and they acquired a phonemic awareness that enabled them to attack any new word they encountered in their subsequent lives. At four years, children began to write words with confidence because of their knowledge of the link between sounds in language and letters of the alphabet. They had learned the processes for analyzing words and for converting them to graphic language. It was new and it appeared to work for all children.

In the teaching of reading, Montessori designed a sequence of new materials and activities to help children learn to read with comprehension, each following his own inner developmental program and timetable. She recorded the results of her trials in detail, along with the description of a child beginning to read as one:

> who has not heard the word pronounced, and recognises it when he sees it composed upon the table with the cardboard letters (movable alphabet) and can tell what it means: this child reads. So until the child reads a transmission of ideas from the written word, he does not read.
>
> (Montessori, 1964: 296)

Knowledge of the relationship between sounds and letters was sufficient for both beginning writing and beginning reading, Montessori averred. In her view, spoken language was 'those little drops of sound [which] had wings' (ibid.: 316). Its counterpart was written language which translated sounds into signs. She was convinced that once an Italian child read a word he had composed, his mind was prepared to say virtually every printed Italian word. That was a large claim but it was reading at a mechanical stage and Italian was mainly a phonetic language unlike English. She emphasized that to be able to read words was the beginning of reading. When children could read words they had composed themselves, they exploded into reading. In one trial, Montessori composed a word (a noun) in silence using a movable alphabet in front of the child who was asked to bring the object that the word represented. After several successful results, a card with one word was presented to the child which he had to interpret unaided and then find the matching object. If he did so, this child could read. With one written word on a card 'we place the child before a new language, graphic language, which served to receive language transmitted to us by others' (ibid.: 301).

For counting, the materials trialed with deficient children were used and Montessori found that normal children 'very easily learn numeration which consists of counting objects' (ibid.: 326). She observed the many opportunities in daily life when children could count objects in their immediate environment. She introduced money so that children could learn to make change but suggested the use of good cardboard reproductions which she had seen used in London for their currency. There were three pieces of materials explained and illustrated for the introduction of zero to ten. Those materials consisted of number rods (represented by red and blue rods, each division measuring 10 cm), a spindle box containing the correct number of spindles for each compartment (marked 0–9), small cubes and number cards for 1 to 10, and sandpaper numerals in preparation for written examples. There was a brief explanation of how to use the number rods for addition, subtraction and multiplication and division by two. Finally, there was an explanation of how to use the number rods for calculations beyond ten using number boards designed by Séguin to record answers. Directresses were to collect small objects and make extension materials for addition, multiplication, and division (ibid.: 326–37). More materials, often referred to as materialized abstractions, were to be developed for mathematics in the next few years.

5 Montessori's System of Teacher Training

The preliminary results derived from the observations and experiments in the first Children's House were to provide the basis of all future teacher-training programs. While much had already been achieved to awaken and excite re-thinking of the educative process, much still lay ahead for Montessori. In 1909, she gave the first of her training courses at the Villa La Montesca home of Barone and Baroness Franchetti near Città di Castello in Perugia. One hundred students attended, the course comprising lectures on Montessori's educational philosophy along with abundant opportunities to observe local children working freely as independent individuals in a Montessori-prepared environment. Montessori herself demonstrated how children taught themselves and the student-teachers witnessed the spontaneous self-development of the individual. Most important of all, they observed and practiced the child psychology she was promoting based on allowing children to take charge of their own work schedules and engage in self-instruction without interruption from the teacher at all. They saw how the prepared environment offered opportunities to study individual children as case studies and keep detailed accounts of their development. An important aspect was that Montessori demonstrated many three-period lessons (Kramer, 1976: 136–8). She was now firmly convinced that experienced state teachers accustomed to the old domineering methods required re-training because of the 'great distance between our methods and theirs' (Montessori, 1964: 88). They had to re-learn when to intervene and to understand that their task was passive, their role being to observe and understand development without interfering in whatever the child was doing (ibid.: 87). They also had to refrain from offering needless help which was 'a hindrance to the development of natural forces' (ibid.: 226) and to desist from talking too much instead of quietly observing. At the completion of the first course, Barone Franchetti persuaded Montessori to compile her qualitative research findings and to write them up for other teachers to share. Montessori stayed on at the villa and within three weeks the volume we largely associate with her life's work was completed under the heading *Il Metodo della Pedagogia Scientifica applicato all'educazione infantile nelle Case dei Bambini* (1909) (or *The Method of Scientific Pedagogy applied to child education in the Children's Houses*). With its translation into English in 1912 as *The Montessori Method*, it became a landmark in the history of education. By 1910, at the request of parents and the encouragement of her friend Donna Maria Guerrieri, she began her experiment with children aged six to twelve years (Montessori, 1974: Preface) and in the same year wrote her second book *L'Anthropologia pedagogica (Pedagogical Anthropology)*.

Montessori's name became known worldwide in education circles through copious articles in newspapers and magazines. Two teacher-training courses had been planned for 1912 in Rome, the first in Italian and the second in English largely because of the interest shown in the United States and England. In both, her successes were widely reported. These courses were held at the Franciscan convent on Via Giusta in Rome. Dorothy Canfield Fisher, a novelist from the United States with a keen interest in education, spent the winter months of 1911 and 1912 with Montessori, attending her first teacher-training sessions in Rome. She shared what she learned at the lectures in her book *The Montessori Manual: For Teachers and Parents* (Fisher, 1913). For her, many of Montessori's observations were simply re-discovered facts, one being 'the old threadbare truism that every child is different from every other child.' In Fisher's words, 'We all knew this and disregarded it while Montessori took it fully into account.' As a contemporary, Fisher's observations take on a special significance not easily accorded the commentator whose knowledge has been derived vicariously from secondary sources. She noted especially that rote-lessons were 'out of the question' (ibid.: 29) in a Montessori class since such lessons may not fit the needs of all children, or for that matter, any child within the group. Her important conclusion was that in such a carefully prepared environment the child could teach himself more quickly and spontaneously with less intervention by the teacher (ibid.: 19, 20). She also pointed out that what was startling about Montessori education was the scientist's integrity of her logic, with its constant admonition that 'if that is the way children are made, our business is to educate them accordingly' (ibid.: 18). In other words, the system had to fit the child, not the other way around. Sixty-five Americans, including university lecturers from Harvard and Yale, traveled to Rome to study under Montessori (Willcott, 1968). William Heard Kilpatrick, a close friend of John Dewey, spent a year in Rome observing Montessori education in action. In 1913, Montessori organized the first international training course in her own apartment in Rome. Participants flocked to attend, not only from the host-country Italy and other European countries, but also from farther afield, including the United States, South Africa, and Australia. Soon the Montessori Method was being put into practice in Italy, France, Switzerland, England, Argentina, America, Asia, and Australia. Montessori was in great demand and was to travel extensively giving lectures and teacher-training courses throughout Europe, the United States, Argentina, and the British Isles but always the center of activity was in Rome where she was to conduct many international courses.

Later in 1913, Montessori visited the United States, giving a public lecture at Carnegie Hall where more than one thousand people were turned away (Kramer, 1976). It was a packed house, with the celebrated John Dewey presiding (Willcott, 1968: 49). A group of influential people formed a Montessori Association with Alexander Graham Bell as president and Margaret Wilson (daughter of US president) as honorary secretary (Phillips, 1977: 57), but critical articles, mostly by academics, effectively halted the momentum in Montessori education in America (Lillard, 1972: 8; Phillips, 1980: 16; Potts, 1980: 41). Despite the negativity of academia, in 1915 she was warmly welcomed back to the United States by her supporters. The demonstration Montessori classroom at the San Francisco World Fair that year was a huge attraction, viewed through glass walls by thousands of visitors. During that visit to America, Montessori conducted a teacher-training course in California. By this time a school had been established in the home of Alexander Graham Bell (Lillard, 1972: 8). The following year there were 189 authorized Montessori schools in the United States and another 2,000 unauthorized, despite the continued attacks by Frances Wayland Parker, John Dewey, and William

Kilpatrick (Edmonson, 1963: 67). Further attacks were responsible for the Montessori star to wane and by the 1920s references to Montessori in American academic circles were 'infrequent.'

Elsewhere throughout the world, Montessori's new education spread, particularly after the publication of *The Montessori Method* in twenty languages in 1912. In Europe, Tolstoy's daughter had visited Rome in 1907 to see the Montessori schools herself (Standing, 1957: 37) and had written a glowing report that same year in a Moscow educational journal (Kramer, 1976: 246). Classes were begun at Vilna in Russia with materials obtained from America following support from the physicist V. V. Lermontov. A classroom was set up in the palace at St Petersburg for children of the Tsar and courtiers. The first Montessori school in Spain opened in Barcelona in 1913 (ibid.: 247) though interest had begun two years earlier with the publication of her methods in an educational journal in Barcelona. In 1914, Montessori published her book for parents entitled *Dr Montessori's Own Handbook* and she ran a second international training course in Rome. In 1916, Barcelona was host city for Montessori's fourth international training course for teachers, and when she was invited to stay by the city's government, Barcelona virtually became her base (Müller and Schneider, 2002: 149). That year a special Children's Chapel was set up. There she supervised a fruitful experiment in which her principles were applied to the religious education of young children. An account of that experiment appeared in her book *I Bambini viventi nella Chiesa* published in 1922. By 1918, the Montessori Method had been introduced into twenty state schools in Naples and Montessori had a face-to-face meeting with Benito Mussolini, which resulted in the Montessori Method being introduced to all Italian state schools, accorded the formal imprimatur of Mussolini. It has been suggested that it was only when Mussolini 'marched on Rome' in 1922 that she took up permanent residence in Barcelona (Kneller, 1951). By 1924, Montessori education was declared to be 'Italy's official educational theory' (Müller and Schneider, 2002: 151). Lectures and teacher-training courses involved her in traveling huge distances throughout Europe, the United States, Argentina, and the British Isles and she continued to travel to Italy until 1934 (Lillard, 1972: 15). When troubles arose at the outbreak of the Spanish Civil War in 1936, once more Montessori was forced to flee for her life. She left Barcelona aboard a British warship for England where she and Mario took refuge (Cohen, 1974: 62). Hitler closed all Montessori schools in Germany in the mid-1930s and when Mussolini joined Hitler, all her schools in Italy and throughout all occupied countries were closed for the duration of World War Two.

Throughout the British Isles, a huge interest had been manifested in the first *Casa dei Bambini* as early as 1909 with glowing reports in the *Times* and magazines. Visitors from Britain traveled to Rome to observe for themselves the young children who were able to read and write at four years. In a number of cases, these visitors 'were so impressed with what they saw that it changed the course of their lives' (Standing, 1957: 36). One was Bertram Hawker who broke his journey to Australia to visit Rome and was so stirred with what he saw that he stayed to have an opportunity to talk to Montessori herself. The more he heard, the more he felt he had to learn, so he canceled his voyage to Australia. On his return to England, he set up the first Montessori class in his house, The Old Hall, in Brixton. Later he founded the Montessori Society in England. Further glowing reports about Montessori's work in Rome saw the establishment of numerous Children's Houses by 1909. Sol Cohen claims that it was Josephine Tozier who, in 1911, introduced Montessori methods to England with her articles entitled 'An Educational Wonder Worker' published in *Fortnightly Review*. That year Edmund Holmes, one of His Majesty's Inspectors of schools, traveled to Rome to investigate. His report was extremely supportive of Montessori education (Cohen, 1974). Montessori classrooms flourished and many schools were soon catering for children up to twelve years as the result of teachers who had attended Montessori teacher-training courses in Rome in 1913 and 1914. Others had read her books or had been inspired by laudatory press and journal articles about her work. Many nuns attended her courses and were credited with introducing Montessori education throughout the British Empire.

It was after World War One, in 1919, that Montessori made her second visit to England. Her first had been in 1899 when she was presented to Queen Victoria. According to Standing 'her reception was almost royal. A banquet was held in her honour at the Savoy Hotel,

London, at which H. A. L. Fisher, President of the Board of Education, took the Chair' (Standing, 1957: 46). There she conducted her first teacher-training course, which attracted over 2,000 applicants. From those, 250 were selected for the two-month course beginning on 1 September at St Bride's Foundation in Fleet Street, London. Lily Hutchinson, who had attended the 1913 course in Rome, acted as interpreter. A public lecture was held at Westminster at which 2,700 attended and there were lectures for 1,500 teachers unable to attend the full course. The course consisted of fifty hours of lectures dealing with children aged three to eleven years, along with the mandatory fifty hours of practice-teaching and fifty hours of observation in established Montessori classrooms. There were also the three obligatory evening meetings per week for debate and discussion, along with the preparation of a manual containing the student's drawings and lessons for every piece of material. At the end of the course, written and oral examinations had to be passed after which a diploma signed by Montessori was presented to the students authorizing them to teach, but not to train others. For all of this, a fee of thirty-five guineas had to be paid, with a reduced fee of twenty guineas for those who already held the Infant Course Diploma (Kramer, 1976: 305). Because of the huge interest shown throughout Great Britain and the wonderful reception she received, Montessori decided to conduct teacher-training courses there every second year.

Eleonora Gibbons from Ireland had attended the London course in 1919 and in 1920 the first three Montessori classrooms opened in Waterford for 110 children directed by Gibbons with one or two assistants she had trained (Fanning, 1994: 14). Several schools were opened in Ireland following a Montessori program with formal lectures given at Dublin's Trinity College during the 1920s. On ensuing visits to the British Isles in the 1920s and 1930s, Montessori conducted training courses and delivered lectures in Manchester, Edinburgh, and Dublin as well as in London. When she traveled to Dublin in 1934 as the examiner of trainees who had attended a six-month teacher-training course, she took time to visit the three Montessori schools in Waterford. During her biennial visit in 1921, Montessori met Edward E. Standing who was to remain a faithful and steadfast supporter. Later he was to become her biographer. It is also clear that by 1921, there was growing restiveness in England with Montessori's exclusive control over accreditation of Montessori teachers and when the London Montessori Society voiced some concerns, Montessori withdrew from the Society as its founding president. Nonetheless, her reputation in the wider community continued to grow. An indication of her standing throughout England was shown by Durham University, which bestowed on her an honorary doctorate in 1923. By 1925, two Montessori training colleges had been established: one (St Christopher's) in Letchworth, the other (St George's) in Harpenden. Both offered courses for younger, inexperienced teachers and either one was a prerequisite for those lacking formal credentials to be admitted to Montessori's own four-month course. The Chairman of St George's, in an appeal for funds, wrote that the aim of the course was to provide England with 'an exact model of the Montessori system, as progressively developed by Dr Montessori, whose word was, and is, to be law in the school' (*The Times Educational Supplement*, 7 February 1925). Neither of these colleges nor the one in Rome (under the aegis of the Italian government) could confer a Montessori Diploma until the student had undertaken the four-month course given by Montessori herself. At the same time, the University of Manchester's Faculty of Education offered a course in the Montessori Method at its Fielden Demonstration School, and in the Borough of Acton in the City of London, primary schools were run on Montessori lines (Kramer, 1976: 298). In 1927, she was received by King George V at Buckingham Palace, London, a telling demonstration of her status at the time.

One ardent supporter was the celebrated Bertrand Russell who sent his three-year-old son to a Montessori school where he 'found that he quickly became a more disciplined human being' (Kramer, 1976: 299). In his *Education and the Good Life* (1926), Russell praised the Montessori method with much warmth. Another notable supporter was George Bernard Shaw who felt impelled in 1928 to direct savage words against upstart poseurs all too keen to exploit her name. His words were prophetic:

If you are a distressed gentlewoman, starting to make a living, you can still open a little school, and you can easily buy a second-hand brass plate inscribed Pestalozzi Institute and nail it to your door, though you have no more idea who Pestalozzi was and what he advocated, or how he did it, than the manager of a hotel which began as a Hydropathic has of a water cure. Or you can buy a cheaper plate, inscribed Kindergarten, and imagine, or leave others to imagine, that Froebel is the governing genius of your creche. No doubt the new brass plates are being inscribed Montessori Institute, and will be used when the Dottoressa is no longer with us by all the Mrs Pipchins and Mrs Wilfers throughout this unhappy land.

(in Kramer, 1976: 299; from *John O'London's Weekly*, n.d. 1928)

By the mid-1930s there were over 1,000 Montessori centers in England alone.

In the meantime, she traveled widely and taught extensively in Spain, Holland, Germany, France, and Austria, and in the European autumn of 1926, she made her first visit to South America, lecturing in Buenos Aires, La Plata, and Córdoba. Then it was back to Europe and Italy, and to Britain for her four-month biennial course. Such an itinerary was typical of her life in the 1920s and 1930s. In the 1920s, a four-month training course was established in Amsterdam. The Dutch Montessori Society started publishing a quarterly journal called *The Call of Education*. In 1928, a collection of her 1923 Brussels' lectures on the child in the family was published in German. In her introduction to *The Discovery of the Child* (1929) an update of her work described in *The Montessori Method* (1909), Montessori commented on the spread of her Method into Asia, where schools had been established in Syria, India, China, Africa (Egypt to the Cape), as well as in the US, Canada, and Latin America. In the Introduction she had a spirited response to criticism that she was unscientific:

My experiences far from being rigid, were logical conclusions corresponding to the application of an exact and positive method. The behaviour of children, being uncontrolled by rigid research, gave new evidence, something living, which issued from my experiments as a spring of water gushes from a rock. In good faith, like the simple Aladdin, I thought I held in my hand a lamp which at the least could lead me to a place hitherto unexplored, but what I discovered unexpectedly was the treasure hidden in the depths of a child's soul, and it is this new and surprising revelation and not what might be called 'the importance of my contribution to official science', which has spread my method so far over the world, so far from the land of my birth.

(Montessori, 1929: ix)

That year, 1929, was also a landmark in the Montessori movement for the commencement of the Association Montessori Internationale (AMI). It was set up by Montessori (jointly with Mario, whom she still referred to as her nephew) during the World Congress on New Education held at Elsinore, Denmark. Helen Parkhurst was in attendance. In August 1929, at the end of her teacher-training course in England, Montessori announced her decision to form AMI as a parent body to oversee activities in all Montessori schools throughout the world (Kramer, 1976: 305). It was a decision that split her followers in England, some groups who wished to preserve 'pure' Montessori education immediately joining AMI, others abstaining. Montessori was to be president of this influential new parent body. Berlin was chosen as headquarters but when Hitler closed all German Montessori schools in 1935, the AMI moved its headquarters to Amsterdam, where it has remained ever since. Amsterdam has played a vital role in Montessori education, not least because of its link with Anne Frank, the heroine belonging to the world at large who had attended an Amsterdam Montessori School. In World War Two, she was captured by the Nazis and deported to Auschwitz, where she died. Today, around the world, Montessori Cycle Three students are encouraged to read *The Diary of Anne Frank*, and in so doing, to keep alive Maria Montessori's dream of a world at perpetual peace.

In the early 1930s 'attempts had already been made in Holland to continue Montessori's approach to education with children twelve years of age to the end of secondary school' (Joosten in Montessori, 1973: ix). Cosmic Education for children six to twelve years was discussed in detail at the Montessori course in London in 1935 and she returned in 1936 for the Fifth International Montessori Congress in Oxford at which she was president. She spoke about the post-primary level, and the education of adolescents. These ideas had been gestating since 1920 and saw light of day in *The Erdkinder* and other essays.

It was thirty years since her first Children's House was established and to mark the occasion, *The Secret of Childhood* (1936) was published during the proceedings. Not all observers who attended the Congress were impressed. On 25 July, *The Times Educational Supplement* reported its concerns:

> There is of course an important educational factor that no application of theory and no formal instruction can provide. As Freud has taught us, the human emotional impacts of early childhood have important lifelong results. Unfortunately, we cannot by deliberation adapt our emotions or those of others to fit needs or expediences. It is on the intellectual, physical and aesthetic planes alone that formal educational planning can help us, and it is a weakness of many enthusiastic educational reformers – including Dr Montessori – that they do not sufficiently recognise this limitation.

Soon afterwards, it returned to the attack, noting other deep-seated reservations about her system:

> The effect of the international short courses which Dr Montessori has held, and the visits she has paid to many countries has been that there are people all over the world who have caught something of her inspiration without understanding its applications. Schools have grown up here and there, and vanished again, in which children have been free, above everything else, to be rude and dirty.
>
> (*The Times Educational Supplement*, 8 August 1936)

Europe and America were not the only fertile fields for the exciting new developments in education. The Montessori Method spread to far-off Australia. Montessori herself never visited Australia but several Australians traveled to Rome to attend her international courses and some left a deep impression on Montessori. As early as 1909, her name was known to Peter Board, Director of Education in New South Wales, through reports in the *Times* and when *The Montessori Method* reached the antipodes in 1912, Board immediately despatched Miss Margaret Simpson, at the time the infants mistress at Blackfriars Demonstration School in Sydney, to journey to Italy to study under Montessori in her very first international course in 1913 (Crane and Walker, 1957;

Petersen, 1971; O'Donnell, 1996). On her return, a total review of infants training took place in New South Wales, with an amalgamation of Montessori principles with traditional Froebelian practices that had hitherto dominated early childhood education. Other states in Australia and all of New Zealand swiftly followed the New South Wales lead. By 1922, all New South Wales children up to nine years of age were receiving Montessori education in state schools (Turney, 1972) but when Board died, other 'new' theories and methods were introduced by his successor and by the 1930s there was little of Montessori education to be found. As occurred in America, it was decades before Montessori was re-discovered.

In Europe, as tensions of war arose in the 1930s, Montessori began preaching with renewed vigor her philosophical concepts on global peace. They were ideas fundamentally unchanged during the whole of the forty years before:

> If man is to overcome war and his own conflicts and complexes, education must be given a scientific basis, one which places at its centre the laws of the child's psychic development, discovery of which will indicate the sensitive periods of growth during which – and only during which – psychic functions can be perfectly acquired.
>
> (*New York Times*, 26 July 1936)

It was a theme she raised at the Sixth Montessori International Congress held in Copenhagen 1937. Representatives from twenty countries attended but there was not one from Germany, Italy, or Russia. Danish papers identified her as 'the greatest living Italian orator' (Kramer, 1976: 337). In her keynote address, she linked her ideas on peace with the education of the child:

> The adult must understand the meaning of the moral defence of humanity, not the armed defence of nations. He must realize that the child will be the creator of the new world peace. In a suitable environment the child reveals unsuspected social characteristics. The qualities he shows will be the salvation of the world, showing us all the road to peace. And the new child has been born. He will tell us what is needed!
>
> (*Time Magazine*, 16 August 1937 in Kramer, 1976: 337)

In 1938, the Seventh Montessori Congress was held in Edinburgh, Scotland and in the same year Montessori conducted a training session in Amsterdam. The following year she was invited by the British Theosophical Society to give a teacher-training course in India where a Montessori Society had been in existence since 1926. Dr Annie Besant, the second president of the Theosophical Society from 1907 until her death in 1933, had long been a keen supporter of Montessori and a close friend of George Bernard Shaw. She was also an ardent supporter of the Home Rule for India movement. At the age of sixty-nine, Montessori left Amsterdam in company with Mario for Adyar in Madras. Sadly for Montessori, the outbreak of World War Two brought about the internment of both herself and Mario for the duration of the war. She was soon released but Mario remained imprisoned until 31 August 1940 when he was released by the British Governor as a special dispensation for Montessori's seventieth birthday. That was when she first publicly acknowledged Mario as her son. Neither was allowed to leave India until the end of war in 1945. During the ensuing years, Montessori and Mario trained thousands of Indian teachers, many of whom traveled long distances just to attend the courses. They trialed some high school ideas as well as education from birth to three years. Mahatma Gandhi, who had already met her several times in Italy, visited Montessori several times. The great man fully concurred with her on education, world peace, and her vision that saw long-term solutions to global problems in the education of young children. Gandhi had even attended several of her courses (Lawson, 1974: 36–49) and well knew her *Education and Peace*, which had been first published in 1932. During her stay in India, Montessori also met Krishnamutri. Both condemned traditional inhumane approaches to education which were not based on love and respect for children (Currie and Breadmore, 1983). Just briefly she was also able to renew her acquaintance with the celebrated Indian poet Sir Rabindranath Tagore, who had established numerous Montessori schools throughout India. Tagore had attended the 1929 Conference in Elsinore, speaking eloquently in praise of Montessori education. He died in 1941. It was during this phase of her life that a number of books under her name appeared. *Education for a New World* was published in 1946 by Kalakshetra at Adyar in Madras and was largely lecture notes. *The Child* and *Reconstruction in Education* (appearing first as pamphlets in 1941 and 1942) were published by the Theosophical Society in 1948. That year twelve of her talks on the Madras station of All India Radio appeared under the title *Child Training* (published by the Indian Ministry of Information). Other titles included *What You Should Know About Your Child* (Colombo, 1948), *The Discovery of the Child* (Madras, 1948), *The Montessori Method* (Madras, 1948), *To Educate the Human Potential* (Madras, 1948), and *The Absorbent Mind* (Madras, 1949).

In 1946, after her exile in India, Montessori returned to England where interest in Montessori education had languished during her eight-year absence (Cohen, 1974: 62). She was met by her faithful followers Margaret Homfray and Phoebe Child and a teacher-training course was organized by them to commence the following year (Kramer, 1976). This gave birth to the famous St Nicholas College destined to play a major role in training Montessori teachers for decades to come. On the occasion, Montessori traveled to Edinburgh where she was presented with an Honorary Fellowship by the Educational Institute of Scotland (Prakasam, 1948). She returned to Rome to conduct her first teacher-training course for teachers of children from birth to three years. There were obstacles even in the land of her birth but as the global story of Montessori education shows, the movement she began survived all adversities. Her commitment to the noble cause of world peace was also demonstrated in her 1947 UNESCO lecture on 'Education and Peace.' At the end of 1948 she returned to India for a planned opening of a Montessori University, but was caught up in the enormous upheaval relating to the newly created Pakistan (Potts, 1980: 40) and returned to Amsterdam where Mario married and settled. In August 1949, she attended the Eighth International Montessori Congress held at San Remo, delivering an inspiring paper on the critical importance of educating children for a changed and changing world desperately in need of their awakened humanity. That year she was nominated for the Nobel Peace Prize, as she was in 1950 and 1951. France honored her with its Cross of the Legion of Honour. In 1950, she made a tour of Scandinavia, as usual accompanied by Mario. She had continued to return to England to conduct her teacher-training courses since she remained the only person responsible for training teachers. In 1951, at the age of eighty, she addressed the Montessori Conference held in London and presented a paper to UNESCO entitled 'The Rights of Children' (Kramer, 1976). The following year while preparing for a visit to Ghana in Africa, this extraordinary woman – champion of children, doctor, feminist, socialist, environmentalist, pacifist, reformer – died aged eighty-one in Noordwijk ann Zee, Holland. She was buried in the local Catholic cemetery. A commemorative tablet on the Montessori family grave in Rome reads:

Maria Montessori 1870–1952

Famous scientist and pedagogue who dedicated her entire life to the spiritual renewal and to the progress of humanity through the child. She rests in the Catholic cemetery Noordwijk (Holland) far away from the country she had profoundly loved, far from her loved ones buried here. This she decided, to give testimony to the universality of her work, which made her a citizen of the world.

Part 2

Critical Exposition of Montessori's Work

The child is the central focus of Montessori education, each one being accorded the status of unique individual. Montessori maintained that children were misunderstood because neither parents nor teachers fully comprehended what happened during each stage of their growth, yet bringing children to full fruition meant nurturing their physical, psychological, social, emotional, aesthetic, and spiritual needs in order to cultivate their unique personalities. For Montessori, the child's personality began to form from the moment of birth and that was when his education should commence (Montessori, 1967: 4) as its foundation was laid by three years. Throughout her life, she stressed that 'the first two years of life are the most important, because during that period, the fundamental features which characterise the human personality are established' (Montessori, 1975: 90). From birth to eighteen years the human personality needed to be considered as one entity, and the utilization of love and respect was the best means of helping that growth. Adults could help or hinder development by the physical and psychological environment they provided.

As a scientist, Montessori took as indisputable that everything in the universe worked according to the laws of nature, with regular cycles for all things in the cosmos, including human life. Rules of the universe never changed, only varied. Since each child passed through observable physical changes, why should the covert human psyche be different, she asked. She had observed that every child passed through the same phases of psychic development and although it was universal, the speed at which each child passed through each phase depended on his intellect. By 1912, she had concluded that physical and psychic development run parallel, noting that 'the general laws which govern the child's psychical health have their parallel in those of its physical health' (Montessori, 1969: 1) and that inner changes of the psyche were as different as the visible changes in the cycle of a butterfly. The psychical growth of a child could be assessed through observations of physical actions. It was not until the appearance of *The Absorbent Mind*, first published in 1949 based on her lectures from 1939 to 1945 that her carefully detailed observations from birth to adulthood were described in detail. That book spelled out the four cycles of development: first, from birth to six years of age (subdivided into 0–3 and 3–6) when children possessed an unconscious absorbent mind; second, from six to twelve years (subdivided into 6–9 and 9–12) when children possessed a conscious mind; third, from twelve to eighteen years (subdivided into 12–15 and 15–18) when children used abstract thinking; and fourth, adulthood from eighteen years (Montessori, 1967: 19). At each stage she told us, 'we have before us a different child who presents characteristics different from those he exhibited during preceding years' (Montessori, 1973: 1). In Montessori education, the first three cycles, or planes of development, became the basis for Montessori arranging children in multi-age groups remaining together for approximately three years. She believed that official education has 'recognised these different psychological types' because children from birth to six years were excluded from compulsory education while primary school was for children 6–12 years, and high school for adolescents was compulsory. She pointed out that 'only a psychological basis common to all children can have made possible this kind of school organization ... but that schools were insensitive to the needs of students particularly at upper levels' (Montessori, 1967: 20, 21).

6 Infancy, the Absorbent Mind, and Sensitive Periods

Infancy, the period from birth to three years, assumed importance in the Montessori world for this was the period when the child possessed what she graphically termed the unconscious 'absorbent' mind which soaked up impressions in the environment that helped bring about 'his marvellous progress' (Montessori, 1967: 21, 24). She recorded in her observations that the infant was able to select all he needed for his 'sensory functions' and his own development according to his own nature (Montessori, 1965: 34). At first, the hand was used unconsciously which helped the development of the mind and later, 'the mind is hand made when the child makes discoveries with something' (Montessori, 1967: 18). From 1896 when she qualified as a doctor, Montessori had observed the physical and psychological development of newborns believing they had a psychic life before birth (ibid.: 165). It was in the critical time after his birth that her attention became focused because while the 'bodily life' of the child was looked after adequately, 'care of his mental life' was neglected. In the early 1930s, it was still commonly thought that a newborn had no psychic life but to Montessori 'the chief characteristic of a human babe is intelligence' (Montessori, 1963: 31). From birth to three years, known in Montessori education as the sensory-motor period, was the most rapid period of development and the most important since the child learned more during this period than in all the rest of his life. But although the child needed the greatest of help during the first period of life, there could be no direct adult influence because the child developed through his own unconscious efforts and by nature's inner urge absorbed 'impressions of life itself' (Montessori, 1967: 24). Each child constructed his memory, his will, his power to reason, and his capacity to adapt to the social environment in which character was formed (ibid.: 28). She pronounced the infant to be 'an unknown being who does not arouse awe and admiration for what he is able to do to create himself' (Montessori, 1975: 49). The newborn, 'a spiritual embryo,' needed to be free to move as nature intended – Montessori informed mothers in those first Children's Houses in 1907 that even excessive swaddling clothes could restrict freedom and prevent the young child from developing every muscle in his body which he needed to do to 'perfect himself' (Montessori, 1964: 172). She told them that confining a child to a cot or imposing artificial restraints could hinder development. Such early observations of infant children pre-dated her more detailed data about the subsequent planes of development through which all children progress. Everything that would develop in future years was based on the foundations laid by the child during this first period of life. Adults could help simply by providing the correct conditions for the child to develop. Mothers were helped to understand the absorbent mind and how each child learned unconsciously. They were advised about the importance of motherhood in the first three years of life and how to provide for a developing infant and of special importance was an anxiety-free environment so each child could develop naturally. She conducted positive parenting talks with mothers.

Montessori claimed that infants from birth to three years acquired knowledge naturally and spontaneously, each creating his own mind, his memory, his intellect, and 'the full totality of his psychic powers' (Montessori, 1967: 21). Nature, for its part, equipped the child with what she called 'an absorbent mind, a marvellous gift to humanity' (Montessori, 1975: 13) because at this stage of development infants could not be reached through verbal help from adults. Her discovery that the newborn child until about six years had a mind able to absorb on its own account induced her to label this phenomenon 'a revolution in education' (Montessori, 1967: 28). Adults could help development by providing a suitable environment to assist the child to create his absorbent mind (Montessori, 1964: 105). It was during this first period of life that character was formed and it was here she saw 'great need for intellectual help' (Montessori, 1967: 28). It was the child's inner urge (horme) which helped him create his mind and build the adult he was to become (Montessori, 1978: 205). In *Dr Montessori's Own Handbook* (1914) for parents, she described the infant's mind as being like a camera, absorbing every detail of information through a process which could not be observed (Montessori, 1965). That development was covert and 'the hidden law inherent in the spiritual embryo is one of the child's secrets' (Montessori, 1978: 209). From the environment, the newborn 'absorbs knowledge, instructs himself, proved by the child's ability to acquire language, a great intellectual feat' (Montessori, 1963: 3). At two years the child 'is capable of miraculous achievements by his unconscious, absorbing power, whilst he is immobile' (Montessori, 1972: 325). At this early age he begins to 'speak the language in his environment with all its phonetic and grammatical peculiarities when he does not yet possess the mental faculties which are necessary in order to learn' (ibid.: 324). No one has taught him and 'he creates not only language but the organs that enable him to speak,' as well as 'every physical movement he creates, every means of intelligent expression' (Montessori, 1963: 16). The child absorbs language through a 'mental chemistry' within his absorbent mind and Montessori reminded us of the magnitude of that power: 'The loss of the absorbent mind is the price we pay for the acquisition of consciousness ... a heavy price, to become a man' (ibid.: 17). She observed that the development in the first three years of life was the same for all children worldwide because it 'is directed by nature' (ibid.: 24). The child's growth and development in this early period she saw as 'an example of perfect obedience to the laws of nature' (Montessori, 1966: 21). In these first three years of life, according to Montessori, the child was 'nature's scholar' who obeyed perfectly 'a natural energy which guides him and sets tasks which he will carry out as nature has ordained,' but how he sets about that inner building was a 'secret he will not reveal' (Montessori, 1978: 210). The baby, she told us, 'has a creative aptitude, a potential energy that will enable it to build up a mental world' (ibid.: 34). At three years a child could walk, run, talk, understand everything in the home and surrounding area and had already formed his personality. For her, the magnitude of those achievements was almost unbelievable: 'No matter where he is born he achieves the same miracle' (Montessori, 1966: 29). Nature was 'a scrupulous and exacting teacher who adheres to a timetable' (Montessori, 1963: 3) and all subsequent development was based on the foundations laid by the child during the first three years of life. The unseen, covert work done by the child with his absorbent mind, satisfied an inner need to achieve 'psychic maturation' (Montessori, 1978: 210). All of this Montessori claimed was 'rendered possible by sensitive periods, one of the greatest wonders of nature' (ibid.: 211).

In *The Secret of Childhood*, first published in 1936, Montessori discussed the sensitive periods of development in children, noting that from the first hours of birth the child's mind remained in a sensitive period. Physically the newborn was incomplete at birth, his motor nerves 'not yet provided with their covering of myelin that enables them to transmit the brain's orders' (ibid.: 72). It was essential that newborns be allowed to move for motor nerves to develop in order to obey the brain. She warned that if a child was unable to move, the connections between the brain and the nerves remained incomplete and died (ibid.). The infant used his hands unconsciously from birth to help him create his mind. Of critical importance in the sensitive periods which she defined as 'a predisposition to a period of growth and transient in nature, occurring for a few weeks, months or years, when a child, guided from within, had an insatiable desire to acquire a skill' (ibid.: 35). It was the child who knew when it was time to learn and that learning was entirely spontaneous. The absorbent mind and the sensitive periods began to fade slowly at three years and by six years the mind had changed and learning became conscious. A skill missed during a sensitive period could be learned later but only with much greater effort on the part of the child. As example, Montessori cited the Wild Boy of Aveyron who had never learned to walk erect nor speak because obstacles within his environment during his sensitive periods prevented such learning (ibid.).

Montessori maintained that it was very important to have knowledge of the sensitive periods and their order of occurrence or 'one cannot understand the construction of the psyche of the child' (Montessori, 1963: 21). To prove her point, she cited examples including the fact that between birth and one and a half years, uncoordinated movement became controlled by exercising the muscles of arms and legs freely, grasping, touching objects within reach, turning the body, crawling, walking, balancing while 'repetition built the inner being' (Montessori, 1978: 209) and established rules of behavior as the child refined movement. From one year to four years the child had a keen interest in the exact detail of small things. The sound of music and his mother's voice always attracted the child's attention from birth while from two to six years there was a spontaneous interest in sounds, rhythms, pitch, melody, and silence. From birth to three years there was a natural progression of language development from babbling, to words, phrases, sentences, with expanding vocabulary. From birth to three years the child showed a love of order, routines, consistency in daily life within a carefully ordered environment. From two years, grace and courtesy, politeness and consideration were learned from the example of others and internalized into the personality. From two and a half years children began to refine their senses through sensorial experiences of touch, sight, sound, taste, and smell.

7 Early Childhood, Childhood, Adolescence/Youth

Early childhood, from three to six years, was a period when the child was continually touching and moving something in exploration of his environment, and Montessori interpreted that behavior to mean that 'he was working out, and making conscious something that his unconscious mind had earlier absorbed' (Montessori, 1967: 27). At three years the child learned without knowing he was learning, but slowly passed 'from the unconscious to the conscious' (Montessori, 1978: 26). The child's mind had been created by using the senses, and with the sense of touch being predominant, unconsciously using his hand until three years, but now the absorbent mind was fading and every action made by the child was an act of will, 'a conscious act . . . an interior labour . . . an exercise of will power' (Montessori, 1969: 140, 141). Montessori education is most often associated with children of these preschool years and the first Children's Houses founded in Rome in 1907 were used for observation purposes to find ways to aid the spontaneous, natural development of 'normal' children. The discovery that the sensitive period for beginning to write and read was four years brought attention to the first Children's House in 1907. That spontaneous acquisition of culture was made possible because the child still possessed an absorbent mind and was given didactic materials which helped him to teach himself (Montessori, 1963: 5). She had helped nurture children's spirits when working with special needs children, claiming all children needed joy and happiness for a healthy life. She continued with her 'experimental investigations with a readiness to accept new concepts whenever experiences prove to us that they are better and closer to the truth that we are seeking' (Montessori, 1913: 22).

It was in the first Children's House when children experienced stress-free physical and psychological conditions that they revealed their natural tendencies. Children were not forced to take up a piece of work or a given task. There was one piece only of each material and children chose what they wanted to do rather than waiting for tasks set by the teacher. To their observant directress, they showed a capacity for intense concentration as they worked, often repeating an activity they were interested in many times. In 1907, Montessori observed a girl repeating an exercise forty-five times before being satisfied and a new concept was fixed in her mind. Children were orderly and they preferred working with materials rather than playing with toys. There was no competition, no fear of punishments because the materials allowed them to self-correct. They had no need for prizes since they gained an inner joy by completing a task successfully. Most possessed a palpable sense of personal dignity and appeared to grow in independence (Montessori, 1964). These natural tendencies shown by the children became Montessori principles and provided for them an underlying goal of Montessori education. They were central to her theory of education in which practice and observation had preference over theory. Out of those detailed observations grew other discoveries that underscored the stark difference between her practices and the work of her predecessors because, unlike them, Montessori began with practice and followed children's development, natural tendencies, and interests, allowing them to select their own tasks, and giving them ample time to complete their chosen activity. When the young disadvantaged children of four years 'exploded' into writing spontaneously and began to read, the results gained by her young students in 1907 were to stun educators and revolutionize educational thought.

Childhood

In 1910, Montessori started her work with children aged six to twelve years when children underwent what she called a metamorphosis (Montessori, 1973: 3). Her work with this age group was published in two large volumes, *The Advanced Montessori Method* Volume 1 and Volume 2, published in English in 1916. By six years a Montessori child was normalized, could read and write, was independent of adults, and could make responsible decisions. At six years, Montessori observed, the child experiences physical and psychological changes. Physical signs were obvious 'when the teeth fall out, the body becomes thinner, curly hair becomes straighter and darker' (Montessori Lecture, Edinburgh 1938). There was 'a great transformation at six years,' the psychic entity beginning to 'become approachable' (Montessori, 1963: 14) because the absorbent mind has faded. During the childhood years there was a calm growth arising from relative physical and mental stability which she called 'a time of serenity and docility' (ibid.: 15) when the child was 'calm and happy' (Montessori, 1967: 19). It was also a period when the child showed a keen interest in culture and morals and wished to use his own judgment even though it often differed from that of the directress (Montessori, 1973: 11). He judged the acts of others and wanted to know 'what has been done well or poorly' (ibid.). It was the age when 'the sensitive period of the concept of justice is born from the interior along with the injustice and legal right concept' (ibid.: 12, 13). Education needed to present 'the natural sense of true justice,' which differed from 'distributive justice about individual rights which is influenced from the external' (ibid.: 13). Moral relationships awakened in this period when children 'do not wish to offend' (ibid.: 18), and social interest developed as each child became part of a social group within the classroom or a team outside the classroom. Each stage of development was based on the foundations laid in the first stage. Montessori points out that if a child is neglected from three to six years he 'is unlikely to have the moral conscience that should develop from seven to twelve years or he may be deficient in intelligence. With no moral character, no ability to learn, he becomes a man of scars, marks of defects of the soul' (Montessori, 1978: 75). At a higher level, children of moral character had an interest 'in aiding the weak, aged and sick' (Montessori, 1966: 6, 17). They needed wider boundaries for social experiences and 'such activities as scouting brought an organized form of life to children' (Montessori, 1973: 9, 11). The Boy Scout movement was reality-based, and seen by Montessori as 'a social response to the needs (natural tendencies) of the child during this phase ... for persons seeking wider social contacts, wider experiences and independence from their families who need wider contacts with both nature and human society' (Montessori Lecture, Edinburgh, 1938). It also had a moral and social dimension and children joined freely, choosing to obey principles in which they found merit. The mind was at an abstract level which 'discovers causes' and the child views things in entirety so everything in the universe needed to be shown to be interrelated. The psychological change that had taken place revealed to Montessori 'the importance of feeding the hungry intelligence and opening vast fields of knowledge to eager exploration' (Montessori, 1961: 6). She suggested much work should be done outside the classroom at this stage. The great outdoors demanded more adaptation and a new environment to be mastered.

Adolescence

The period of adolescence from twelve to fifteen years was a period of great physical change and therefore of psychological change. Montessori pointed out during the 1930s that 'from a psychological viewpoint this is a critical age,' with so many physical changes it called for as much care and attention as the newborn. The young adolescent needed very special care, less physical exercise and less intellectual work because during this period he experienced 'doubts and hesitations, violent emotions, discouragement and an unexpected decrease of intellectual capacity occurs' and the difficulty of studying arose from 'a psychological characteristic of this age.' Physical health during puberty could be a dangerous time but was seldom recognized as such, especially by schools (Montessori, 1967: 19). The child at this stage is 'as prone to tuberculosis and other diseases, as in the first stage of development, yet was expected to continue with guided studies' (Montessori Lecture, Edinburgh 1938). All of a sudden the adolescent became 'very sensitive to rudeness and humiliations he had previously suffered with patience and indifference' and reactions were 'often rebellious' (Montessori, 1973: 101). At the same time he felt empathy with others whom he had never seen, an abstract love without retribution because it is directed at those never seen. 'These children want to give their direct contribution to society,' Montessori explained in her Edinburgh lecture of 1938. She recognized that secondary schools desperately needed to reform (ibid.: 97), and there was one thing that education could take as a sure guide, she wrote, 'and that is the personality of the children who are to be educated' (ibid.: 99). The special needs of adolescent children simply had to be addressed.

Adolescence/youth

The three years from fifteen to eighteen were the final period of development before adulthood. These years were calmer than the first three years of adolescence and students were better able to study than during the first period of adolescence (Montessori, 1973: 100).

Serious study could be done by those who wished to prepare themselves for university entry. It was essential for students to understand that 'life must not remain an unknown quantity ... for success in life in every case depends on self-confidence and knowledge of one's own capacity' (ibid.: 102). Success in life also depended on the ability to adapt (Montessori, 1964: 271) as 'adaptation is the most essential quality: for progress of the world is continually opening up new careers' (Montessori, 1973: 99). She suggested boarding school for adolescents where they could experience living together in harmony within a democratic society and working together co-operatively. The school for adolescents, twelve years to eighteen years, which she proposed required adolescents to leave home for a type of self-sufficient boarding school in the country. She called it an *Erdkinder* (earth school) where they could learn to become independent economically through their own labor, and suggested work experience including working the land, caring for animals, and running a section of the school as a hotel where parents could visit and pay for their accommodation while students learned how to run a hotel, making and serving meals. A shop was another suggestion where students could sell their home-grown produce or their own handmade products. Projects proposed by the students were always considered by the group and votes taken on what could be viable financially. Being separated from parents during these years would avoid conflict because Montessori observed that many parents did not understand development during adolescent years. She proposed very different conditions and choices for teenage students from choices offered in other high schools. Her hope was for each independent, well-adjusted, reliable, responsible, adaptable adolescent to reach his potential and take his place as a contributing member of society prepared to meet the challenges of a new world.

8 The Montessori Learning Environment and Didactic Materials

Learners, three to six years of age, found themselves in a large room with Montessori materials displayed on low shelves for easy access. There was space to move and lightweight, child-sized furnishings which could be moved easily. In many ways it was a controlling environment, suitable to help clumsy children take more care and so refine their movements. There were child-sized practical life materials designed to help each child refine his motor development. Children were free to move about and talk to each other as long as they did not disturb others at work. Montessori helped nurture each child's spirit by providing stress-free living conditions resulting in a group of successful, happy learners. These children, who chose their own activities, were encouraged to think for themselves (Montessori 1967: 257), which helped them become self-confident and self-directed. Each followed his own agenda as there was no set curriculum or timetable to follow because each child knew what was best needed 'to help him construct himself' (ibid.: 223). Young children were always the best judges of what their needs were for their own development and 'were drawn to pieces of material like a bee to a flower.' That awareness of his own needs, and the capacity to act on them, was what constituted 'an autonomous individual' (Montessori, 1969: 71). In her words, 'the young child thinks and reflects and the hand is directed by the child' (Montessori, 1967: 222). Only he could organize his psychic life. One notable discovery made by Montessori completely by chance in 1907 was that children loved silence. It happened when she unexpectedly met a mother with her four-month-old child in the courtyard of the first Children's House. When Montessori took the infant into the classroom, children ran to greet her but no one touched her, no one spoke aloud, out of respect for the sleeping child she held. She invited the children to be as still as the sleeping child. There was a great silence and the children suddenly became conscious of being quiet and still. When they moved, they walked on tiptoes, without instruction to be quiet. They had achieved complete self-control. Each child revealed he had the will to be master of himself. The silence games she devised were popular and she was soon to discover that freedom and self-discipline were two sides of the same coin (Montessori, 1964).

Montessori materials are extremely important in Montessori education and each must be used for its designed purpose. Each child was to enjoy a spiritual experience through successful use of the materials, which were not to be used in a mechanical way, as Montessori had observed had happened with Séguin's materials. Practical life materials, designed for motor education, were part of the environment and Montessori designed these materials to help the development of each child's sense of order, co-ordination, and independence through daily activities. Some were similar to those she had used to help children within the asylum care for their environment and personal needs and all were introduced to each child individually through demonstration, without words. Silent demonstration allowed a normal child to concentrate on the activity and not be distracted or confused by language. Every activity focused on respect for each other by not interrupting others at work. Social graces, social courtesies, and socially acceptable behavior became an obligatory way of life in every Children's House. The purpose of the practical life activities was to help co-ordinate all gross and fine muscular movements. Simple activities using specially made child-sized household materials involved the use and development of large and small muscles as the children tidied the Children's House. Other activities cultivated a sense of responsibility as children cared for pets and plants in the garden, or prepared and served food for their pets, or weeded and watered plants, or prepared food, set the table, and served lunch for the whole group. Many practical life experiences were shared experiences introducing children to the social life within the classroom. Montessori noted how calmness of the nervous system and concentration were developed as children polished brass objects or worked on other activities. As well, they learned about personal hygiene, the importance of washing hands, grooming needs, and dressing themselves. Their tiny fingers developed dexterous co-ordination when they did buttoning and bow-tying exercises. Montessori's underlying aim was that mastery of such basic skills allowed children to become more independent of adults. For her, no one could be free unless he was independent. She emphasized that all free movement was synonymous with 'spontaneous development' (Montessori, 1964: 230). Many practical life activities were designed 'to help the development of co-ordinated movements of the fingers' (ibid.: 145) especially the co-ordination between the thumb and the first two fingers. It was with the observations of the movements of the hand that Montessori made her point since it was with the hand that the young child made his growing knowledge most evident. For Montessori, the hand was 'companion to the mind . . . connected to mental life' (ibid.: 151,152). Activities for motor education allowed observation of the steadiness of the hand, which indicated the state of the nervous system. She differentiated between motor education and muscular education (gymnastics) that was 'to aid the normal development of physiological movements (such as walking, breathing, speech)' including 'walking the line,' which Séguin had first suggested for development of equilibrium, poise, and graceful, co-ordinated movements. Muscular education improved circulation and thereby health. Through observation of children and their movements Montessori designed a type of jungle-gym to allow them to move along sideways and kick their legs freely. It was 'a proper outlet for his individual activities' the varied exercises 'tending to establish co-ordination of movements' (ibid.: 138, 141–4).

Sensorial (didactic) materials were introduced to each child individually in silent demonstration and only then was he allowed to work with the materials himself (Montessori, 1964). The rewards with these self-instructive materials lay in 'the spontaneous reaction of children,' which were easily observed. Each piece of material was designed to isolate a general principle or idea and so transfer non-specific knowledge which 'could be used as a basis for recognising special cases or applications of it' and through practice, as each child gained insight, 'the general principle or idea is felt as a personal discovery' (Montessori Jr., 1976: 69). The aim of the experiments was to focus the child's attention and 'so cause him to exercise his senses because little children must proceed to the making of trials and must select the didactic material in which they show themselves to be interested' (Montessori, 1964: 168). Every exercise required the child to concentrate on the task at hand while developing control over his body and will. The final step using sensorial materials (except the color activities) was to blindfold the child, depriving him of the sense of sight. Montessori found that the actual deprivation of sight (brief as it was) aroused even deeper interest in the activity and sharpened the child's sense of touch in order to complete the activity.

Montessori observed that 'normal' children focused on the didactic materials which allowed them to teach themselves (ibid.: 171). In all her training courses, she fully explained her didactic materials and how she expected them to be used. In Lecture 14 of her training course in London, May 1921, she emphasized the correct procedures to be followed in presenting the materials to children. 'First of all, let us consider the presentation of the material, which consists in using it in the precise way when placed in front of the child,' she told the trainees:

> In this particular case it consists in the displacing and replacing of certain objects. Sometimes the correct presentation of material requires the preparation of the individual. For instance, the preparation of the fingers for the tactile exercise, or the temporary impeding of some other sense, such as the sight, may be required. Sometimes it is necessary to demonstrate a certain mode of procedure in the presentation, such as the lightness of the hand in touching surfaces and the almost imperceptible movement of the hands when weighing the baric tablets.
> (Montessori in Chattin-McNicholls, 1991: 53–4)

Each child followed his own agenda choosing the materials, working with them for as long as he wished and returning them to the place they were found. She observed how this work cycle brought inner joy and satisfaction to the child on completion of the task. The number of times a child repeated each exercise was carefully recorded because in order to repeat there must first be an idea to be repeated. A mental grasp of an idea was indispensable to the beginning of repetition (Montessori, 1964: 358). Montessori concluded that with repetition the child perfected psychosensory processes.

9 The Three-period Lesson

The three period lesson was a critical aspect of Montessori education. It obliged the directress to intervene after a child had experimented and exhausted the use of a piece of sensorial material and it helped 'to lead the child from sensations to ideas, and to the association of ideas' (ibid.: 224). She was to lead the child from the concrete to the abstract by introducing him to the correct nomenclature or vocabulary. With the exact words to use, the child could think and talk about ideas in the abstract because a word fixed an idea in the mind. For example, in introducing vocabulary for the knobbed cylinders (a sensorial activity which attracts very young children from two and a half years of age), vocabulary was presented with two contrasting pieces of the same material. Words describing opposites were introduced with words for comparison, such as tall–short, tall–taller–tallest, short–shorter–shortest, wide–narrow, deep–shallow, and so on. At this age the child was in a sensitive period for needing to know the exact words of objects and the words to describe the objects. Using sensorial materials, vocabulary was introduced to each child individually using the brief three-period lesson originally designed by Séguin, which had three distinctive ingredients: brevity (the teacher used few words), simplicity (the teacher spoke only the bare essentials), and objectivity (the child could concentrate on the materials being demonstrated without any extraneous talking) (ibid.: 107, 108). Montessori felt that 'the association of the name with the stimulus was a source of great pleasure to the normal child' (ibid.: 178). She was conscious that many teachers were greatly surprised at the simplicity of the lesson believing that

> everybody knows how to do that but the truth is that not everyone knows how to do this simple thing, to give a lesson with such simplicity. To conform to these standards of clearness, brevity and truth, is particularly a very difficult matter.
>
> (Montessori, 1964: 109, 110)

Montessori was insistent that although countless three-period lessons have to be given individually, each must be presented exactly. Every lesson was 'an explanation of the object and of the use the child can make of it,' its fundamental purpose being to focus the full attention of the child without distraction (ibid.: 177). In 1916, she pointed out that the actual duration of each three-period lesson was about thirty seconds since 'every lesson infringes the liberty of the child and for this reason we allow it to last only a few seconds' (Montessori, 1969: 43). In May 1921, she told trainees in London that with a three-period lesson the teacher initiates the child and it is almost as though she gives him a key to the secret of the modification or development of himself of which he is in need. We do not in effect teach him anything in the presentation. In order that this material will have the desired effect, that the child shall be stimulated to the exercise, it is necessary that the teacher should know the technique of correct presentation.

(Montessori in Chattin-McNicholls, 1991: 54)

The three-period lesson allowed careful observation, and anecdotal notes were kept of each child's natural development using the materials. This sound information provided every check necessary because the real development was 'inner.' Every three-period lesson gave the directress an opportunity to be a researcher. Itard's injunction that 'each lesson corresponds to an experiment' (ibid.: 107) was closely followed. From an instructional point of view, there was immediate feedback for the directress from the pupil and it was clear to both whether learning had taken place. It was imperative that a directress knew how to give a three-period lesson exactly since it was an experiment. In Montessori education, it was critical that all materials be demonstrated in exactly the same way in order to obtain the same outcome. Statistics were not compiled. Observations and detailed notes were made to gauge each child's stage of development. Montessori education was based on the spontaneous interest of each individual child; therefore 'collective lessons are of very secondary importance (for children 3–6 years) and have been almost abolished by us' (Montessori, 1964: 108). On completion of any activity, the material was to be replaced by the child exactly where it had been found on the shelf, and in perfect condition, with no missing pieces. This was out of respect for the next child who wished to work with the same materials. Some children, Montessori had observed, became upset or agitated if materials or objects were not in exact order since they were in the sensitive period for order. She claimed that an orderly classroom helped the child construct an orderly mind. It was important that the child should enjoy success when using the materials for the first time. After that, he was left to repeat the exercise as often as he wished, experimenting with its uses and applications for himself. If he wished to be introduced to another piece of material, he took it to the teacher and asked for a lesson. There was no specific order for the introduction of practical life and sensorial materials.

A directress could test her judgment of a child's stage of development. If the material she introduced to a child proved to be too easy or too difficult, the child showed little or no interest in it, but if it suited the child's stage of development, the child 'could confirm something in his mind for himself' (Montessori, 1964: 226), and he became interested, absorbed, concentrated, and repeated the activity a number of times. She then knew that she had chosen the right psychological moment to introduce that new piece of material using the three-period lesson. Most Montessori didactic materials controlled errors and the child could self-correct. This meant errors became a private experience because only the child concerned (or an observant teacher) knew a mistake had been made. Errors could provide valuable educational experience by allowing a child to exercise his intelligence in any number of trials.

If errors were made, or if the child did not make the correct association at any point during the three-period lesson, the directress was not to correct him, instead finishing the lesson at that point and helping the child pack the material and place it back on the shelf. Montessori's explanation was that 'he was not at that instant ready for the psychic association which we wished to provoke in him, and we must therefore choose another moment' (Montessori, 1964: 108). Moreover, the directress was to realize that she had made a mistake by 'not choosing the correct moment and must not repeat the lesson nor make the child feel he has made a mistake' (ibid.: 109). If possible, the inhibiting sense of failure was to be avoided. Montessori observed how corrections had 'a lowering effect on children and as a result they lose interest, while scolding humiliates, insults and offends' and children become discouraged (Montessori, 1967: 145). The directress had to possess 'great respect for the interior construction of personality' done by the child as it was of 'greatest importance' (Montessori, 1973: 111–13).

When a child confidently performed an activity correctly every time, that piece of material became of no further use to him and he would no longer choose that activity. Self-correction led the child to concentrate his attention on the comparisons of the various pieces:

'the psycho-sensory exercise lies in the comparison' (ibid.: 171). Montessori stressed in 1939 that the directress should present new materials 'when the child has exhausted all the possibilities of those he has been using before' (Montessori, 1967: 256). Sensorial materials were designed specifically to attract each child's attention to one definite quality such as dimension, color, sound, texture, weight, or temperature.

10 The Active Learner and Normalization

In all of Montessori education, there was only one variable. That was each active learner. Montessori did everything in her power to control the constants of each experiment. The materials and the directress's spoken words for the three-period lesson were to be the same in every environment, and the only variable was the individual child. Not only was every child regarded as unique, but it was fully appreciated that every single one would emerge from the experience of a three-period lesson in a different way from his neighbor because new information had been added to each individual child's schemata. Every human mind was different, ever-changing with the absorption of new knowledge. It was the role of every directress to foster self-growth in children without incessant interruptions, 'her duty to the child to give a ray of light and go on her way' (Montessori, 1964: 115). Intervention by the directress (nurture) was in delivering the short three-period lesson while the learning was left to the child (nature). Montessori also observed that when a child became interested in a particular item of material introduced to him and he focused his attention repeating the process as many times as to satisfy his inner need, his nervous system became relaxed and a calmness took over his behavior as he experienced spiritual inner peace. That simple discovery about behavior change was what she was to term the process of normalization.

Although considered unscientific in 1907, Montessori's observations led her to interesting and valuable discoveries about child behavior. In the three Children's Houses opened that year, she observed children with regard to behavior noting that when children were free they revealed their personalities. Some children remained 'quietly in their seats, apathetic and drowsy,' some left their places to quarrel or overturn the various blocks and toys and others 'set out to fulfil a definite and determined act' (ibid.: 95). While such behavior was increasingly accepted by adults as normal, to Montessori it was 'deviant' and abnormal, every deviation having been learned through negative social experiences at home or at play. Thirty years later she described her findings in more detail, noting that at three years of age, children's behavior could be classified into two types: deviant and normal. Deviants were children whose true course of development had been blocked by adults with obstacles to spontaneous activity caused by lack of freedom. If deviations were not corrected, they became fixed in character for life. In general, children with deviations fall into three categories. The first, 'strong' children were rebels who fought back against adults; sometimes had violent tantrums, were defiant, cruel, and identified as 'bad'. The second, 'weak' children had given up the fight and were submissive, quiet, and often labeled 'good' except for some who lied. The third, 'bright' children were highly imaginative, intelligent but were restless with poor control of movements and had chosen not to fight and not to give in. Montessori pointed out that members of society were so used to some of these abnormal behaviors that they applauded, even valued, some of these deviant traits. For example, the 'weak', quiet, submissive child was good and the 'bright' imaginative child who described incredible things or creatures was seen to possess valuable traits (Montessori, 1967). Montessori averred that if a child was 'scientifically treated from birth he should at three years be a model individual, but this never happens' (ibid.: 195). She was adamant and showed how all such deviations could be cured. Every 'free' child with normal intelligence became self-disciplined as he worked with Montessori materials. The behavior became 'normalized,' which Montessori claimed to be the way nature intended children to be, and it was possible to observe and record the moment the change happened. 'Normalized' children acted in a calm manner and revealed their true personality. The conversion in behavior did not happen gradually but appeared all of a sudden, after a spell of deep concentration on an activity. One by one the children became 'normalized.' In her words:

A room in which all the children move about usefully, intelligently and voluntarily, without committing any rough or rude act would seem to me a classroom very well disciplined indeed.

(Montessori, 1964: 93)

To Montessori, normalization was the birthright of every child. The true natural characteristics of normal behavior were recognized in a child who was calm, self-controlled, willing, obedient, affectionate, cheerful, and lively. Such a child enjoyed stillness and was independent of adults.

It was Montessori's aim that every child in the prepared environment would become normalized by six years. It was a theme she returned to regularly from 1907 until her death in 1952. At a course given in London in 1933, she spoke of the children in the first Children's House where each child had revealed a personality different from the one he had been previously known by, and how she had observed children's behavior change from 'deviant' to 'normalized' when they were given freedom. She described this view of childhood as one hitherto unknown in education, stressing that 'the foundations of all that we are doing consists of being able to distinguish between these two natures (deviant and normal) of the child' (Montessori Course, London, 1933). In her words:

I was made to realise that certain conditions which fulfilled psychic needs had evidently also influence upon the physical body . . . health and happiness were closely linked and the time came when doctors recommended our Casa dei Bambini as a sort of health resort.

(Montessori Course, London, 1933)

Montessori claimed that the concept of normalization was her greatest discovery. 'Normalization was repeated unfailingly in all our schools with children belonging to different social classes, races and civilizations' and 'it is the most important result of our whole work' (Montessori, 1967: 204). As a telling embellishment to her thesis about the child's ultimate place in the destiny of man, she added, 'It is the child's contribution to society' (Montessori, 1967: 201).

11 Beginning Writing, Composing, Reading, Mathematics

Montessori observed children at three and a half years to be in a sensitive period of language development when they were attracted to and responded to writing and reading materials. They used the metal insets she had designed for learning to hold and control a pencil. 'With practice,' according to Montessori, 'the child became master of the pencil as muscular mechanism is established' (Montessori, 1964: 273). She demonstrated the correct use of the metal insets and how to draw parallel lines from left to right to each child individually and then he repeated the exercise. She recorded that by filling one figure the child repeated the same movement of manipulation which would have filled ten copybook pages and so there was no need for copybooks. Each child acquired a collection or portfolio of the inset designs which 'grew more and more perfect and of which they are very proud' (ibid.: 375). Such preparation for handwriting is unique to Montessori education. These young three-year-old children were also attracted to the sandpaper letters and soon knew the sounds each represented as well as how to trace the shape of each carefully, even when blindfolded. Their hands and minds were prepared for writing through practical life and sensorial materials. By four years, children compose words using a movable alphabet. Their ability to hear a sound and to recognize a letter was the basis for a Montessori child to be able to compose a word, a unit of meaning. If a child did not recognize a sandpaper letter, he was invited to trace it with the first two fingers. His muscular memory (named the stereognostic sense by Montessori) helped the child to recall the sound associated with the letter because muscular memory is very strong at four years. In Montessori's study, the four-year-old child was helped to focus on listening for one sound within a word and to become aware of its position in words – at the beginning, at the end, or in the middle. Children began this work when she found them to be in the appropriate sensitive period to learn to begin to write and read, when they were able to hear sounds and identify letter shapes. She discovered that children generally did not experience difficulty in hearing sounds in words because their ears had been prepared earlier to distinguish and pair sounds using different sensorial materials including soundboxes and bells. The final test for each child was to identify every sandpaper letter when blindfolded, by tracing the sandpaper letter with his first two fingers and saying the sound it represented.

Sandpaper letters offered the directress an opportunity to correct speech defects. Because each child perfected the mechanism of articulate language between the ages of two years and seven years, the pronunciation by the directress of the sound each letter represented had to be meticulously accurate. Montessori stressed that errors in articulate speech should be corrected early and so eliminate the need for subsequent remedial work. Speech defects produced poor spellers while children who pronounced words correctly were more successful spellers. It was further proof of that direct connection between spoken language and written language. She introduced directresses to the practice of correcting the defects in children's language (ibid.: 323) when introducing sandpaper letters. A record of each child's progress in pronunciation was kept since it was 'a necessary part of learning graphic language' (ibid.: 280).

Children progressed to composing words then sentences using a movable alphabet, reaching the final step of being able to communicate through writing (see Part 1). Children 'exploded' into writing, which Montessori explained was the result of the absorbent mind and a sensitive period working together. She saw writing as being a cultural, socially constructed activity needing 'new mechanisms' to be established permanently in the nervous system. The movements required by a writer using a pen were 'performed by large muscles, all external, established by psycho-muscular mechanisms upon which we can directly act' (Montessori, 1964: 318). The hand needed to be prepared because children were under 'immense strain when we set them to write directly without a previous motor education of the hand' (ibid.: 288). They experienced 'all sorts of depressing feelings' because they produced 'imperfect and erroneous signs' (ibid.: 294). Each child's hand, using thumb-, forefinger-, and middle finger-grip, was already prepared using the sensorial materials, including the metal insets and sandpaper letters. Montessori argued that there was 'educational value in the idea of preparing oneself before trying and of perfecting oneself before going on' (ibid.: 260), claiming that it was a mistake for a child to continue 'to go forward boldly attempting things which he does imperfectly [because it] dulls the sensitivity of the child's spirit toward his own errors' (ibid.: 292). She was convinced that a child prepared for handwriting at four years developed character traits which helped him perfect his personality. Handwriting contained 'an educative concept, teaching the child prudence to avoid errors, dignity to make him look ahead and guide him to perfection, and humility to make him strive to do better' (ibid.: 292). At any stage when a Montessori child needed to know the genre for some social function of writing, that child was given the help he needed to complete the task. A copy of a letter written to Eduardo Tamalo in 1909 by a child of five years is shown in *The Montessori Method* (ibid.: 309). Montessori found that while four-year-olds were bursting with keenness to write, six-year-olds struggled. They were no longer interested in working with the sandpaper letters since they had passed that sensitive period. They experienced more difficulty in co-ordinating their muscles and Montessori observed six-year-olds were never able to write letters as perfectly as they could have if training had started at four years. Montessori had the children write sentences and passages she dictated, which materially translated sounds into signs. 'It was,' she wrote, 'always easy and pleasant for a child to do, analogous to the development of the spoken language which is the motor translation of audible sounds' (ibid.: 267). Dictated writing was 'a perfect parallel with spoken language since a motor action must correspond with heard speech' (ibid.: 317) and offered an opportunity to observe progress both in handwriting and in spelling.

Reading

The sensitive period for reading was from three and a half years to five years when the child began spontaneously to read word cards silently, progressing to reading phrases then sentences. Knowledge of the relationship between sounds and letters was sufficient for both beginning writing and beginning reading. Written language translated sounds into signs 'a motor translation of audible sounds' (Montessori, 1964: 266). Some four-year-old children remained in this stage of development for a length of time before learning to listen for the sounds in words they said aloud or in their inner voice. When they could do so, they exploded into reading words they had composed. In one trial, Montessori composed a word (a noun) in silence using the movable alphabet in front of the child. The child had to interpret the word then find the object. After several successful results, a card with one word was presented to the child which he had to interpret unaided and find the matching object. If the child could interpret the word and find the object, that child could read, Montessori claimed. She found four-year-old children were interested in words, a sensitive period in language development. Many boxes of words, classified in family groups were made which 'helped develop schemata in each child's mind' (ibid.: 299). Each child had to construct schemata himself so hundreds of reading cards were made by Montessori and her directresses in 1907, including the names of children, animals, flowers, insects, birds, cities, objects, colors, quantities, and fruit. The directresses wrote more and more names but they could not satisfy the children's 'insatiable desire to read' (ibid.: 300). The activity was duplicated successfully in Milan where the directress reported she had been writing cards for one and a half hours and the children were 'not satisfied yet' (ibid.: 301).

The approach to reading introduced by Montessori in 1907 did away with primers for beginner readers. Children practiced reading words mechanically before reading 'logical' text. These embryonic readers were introduced to the many beautifully illustrated books (Montessori, 1964) and directresses claimed the children read the books 'much more perfectly than children who had finished second elementary' (ibid.: 303). The four-year-old children did read the words accurately but when they could not retell the stories, it showed 'the complex thoughts of the writer had not been communicated to them and was to be one of the beautiful conquests of the future, a new source of surprise and joy' and so Montessori stopped the reading of books 'since they were not suited to our method' (ibid.: 301). She recommended non-fantasy books for children and she made an appeal to authors to write such books for young children as no published material was available to suit her beginner readers. A number of extra materials were designed for learning to read English, a non-phonetic language, before children could continue with subsequent activities. She discovered that the sensitive period for beginning to write and read spontaneously was at four years. This was possible because the child possessed an absorbent mind and was given specially designed didactic materials which allowed him to teach himself (ibid.: 173). The discovery showed that 'the mind of the child is capable of acquiring culture at an incredibly early age, through own unaided activity' (Montessori, 1963: 71). In the early 1900s, children aged four years were considered to be 'too young for school to be taught ... and teaching was identified with education' (Montessori, 1967: 25). Montessori had shown these prejudices to be wrong because young children with absorbent minds learned spontaneously when given the correct conditions for learning and didactic materials. By the sixth year the absorbent mind began to fade and there was 'psychologically, a decided change in personality' (Montessori, 1961: 4), as he moved into the second plane of development. Montessori pointed out that at each stage of development 'we have before us a different child who presents characteristics different from those he exhibited during the preceding years' (Montessori, 1973: 1).

Several other discoveries were made and Montessori recorded them in detail. Writing compositions and reading with comprehension she discovered developed together and she explained how she observed four children who 'had arrived spontaneously at the art of composition just as they had spontaneously written their first word' (Montessori, 1964: 305). The children wrote and read, communicating with each other silently because 'graphic language does not need spoken words' (ibid.). Another silent reading experiment using commands was devised by Montessori. Long sentences were written on cards describing actions which the children acted out exactly. They read these cards 'with intensity of attention amid the most complex silence' (ibid.: 306). Unexpectedly, the command card game produced spontaneous discipline 'like some magic force, the magic of graphic language, the greatest conquest of civilization' (ibid.: 307). Command cards were the answer to the key problem of having children read aloud in schools in order to show they understood what they read. When Montessori discovered that 'children could read Gothic script on a calendar ... there remained nothing to do but the presentation of a book' (ibid.: 301). By reading silently, the child was able to attend to thinking about meaning and did not need to attend to the pronunciation of the words. Reading in Montessori education was a silent activity from the very start. At no time were children asked to read aloud a passage sight unseen. They read orally only when they chose to do so and after they had an opportunity to practice. To Montessori, oral reading was extremely complex because it combined reading with comprehension and oral expression, these two processes being connected to articulate language and written language in a complex, covert manner. Montessori materials led children to read spontaneously with little intervention by the directress. The length of time for the process depended on each child's intelligence and interest in learning to read along with the ability of the directress who intervened at the exact psychological moment. Children did not follow the program in a linear fashion but took leaps forward using the materials they chose. The directress followed each child's path respecting the inner work of each child by providing time to master the complex processes of learning to read in his own way. Montessori concluded that learning to read was a long complex journey.

Mathematics

New materials were designed for mathematic activities to consolidate the concept of number to ten. There were long rods, the spindle box, counters, and cards to consolidate the values zero to ten and colored bead bars for simple addition and subtraction to ten. Golden bead material allowed children of four to six years to understand the processes of addition, subtraction, multiplication, and division to 9,999 by knowing numbers to nine and then understanding hierarchies. New materials were continually trialed as Montessori continued her research experiments into child development following children's interests.

12 Fantasy, Imagination, and Creativity

To Montessori, the experiences working with all the different sensorial materials helped the child's mind to develop normally, but for the child who did not work with materials she noted, 'the mind that should build itself up through experiences of movement, flees to fantasy' (Montessori, 1978: 164). She observed such children were never still, their movements disordered and without purpose yet the adult 'admires and encourages their fancies, interpreting them as imagination' (ibid.). For her, 'fantasy involved unreal mental images and allowed the mind to wander rather than become ordered' (Montessori, 1969: 189) and the child's mind 'escapes and loves to wander in the fascinating worlds of unreality . . . a tendency characteristic of savage peoples' (ibid.: 255) who were attracted to the supernatural and the unreal. Any form of this kind of imagination was 'universally recognised as creative imagination by which children attribute desirable characteristics to objects which do not possess them' (Montessori, 1967: 256). Adults perpetuated 'the savage state' by writing and reading stories for young children in which animals talked or they had children pretend they were playing the piano, a violin, or a drum. Montessori pointed out that some of Froebel's games are 'based on similar beliefs' and gave many examples. Among these, a wooden block is given to a child with the words 'This is a horse'. Bricks are arranged in a certain order and the child told 'This is a stable: now let us put the horse in the stable' (Montessori, 1969: 258). The bricks were then rearranged to represent something else. These children did not imagine spontaneously but had to see what the teacher suggested (ibid.). Adults supposed they were developing children's minds by 'making them accept fantastic things as realities'; for example, Santa Claus and the tooth fairy. These were the fruits of our imagination and though some children believed them to be true, their 'credulity is a characteristic of immature minds' (ibid.: 259). There was to be no place at all for fantasy in the three-to-six-year Montessori environment. With Montessori materials children developed spontaneously and their minds became ordered, contributing to good mental health. Fantasy did not help the child gain a realistic view of his environment and hindered his perception and understanding of the world. Montessori's first concern was always the mental health of children and she considered such practices could confuse a young child's mind. Once when visiting an orphanage, some teachers told Montessori that the children performed the practical life exercises 'which you describe.'

These children 'with expressionless faces, were laying the table for a dolls' meal.' The teachers 'evidently thought that there was no difference between laying a table in play and laying a table for an actual meal: for them imaginary life and real life were the same' (ibid.: 265). In 1939, she wrote about fantasy and that it must not be confused with imagination. She called the early years 'the blessed age of play' (Montessori, 1967: 168) but she observed that 'active children left to themselves [with no materials] have rarely a good result because it does not aid development ... there was no grace, no natural impulse towards perfection.' The active child 'needed help to develop the formation of his person, his personality was complex' (Montessori, 1969: 116, 118). She observed many parents and teachers continued to encourage children to respond to suggestion and to develop credulity and emphasized that 'education should not develop the savage state, nor keep the child therein but should help each child to overcome it' and 'should not be directed to credulity' (ibid.: 255, 260). To her, imagination was to be used for 'real' things and as an example she wrote of her observations. A three-year-old looked at a globe and declared now he understood what his uncle meant when he said he had been round the world three times. He had grasped that the globe was a model. She encouraged children to imagine real things in their minds and she wondered why adults told young children fairy stories because if they could imagine fairies and fairyland 'it was not difficult for children to imagine America' (Montessori, 1967: 176, 177).

Imagination

Imagination was important because it was 'a higher mental function, and helped children develop mentally' (Montessori, 1967: 186). For Montessori, there were two types of imagination: first, 'creative imagination of art which was extrapolated from the senses' and second, 'creative imagination in science which was derived from truth' (Montessori, 1967: 186) which were not to be confused with fantasy. Imagination was described by Montessori as a tool, 'a great gift' (Montessori, 1967: 177). It helped each child understand any topic based on reality and now it would be used to imagine everything in the cosmos. It had a sensory base as well as a solid foundation with sensorial materials (ibid.: 168) invaluable for children learning anything that was not within sight. In her copious writings, Montessori gave many examples of children revealing their powers of imagination. One example was when she introduced a globe, 'the world,' for the first time. She wrote about 'the effect of presenting the whole world at once' and when a three-year-old child showed 'he was able to form the idea that the globe represented the world,' she concluded that it was possible 'by virtue of an intangible power of his mind, an imaginative power' (ibid.: 176). Creative imagination of science was to be used for 'real' things and used constructively in young children's learning because it assisted him to picture in his mind what could not be seen. The prepared environment contained carefully designed materials to order each child's mind. Creative imagination in science was 'a tool to discover truth' (Montessori, 1967: 161). The solid foundation of children's sensory experiences within the prepared environment was the basis for all future learning.

Creative imagination of art was defined as 'the extrapolation of the senses' (ibid.: 189). Montessori had devised sensorial material precisely to aid and educate the senses 'to awaken creativity [which was] firmly allied to reality' (Montessori, 1969: 248). The great artist she defined as 'able to recognise the beautiful in detail ... possesses the absolute sense of the beautiful and readily perceives any disproportion of form' (ibid.: 338, 339). The sensorial materials aided the development of creativity and in turn 'creation of art is constructed with materials' (ibid.: 245). Montessori described the various materials for creativity in 1909 in *The Montessori Method*. In the first Children's Houses, children drew with chalks, crayons, and colored pencils, painted with water colors and worked with clay. Professor Randone's exercises for pottery to make vases and bricks were incorporated (Montessori, 1964: 162). The bricks were used to build low walls round the garden plots. Attempts were made by some children to build small houses. From this, children learned to appreciate objects and constructions in their environment (ibid.: 162, 166). Twenty years later Montessori wrote about the new 'free' drawing in 'modern schools of advanced ideas' but children in Montessori schools 'do not produce of their own accord ... those dreadful drawings which are displayed and lauded ... nor those strange daubs where the child has to explain what he intends to represent by his incomprehensible attempt' (Montessori, 1967: 284, 285). She explained that Montessori children learned indirectly about form and color and how their drawings and paintings were clear and harmonious. Dr. Revesz, a psychologist dedicated especially to art, commented, 'the Montessori school does not repress free drawing ... it makes children find the greatest pleasure in free drawing along with the free development of their sense of colour and form' (Montessori, 1969: 288). Children 'compose artistic representations by cutting out coloured paper like those of Oswald, the famous Viennese physicist' (Montessori, 1967: 285). The editor of *Communications* (Carr, 1969: 9) noted that Montessori 'began guiding children to the artistic skills and artistic appreciation in 1912.' She declared that 'there can be no graduated exercises in drawing (or painting) leading up to an artistic creation ... children can be prepared indirectly.' The artist 'perfects himself by refining powers of observation' by working with sensorial materials. Creation itself is constructed with materials (Montessori, 1969: 251, 254).

13 Abstract Thought and Curriculum

During childhood the mind used 'both imagination and abstract thought as useful tools to discover the truth' (ibid.: 161). About seven years of age, he found 'a need for abstraction and intellectual activity' (Montessori, 1961: 6) and 'the burgeoning of imagination that needed to be built and organized' (Montessori, 1973: 38). Montessori education between six and twelve years called for great reforms. The content of curriculum was not to be what adults thought it ought to be but based on the children's interests and Montessori discovered that they were interested in everything, therefore a wider and more varied selection of books and materials was required. Learning experiences at every stage of development were to promote the development of the children. They had different needs and thought differently at each stage of development. What each child learned depended on experiences during the previous stage.

The idea of cosmic education began in 1912 when Montessori extended her approach for children aged six to twelve years, introducing a wider curriculum and a full description of her materials was published in 1916 in *The Advanced Montessori Method Vol. 2* which developed into cosmic education. Introducing young children to the universe meant 'all the factors of culture could be introduced but not in a syllabus to be imposed on him, nor with the exactitude of detail but in broadcasting the maximum number of seeds of interest' (Montessori, 1963: 5). At six years 'if the idea of the universe be presented to the child in the right way, it will do more than arouse interest, it will create in him admiration and wonder.' The child's mind 'will no longer wander, but become fixed and can work' (Montessori, 1961: 9). Imagination 'could help young children understand ideas and concepts bringing them to a level of abstraction' (Montessori, 1973: 38) and Montessori maintained that it was the correct use of imagination based on reality which helped each child to understand any topic.

The method was relating five 'Great Stories' based on scientific evidence, anthropology, and history which were to be continually updated as new information was found. The stories comprised of The Creation of the Universe (scientific with all religious views studied), The Coming of Life, The Coming of Human Beings, The Story of Communications and Signs, and The Story of Numbers. The five stories were heard by children once every year from the age of six to twelve years. Imagination had to be roused and the best way to do that 'was to present the whole with grandeur and mystery' (Montessori, 1973: 37). For the development of the mind a study outline presented itself to Montessori. By introducing the cosmos, children were required to use their imaginations. Now she could bring 'the whole' to the child 'by means of the presentation of detail' (ibid.: 39) through the classification of all living beings which would help memory and order the mind. Montessori found young children displayed a keen interest when they were introduced to cosmic education because 'a young child is interested in everything if put in an acceptable manner, suited to the child's psychology' (Montessori, 1961: 28).

In 1935, at a conference in London, Montessori spoke of 'cosmic' education including cultural studies in history, geography, botany, zoology, science, art, and music. Her materials were to help the mind which 'bases itself on the imagination' at the abstract level and 'has need of support. It needs to be built and organized. Only then can the mind attain a higher level ... penetrating the infinite' (Montessori, 1973: 38). Cosmic education 'provides answers to children's questions about their world and Man's place in it' (Montessori, 1961: 2): the cosmic plan. If a child studied a part of anything, he knew it to be part of the whole universe because he grew to understand that everything in the world was interrelated.

Montessori averred that 'we enlarge the mind' (Montessori Course, London, 1946) when the curriculum is decided by the interests of children. Introducing young children to the universe meant 'all the factors of culture could be introduced but not as a syllabus to be imposed on him, nor with the exactitude of detail but in broadcasting the maximum number of seeds of interest' (Montessori, 1961: 5). Montessori planned to bring the world into the classroom by introducing children six years to twelve years to history 'giving living documented truth' using 'prepared moving film' (Montessori, 1974: 199). This idea was 'beyond resources' so it was decided 'different school books to show complete pictures of reality and factual situations' were needed to be written and published (ibid.). Children could be stimulated by 'attractive literary and pictorial material, all correlated to a central idea of greatly ennobling inspiration' (Montessori, 1963: 1). Geography was to be introduced through travel stories and natural science through true stories about insects and other creatures (ibid.: 200). The new proposal was decided because there was 'a plan to which the whole universe is subject ... a universal plan' and the child was part of it (Montessori, 1969: 121). The cosmic plan could be presented to the child as a thrilling tale of the earth we live in, the child being 'led through thrilling epochs of world history' (Montessori, 1974: 2, 3). All of this was possible because the child possessed a natural gift – imagination.

14 The Directress

The role of the directress evolved over a period of forty years of experimentation and is complex. Understanding development was a key feature of Montessori education and Montessori had conducted a scientific study of each child to explain child development within the Children's House between the age of three years and six years over a two-year period. The directress understood child development and her fundamental task was to assist each child's natural development. Montessori was convinced that to be able to help life 'we must be able to understand the laws that govern it. We need an education based on the care of the living' (Montessori, 1967: 12). The directress was to put Montessori principles into practice, all of which were based on the natural tendencies of children which Montessori had observed in 1907. The fundamental function of the directress in the Montessori environment was to have 'techniques analogous to those of a valet; they are to serve, and to serve well: to serve the spirit' (ibid.: 281). In order to serve the spirit she was required to remain patient, calm, dignified, tolerant, self-controlled, non-judgmental, and humble, all the while learning from the child. She catered for the spiritual needs of the children by maintaining a classroom climate where children could be happy, confident, and loving. She prepared herself spiritually and instead of being proud and claiming to be infallible 'she assumes the vesture of humility' (Montessori, 1969: 100), realizing children taught themselves and recognizing that she was successful when 'free children are working as though I do not exist' (Montessori, 1967: 283). She understood that the spirit of the child could be nurtured by allowing him to explore and experiment with the materials, making discoveries through trial and error and being a successful learner. She had no ambitions for herself, her spiritual happiness deriving from helping each student reach his potential (Montessori, 1963: 89).

As classroom custodian yet 'unobtrusive part of the environment' (Montessori, 1975: 39), each directress prepared and maintained the environment, with all materials meticulously in order, in beautiful, shining, perfect condition. There, active, exuberant learners, three to six years old, were to experience physical, psychological, and spiritual freedom. She was to help the development of the whole child to enable each child develop his personality by keeping in mind the basic principle of Montessori education which was 'the liberty of the pupils in their spontaneous manifestations' (Montessori, 1964: 80). The beautiful appearance of the directress was the first step in gaining a child's confidence and respect, and it was desirable that she also possess excellent speech standards, grace in her movements, unfailing courtesy, and a sensitive, sympathetic nature. Twenty years later these attributes were substantially unchanged: the directress should be 'attractive, preferably young and beautiful, charmingly dressed, scented with cleanliness, happy and graciously dignified' (Montessori, 1961: 87), all of which helped nurture the spirit of the child.

As 'the facilitator of the child's learning' she acted as the *trait d'union* between the materials and the child (Montessori 1975: 39). Because she understood child development she judged the appropriate time to introduce a new piece of material to a child and she knew through her teacher preparation how to introduce the material by exact demonstration to each child. The principle which brought success to the directress was this: 'as soon as concentration has begun, act as if the child does not exist' (Montessori, 1961: 87). The advice to directresses in 1909 was 'our duty to the child was to give a ray of light and go on our way' (Montessori, 1964: 115). To be successful using the materials was extremely important to the child because 'the material is the base from which the spirit soars' and 'the staircase (scaffolding) for the student to ascend' (Montessori, 1969: 64) to a higher plane of development. She supported each child 'by standing behind him and allowing him to go forward as far as he can,' which was very different to the general teaching method of 'standing in front of the child and preventing him from going further than the limits imposed upon him by the teacher' (Montessori, 1961: 65) who followed a syllabus.

As 'caretaker' of the children, she provided the stress-free environment to nurture each child's development and had faith that she would witness and help each child's general development (Montessori, 1967: 252) because of her knowledge of the absorbent mind and sensitive periods. Further observations by Montessori revealed that 'nature lays down a plan for construction both of personality and social life' (ibid.: 133). Social and emotional development evolve together and are helped by the social conditions provided by the directress.

As 'scientist and skilled observer' she would witness 'children working with materials in silent fascination' (Montessori, 1967: 252). She must be 'interested in the development of life' and 'be a lover' of nature (Montessori, 1964: 104). She was to prepare herself spiritually through self-analysis, by eradicating obstacles from the environment which impeded children's development and by being willing to accept guidance and be taught by the children and others (Montessori, 1978: 149). As an objective observer she was to give a large proportion of her life to her work as she discovered cures for any deviations in the behavior of children in her care. She would carefully observe children making discoveries for themselves and be totally open-minded, non-prejudicial, inquiring, and humble (Montessori, 1969: 131).

By 1916, Montessori had a list of important factors to be studied in the observation of each child. In a study to be conducted over a period of time, the materials were to be introduced in order, so individual differences, development of abstraction, stages of intellectual development, and the acquisition of self-discipline could be recorded objectively. The constant aim was to help each child become normalized. This six-point scientific instrument could identify differences between students which could be attributed to either nature or nurture (ibid.: 87–9). Thirty years later, when questioned about how to observe children, Montessori responded:

> When I am in the midst of children I do not think of myself as a scientist, a theoretician. When I am with children I am a nobody . . . this enables me to see things one would miss if one was a somebody, little things, simple but very precious truths.
>
> (Montessori, 1972: 101)

As 'a researcher' there were important factors to be observed in the study of each individual child over a period of time. Notes were made of the materials selected and how long he worked with them, individual differences, development of abstraction, stages of intellectual development and acquisition of self-discipline, normalization, and independence were recorded objectively. Character development was observed and attributed to nature or nurture (Montessori, 1969: 87–9). The directress knew where each child 'was' developmentally (Montessori, 1978: 150). Every individualized three-period lesson gave her the opportunity to be a researcher. She received immediate feedback as to whether the child had understood the lesson or not, by observing how the child worked and explored using the materials.

To help children gain independence, the directress relinquished power by not forcing her will on children by selecting everything they did all day. She understood and helped each child develop his will by empowering him to choose his own experiences. To make a decision was an act of will, 'a conscious act ... an interior labour ... an exercise of will power' (Montessori, 1969: 140, 141). Children chose their own activities and were encouraged to think and act for themselves (Montessori, 1967: 257). Each child followed his own agenda as there was no set curriculum or timetable to follow and it was each child who knew what he needed to help his development, 'to construct himself' (ibid.: 223). And he was better able to choose the material to match that need. Montessori saw that by empowering children in this manner, all reached a higher educational level. The directress respected the child, did not interrupt his concentration by praising him nor did she correct mistakes or punish him. Observations showed that 'prizes and punishments offended freedom of the spirit' and obstructed the spontaneity of children's learning. Corrections had 'a lowering effect on children and as a result they lose interest, while scolding humiliates, insults and offends' (ibid.: 145). Such actions she found lowered the 'general quality of social life' (ibid.: 240) especially the relationship between the directress and children. There was always to be respect and trust between directress and student (Montessori, 1964: 13) along with relationships between student and student (Montessori, 1961: 89). Instead of correcting, notes were taken and individual lessons planned to be given privately to help overcome learning problems. The directress had to possess 'great respect for the interior construction of personality' done by the child as it was of 'greatest importance and must be done in practice'

(Montessori, 1973: 111–13). In a Montessori environment, free children co-operated and helped each other. They admired those who
did better than they did. These were natural developments in children when 'rivalry, emulation and ambition were not encouraged'
(Montessori, 1967: 242). As a result of 'reciprocal helpfulness,' the
group 'gets cemented by affection' (ibid.: 206). The change to a society through cohesion occurred when a child 'puts the group first'
(ibid.: 213).

Social relationships within a Montessori environment underwent
radical change in 1907. While the directress's basic role was to
empower each child by allowing him to choose his own activities
within the prepared environment, she was to treat each child with
the respect due to a fellow human being with his own social rights
and promote the 'keys of life' which were the simple pleasures of
joy and happiness derived from harmonious and pleasurable experiences within the prepared environment. As the directress worked
with each child individually, so they grew to know, trust, and respect
each other (Montessori, 1964: 12, 13). There was respect and trust
fostered between children and directress partly because of the three-
period lessons which presented opportunities for her to work with
each child individually every day. It was not a laissez-faire environment or a cavalier abandonment of standards leading inevitably to
chaos, aggression, and confusion. The clearly defined boundaries
inculcated a keen awareness of responsibility and even those as young
as three years swiftly realized their obligations to others within the
group. Every child learned to co-operate and to work and live together
in harmony. The role of the 'new' Montessori directress from 1907
demanded a dramatic change from the strict, domineering dispenser
of punishments of the past. She had to be interested in the development of life, worship life and respect the development of the child
(ibid.: 104).

15 Multi-age Grouping

Significant observations were made by Montessori over a number of
years about the advantages of multi-age grouping of children. Tasks

were matched to each child's stage of development and so a fast developer was extended while still working alongside his peers. There was no envy among them because there was no competition for marks and prizes and as a result they admired those who did better than they did. These were natural developments in children when 'rivalry, emulation and ambition were not encouraged' (ibid.: 242). A slow developer never felt he could not achieve because his task matched his needs. Montessori observed that 'children of different ages help one another' (ibid.: 206) and sometimes 'there may be things a teacher cannot convey to the child of three but a child of five can do it with utmost ease.' There were opportunities for peer/cross-age tutoring which were enjoyable and rewarding experiences for children. Vertical grouping led to group solidarity with a responsibility toward each other. Montessori affirmed that human evolution 'had advanced when society began to help the weak instead of oppressing and despising them' (ibid.: 210). The change from a class to a society through social cohesion occurred when 'a child did not put himself first but rather the group first' (Montessori. 1967: 213). All social experiences within Montessori environments were extremely important for daily living because students 'lived' in an active community. They lived in harmony without any inferiority complexes. It became habitual for them to be polite and respectful, to wait one's turn, and to solve social problems themselves during every day of school life (ibid.: 227). Multi-age grouping allowed for daily lessons about society at its best. The society of mixed-age children 'added charm to social life because of the numbers of different types (of personalities) one meets' (ibid.: 226). All were equal, and the mutual respect brought harmony and cohesion leading to affection and joy in each other's company. Social problems were resolved by the children themselves. They were free to discipline each other. This occurred if a child did not respect another child's space or when a child interrupted another child at work. Peer intervention was effective because of the feeling of equality and understanding, while teacher intervention was not taken in the same light. It is axiomatic that well-adjusted children live harmoniously together, and in Montessori's words, normalized children unaided 'can construct an orderly society within the classroom and solve their problems peacefully' (ibid.: 258). Vertical groupings in three-year spans were found in all Montessori environments for children in elementary and high-school years. Segregation by age is, according to Montessori, 'a fundamental mistake which breeds a host of evils' (ibid.: 205). Central to Montessori education was the need to follow children's interests. She observed 'that mentally, small children are able to do things far above expected capacity' (Montessori, 1966: 108) so more and more materials were introduced into their environment and she perceived how young children accepted everything if 'put in an acceptable manner, suited to the child's psychology' (Montessori, 1961: 28). For children three to six years she introduced materials for music, movement, history, geography, botany, science, and art which she designed and trialed. It was her goal that parents and teachers should fully understand child development and how children learn so that they could assist each child's natural development. Galloway (1976) noted that Montessori found support in Plato, Comenius, Rousseau, Pestalozzi, Owen, and Spencer, all 'naturalistic' educators who were concerned with the child's natural stages of human growth and development. What Montessori proposed was similar in some respects to the work of these naturalistic educators. In ensuing decades on different continents, she confirmed in her own mind that development occurred following the same time frame for every child.

While Montessori's experiments in the first Children's Houses in 1907–08 had convinced her beyond doubt that education needed a drastic overhaul, thirty years later she was still bemoaning the indisputable fact that this supremely important field of human endeavor was loathe to embrace change. Observe her views in 1939:

> The method and theory of education is quite old and not very willing to change. Education needs to change at all levels. It must be rearing students for a better life, decreasing deviations and crime.
>
> (Montessori, 1967: 11)

Seventy years on, her words still ring true.

Part 3

The Reception and Influence of Montessori's Work

Around the world, massive interest was aroused in the first decade of the twentieth century by reports of educational innovations coming out of Rome. Many, on all continents, were captivated by the new methods, and when children's spectacular successes in the first Children's Houses were reported in the London *Times*, foreign newspapers and American magazines, educators everywhere felt they had to travel to Rome to meet Montessori and visit the Children's Houses. Reports were mixed from the very start, with supporters and critics around the world.

16 Europe

Among the very first nations to manifest interest was Switzerland, largely through the endeavors of Teresina Bontempi (1883–1968) and the University of Geneva. Bontempi had closely followed Montessori's first course in 1909, and within two years, established a number of Children's Houses in Switzerland. The University of Geneva, already with an international reputation at the cutting edge of contemporary educational practices, invited Montessori to demonstrate her method in person with a group of young children (three to six years) at its Jean-Jacques Rousseau Institute, in the presence of three of its teaching staff – Professors Pierre Bovet (1878–1965), Edouard Claparède (1873–1940), and Adolphe Ferrière (1879–1960). At that demonstration, Jean Piaget (1896–1980) first came in contact with Montessori's educational innovations (Association Montessori Suisse www.montessori-ams.ch/). He was deeply impressed and it was the start of his distinguished career in education. Out of his own detailed observations emerged his ideas of cognitive development. It is worth noting here that Piaget took part in the Second International Montessori Congress in Nice (1931) and in the Fourth in Rome (1934) where he presented a paper entitled 'On the development of the geometric thought of the child.' Pierre Bovet also took part in that Congress. In 1932, Montessori visited Switzerland, including in her lecture tour Geneva, Lausanne, Berne, Zürich, and Bellinzone. Her book *Education and Peace* appeared in Geneva at that very time, along with the birth of the Swiss Montessori Society with Piaget as its first president and Elisabeth Rotten, the celebrated pacifist, first vice-president. Rotten became the vice-president of AMI in 1939 (Association Montessori Suisse www.montessori-ams.ch/). Montessori herself noted in 1909 that all Swiss kindergartens were to become Montessori environments in 1910, and by 1911 Montessori education was introduced into Swiss schools (Müller and Schneider, 2002).

As in many other countries, it was women who introduced the Montessori system into Denmark, the first Dane being Marie Helms in 1911 with 'a charming and comprehensive article on Montessori's Kindergartens in Rome' (Nasgaard, 1929: 61). Thora Constantin-Hansen read this article and began to convert two of the classes in the school for crippled children, 8–10 years of age, into Montessori classes. According to Constantin-Hansen, the invalid children became 'quieter and better balanced, and sank themselves in their work.' She proposed the whole school of one hundred children be converted to Montessori but met opposition from the Committee of the Crippled Children's Home, so Montessori's practices could not be trialed there. In 1917, she helped to found the Montessori Society in Denmark and with two colleagues the following year opened the Danish Montessori Society's School at Frederikssund in a quiet, remote villa looking out over the Roskilde Fjord. There 'the most radical educational reforms in Denmark were carried out.' Soon she began to help establish other Montessori classes throughout Denmark. There were other champions of the Montessori movement mentioned in this article. Sofie Rifbjerg who attended the training course in London in 1919 later 'converted her own class for feeble-minded children into a Montessori class.' Elna Marstrand also 'greatly helped the work in Denmark' as did Fru V. Sveistrup who in 1928 converted her kindergarten into a Montessori school. Schools opened in Copenhagen and other major towns, and keen interest was shown in the Fifth International Congress to be held in Denmark in 1929 (ibid.: 66). Erik Erikson, another devoted supporter of Montessori education in Denmark, was later to participate with distinction in another arena.

Criticism of Montessori's work began as early as 1909 after the publication of *Il Metodo* when psychologists challenged her spectacular results in reading and writing with young children aged four years. Montessori responded tartly that such critics appeared to question 'if the mental life of the child ought not to be immolated in favour of useless results because a little later on, a child over six years can learn to read and write' (Montessori, 1975: 22). In Vienna in 1914, Charlotte Bühler, an authoritative exponent of experimental psychology, reached the conclusion that the mental faculties of children under five years of age were 'impermeable to any form of culture.' For Montessori, such an assertion in the name of science 'was like a kind of tombstone placed over our experience' (ibid.), the failure of official education to attain similar results an indictment of their methods. As she put it later, the 'miracle' of children learning to read spontaneously at four years was 'relegated to oblivion,' thereby obliging her 'to deal with the task of investigating the secrets of child psychology' (ibid: 23). In 1909, she was virtually alone among psychologists with little or no support for her work since they were 'concerned not in inner patterns or powers of the mind but concentrated on external activities concerned in developing children' (Montessori, 1966: 108). By 1938, however, she was able to note that psychologists 'were starting to concentrate on the development of the very young from the earliest stage,' among them being the German Charlotte Bühler (Montessori, 1967: 4).

From 1914, Berlin became the heartland of Montessori education in Europe as a consequence of the work of Hilde Hecker, Elsa Ochs, and Elizabeth Achwartz, all of whom had attended Montessori's second international course in Rome in that year. They were later supported by the educator Clara Grunwald. Both Ochs and Grunwald were ardent supporters of Montessori education and joined the Association of Resolute Schools Reformers in Berlin where the principles of Montessori Method were discussed. In 1919, Grunwald established the German Montessori Committee, which swiftly set up Children's Houses for children of working-class families. Three years later the Society of Friends and Sponsors of the Montessori Movement were also established in Germany. In 1925, the two bodies merged to form the German Montessori Society with Grunwald as its head. Montessori herself boosted the fledgling movement in Germany with visits in 1922, 1925, 1926, and 1927. But the shortage of funds in post-World War One Germany, still struggling from crippling debt, along with a conservative reluctance to move too far from accepted Froebelian principles and a dearth of trained Montessori teachers, militated against wider acceptance. By 1923, the demand for Montessori education outstripped the capacity of the limited number of teachers to satisfy the need and Elsa and Clara ran the first teacher-training course in Germany. By 1927, differences between Montessori and Grunwald over the latter's organizing of her own training workshop flared up and a faction formed within the Berlin group. Montessori refused to sign the certificates to those who had attended Grunwald's training courses. When another body, the German Association of Montessori Education, formed in 1929, Montessori took over the presidency and Grunwald was denied membership. It is of enormous historical interest to know that the honorary committee included Konrad Adenauer, then Lord Mayor of Cologne and later celebrated figure on the post-World War Two international stage. It was that very year, 1929, that Montessori established the Association Montessori Internationale (AMI) with headquarters in Berlin. When the Nazis came to power in 1933, all schools run by the national body headed by Montessori in Berlin, Breslau, Guben, Jena, Leipzig, Cologne, Aachen, and Freiberg were closed along with others run by Grunwald and private Children's Houses. It was at a time when the persecution of Jews and Jewish sympathizers was beginning in earnest. Elsa Ochs migrated to the United States, while Clara Grunwald, a Jew and a socialist, was forbidden the right to teach at all. She continued to do so and in 1941 was sentenced and sent to a re-training farm. In 1943, Grunwald and the children in her care were deported to Auschwitz where Grunwald died (Müller and Schneider, 2002: 37).

Of special interest in the German connection with Montessori is the unique contribution of the firm of P. Johannes Müller, which in 1913 translated Montessori's *Il Metodo* into German. It was an instant best seller. In subsequent years, the firm held 'exclusive manufacturing and sales rights for Maria Montessori's teaching materials in Germany, granted by Montessori herself' (ibid.: 41). The ready availability of quality materials was a significant part in the success of the movement and the company played an active role at the second International Montessori Conference held in Nice in 1932, particularly with regard to the display of new materials for mathematics and language along with building and classroom designs. By 1936, the Montessori Movement in Germany was 'crushed' (ibid.: 53). All Montessori schools in German-occupied countries were closed. At the end of World War Two, Grete Aurin tried to revive Montessori education in Soviet-occupied East Berlin in 1946 before she fled to West Berlin, while Irene Dietrich was able to open a Montessori class in the British sector of Berlin in 1947, and, soon after, Montessori education was practiced in secondary schools (ibid.: 139). Montessorian Hélène Helming first published her *Montessori Pädagogik. Ein moderner Bildungsweg in konkreter Darstellung*, in 1958. It is currently in its seventeenth edition. Another worthy of mention is Dr. Theodor Hellbrügge, a Munich pediatrician who set up a diagnostic treatment center for children with multiple disabilities. Against huge opposition, he managed to establish the first school class which integrated disabled children with normal children in 1970. There he achieved remarkable results and other classrooms soon followed. Hellbrügge's description of his new school mirrors the very words of his mentor seven decades earlier:

> A school without grades, where the misery of having to repeat a year does not exist, where they are not forced to cope with an impossible homework load, is perfectly possible and does not lead to even the slightest lowering of school achievements, indeed the children's achievements are higher when they have free choice.
>
> (Müller and Schneider, 2002: 129)

Hellbrügge was firmly of the opinion that the educational principles he incorporated into his school were identical to those used in Montessori's Children's Houses – the same practices, same materials, same individualized methodologies – and moreover, the smooth transition from his nursery school to his newly opened primary school were totally in line with current pediatric thinking in the 1970s. He wrote in 1977: 'A child's development is never intermittent or disjointed. Each developmental stage always builds on the one before it' (ibid.: 130). The words are a ringing endorsement of that earlier pediatrician – Montessori herself.

There was a renewed interest in the place of the church in Montessori education. It was Anna Maccheroni who had established a children's chapel, or 'Atrium,' in Barcelona in 1916 for children three to six years. In 1954, Sofia Cavalletti, Hebrew scholar and biblical scholar, was approached to introduce Scripture lessons for young children in Rome. With the assistance of Gianna Gobbi, who had worked with Montessori in 1951, they established The Catechesis of the Good Shepherd (Lillig, 1998). Both women traveled widely and were invited to the US in the mid-1980s. Interest has spread worldwide.

By the middle of the twentieth century, a number of theories of development appeared. Among these were the theories of development proposed by students of Montessori including Erik Erikson, one of her first students, who migrated to the US and worked on his theory of developmental progression of personality. Lawrence Kohlberg also in the US worked on a theory of moral development, while Jean Piaget in Switzerland studied cognitive development. A trained observer, Piaget believed children passed through stages of development according to their age and during the first period children showed their intelligence through activity with concrete materials which could be observed easily. His theories became popular in the 1960s when his writings were published in English. Much of his theory matched Montessori, even the language he used to describe his findings being similar. However, Montessori and Piaget had parted at least twenty years before the publication of his work when she discovered his research was done using his own three children on a one-to-one basis and not within a classroom setting. Another point she strongly disagreed with was his method of including long, involved questions. Montessori believed in the art of few words, expecting the children to ask questions. It was Margaret Donaldson, a psychologist who worked with Piaget in Switzerland, who was able to show why the findings of his experiments were not reliable. She found the spoken questions confused many children (Donaldson, 1978). Donaldson's conclusion substantially supported Montessori. It is an interesting comment on current teacher-training programs around the world that the names Erikson, Kohlberg, and Piaget and their theories of development are well known to education students, while Montessori is not. What is important, however, is that psychologists have continued their research into the best ways of helping child development. In an interview in *Communications*, Dr. Lee Salk remarked in 1975:

> I am very impressed with Montessori education especially the understanding and sensitivity directresses have for the developmental stages of children and how they create an educational environment. It is structured yet gives children a sense of freedom which is good for ego development. But Montessori is misunderstood and educators steal her ideas and use the equipment in their own way.
>
> (Salk, 1975: 16)

Individuals and organizations have promoted Montessori education in Europe from 1909. Catholic nuns have been responsible for introducing Montessori education to many remote places in distant lands as well as teacher training. In 1920, Montessori spoke of her fundamental ideas of secondary education at the University of Amsterdam, and by 1930, the first Lyceum (grammar school) had opened. In 2000, the Montessori College Oost, designed by Herman Hertzberger, a former Montessori pupil, 'is the first building in the world to have been specially built as a Montessori secondary school' (Müller and Schneider, 2002: 139). The 1,600 multi-national students enrolled are aged twelve to eighteen years. In the Netherlands and Belgium, students have the option of attending a state school or a Montessori school because Montessori education is officially recognized by their Departments of Education. The Association Montessori Internationale (AMI) has continued to show the flag since its birth in 1929 with headquarters in Amsterdam since 1936. Mario Montessori, his son Mario, and daughter Renilde have continued a close association with AMI and teacher training.

At Bergamo, Italy, AMI teacher training continues. Longstanding Montessori supporter, Camillo Grazzini, who assisted Mario

Montessori for many years with teacher training, was a founding member of the International Centre for Montessori Studies Foundation at Bergamo, Italy, in 1961. As a member of the Pedagogical/Material Committee, historian, researcher, and lecturer he continued to make a fine contribution to Montessori education as AMI director of teacher training at Bergamo from 1982 until he died in 2004. Dr. Silvana Montanaro, director of training (birth to three years) and author of the important text *Understanding the Human Being – The Importance of the First Three Years* was a keynote speaker at the International Montessori Congress in Sydney, 2005.

17 United States of America

Montessori education made a huge impact in the United States even before Dr. Montessori visited in 1913. Anne E. George visited San Lorenzo in the summer of 1909, having heard from a friend about the Children's Houses in Rome and Milan (Kramer, 1976: 162) and she returned to Rome in 1910 to enroll for the eight-month course. She was the first American to do so, and on returning home opened her Montessori school in a private home overlooking the Hudson River in Tarrytown, New York, in October 1911. The opening was reported by *McClure's* magazine. Twelve children made up that first class, a far cry from the slums of San Lorenzo (ibid.: 163) but one vital lesson was to emerge nonetheless. The Montessori Method worked equally well with children from affluent or socially deprived backgrounds. The first word written about Montessori in the USA appeared in the *Kindergarten Primary Magazine* of December 1909 in an article by Jenny Merrill (Hunt in Montessori, 1964: xii). That was swiftly followed by a second article by the same author in the March 1910 edition. Six more reports were published in other places in 1911 and fifty-four the following year – there was what was later called a 'frenzy' in education in response to articles published about Montessori's work.

When word of Montessori's first training sessions filtered out of Italy there was such interest that Montessori was induced to commence her first international course in 1912 and sixty-five Americans traveled to Rome. The publication of *The Montessori Method* in English in 1912 had a huge impact on America. Dorothy Canfield Fisher, an American author who had attended one of the first teacher-training sessions in Rome and had been converted to Montessori education, declared that Montessori had 'a purely medical interest in children's brains' and had 'discovered certain laws about the intellectual activities of childhood in general' (Fisher, 1913: 17). For Fisher, there was nothing actually new in Montessori's discoveries, 'nothing that we do not admit in theory, although we do not have the courage to act on them' (ibid.: 18). But it is of importance to note that Montessori did not begin with theory at all. She acted on what the children revealed to her through observation. By 1913, there were over sixty Montessori teachers working in private schools, some with special classes, in Los Angeles, Boston, and New York. A National Montessori Association was set up in Washington 'with powerful backing' and there was much interest from school boards across the country. From afar, the London *Times* voiced the opinion:

> This enthusiasm is natural. The United States is a great educational laboratory and the passion of Americans for improvement of all kinds guarantees a fair field for new ideas.
> (Washington correspondent, London *Times*, 28 January 1914, cited in Kramer, 1976: 203)

The report also quoted Montessori on the essential differences between her system and Froebel's. Her's was much freer, she explained, since Froebel imposed his will and his imagination on the pupils. As well, he confused the child with a false psychiatry. 'Not in that way was a Dante made,' she told the London reporter:

> The imagination must be the child's. He must first of all see clearly. Then out of the whole world of metaphors and comparisons he may choose what he likes.
> (London *Times*, 28 January 1914, in Kramer, 1976: 203)

On Montessori's first visit to the USA in 1913, she was greeted by a party of admirers and supporters. Among them was Erik Erikson who had first met Montessori when he studied under her at a course in Europe and then again later when he lived in Vienna. Both he and his wife were supporters of Montessori education and when they moved to the US, they set up a classroom in their home. There were detailed reports of Montessori's 1913 visit to the White House and the public lecture at Carnegie Hall where more than 1,000 people were turned away. At that meeting, she lectured in Italian to a full house at which the celebrated John Dewey himself presided (Willcott, 1968: 49). Many other influential people attended including Thomas Edison, Alexander Graham Bell, Margaret Wilson, William Heard Kilpatrick, and Adelia Pyle, who was to become her friend and interpreter. So much interest was manifested that a Montessori Association was formed with Alexander Graham Bell as president and Margaret Wilson as honorary secretary (Phillips, 1977: 57). In Chicago, Montessori resided with the wealthy Kellogg family, and on her departure, she was bid farewell by the McClures and all the executives of the newly created Montessori Education Association (ibid.). An indication of her success was the big write-up of her visit in the *New York Times* (9 December 1913) and the *New York Tribune* (9 December 1913). Soon after, the London *Times* reported:

> There are abundant signs that the United States will be the first country to experimentalize with the Montessori system on a large scale. It is clear that she has compelled the interested attention of specialists the country over.
>
> (London *Times*, 28 January 1914, in Kramer, 1976: 203)

Not every word written about her visit to the US was complimentary, by any measure. There was considerable opposition from influential establishment figures strenuously opposed to her. In one article in the influential *National Educational Association Journal* in 1912, Elizabeth Ross Shaw denounced Montessori because she taught children to read and write before six years (Willcott, 1968: 50). Montessori had now been attacked on both sides of the Atlantic for having children read spontaneously at four years. John Dewey was not an ardent admirer nor was William Heard Kilpatrick, his close colleague. At the annual meeting of the International Kindergarten Union in 1913, Kilpatrick argued that there was nothing new about her ideas at all. She simply belonged to the Rousseau–Pestalozzi–Froebel tradition, and 'some fifty years behind the present development of educational theory' (Kilpatrick, 1914: 63). He discredited her in his book *The Montessori System Examined*, published in 1914 comparing her unfavorably with Dewey (who was his 'guiding light') and declared that to teach the 3Rs before the age of eight was 'at best a waste of time, and might possibly be harmful' (ibid.). As a result of his book and comments, Montessori lost many supporters. Kilpatrick effectively helped stop academic interest in Montessori education in the United States (Lillard, 1972; Kramer, 1976; Phillips, 1977; Potts, 1980), especially with his strenuous argument that Montessori education offered nothing that was new. Rita Kramer (1976: 259) has noted that when Montessori was shown a copy of Kilpatrick's book, she replied 'I suggest that he should open his eyes. I can't help it if things he says are impossible, continually happen'. Kramer raised Kilpatrick's criticisms that Montessori had 'the spirit but not the content of modern science,' that her much-vaunted didactic materials were 'based on so erroneous a psychology that we must accordingly reject the apparatus itself' (ibid.: 231). On that point, Kramer cited Kilpatrick's devastating put-down that by rejecting Montessori materials: 'we discard probably the most popular feature of the Montessori system, a feature popular both because it can be mechanically applied and because it costs $50 – two characteristics which suffice to commend any system to the unthinking American public' (Kilpatrick, 1914: 49).

That same year, 1914, Montessori's second book *Dr Montessori's Own Handbook*, was published in English. It was a guide for parents. In it she explained clearly to parents how the Method 'followed the natural physiological and psychical development of the child' (Montessori, 1965: 17).

Despite the negativity of academia, Montessori was welcomed back to the USA in 1915. By this time a school had been established in the home of Alexander Graham Bell (Lillard, 1972: 8). He had been interested in Séguin's work with the deaf (Montessori, 1969). Montessori had returned to attend the World Fair held in San Francisco where a Montessori classroom enclosed by see-through glass walls was observed by thousands of visitors. The directress was Helen Parkhurst who had studied under her in 1913, in Rome, and was later to earn her own place in the pantheon of educators for her famous Dalton Plan.

Before leaving California, Montessori conducted a teacher-training course. By 1916, there were 189 authorized Montessori schools and 2000 unauthorized. In this period of American education, Montessori was at its height. Rita Kramer has pointed out, it 'would never again in her lifetime be as great' especially with her falling out with the millionaire McClure when she declined his offer to set up a Montessori establishment in America (Kramer, 1976: 203, 208). Montessori schools in the United States spread despite continuing attacks by Frances Wayland Parker, John Dewey, and William Heard Kilpatrick (Edmonson, 1963: 67) but they helped to diminish her influence in academic circles in America and by 1916, Montessori was off the American education agenda. Some 200 books and articles on her in America and England had been published between 1909 and 1914, seventy in 1913 alone, and about sixty between 1915 and 1918, but there were only five in 1918 (Kramer, 1976). For the next few years, Kilpatrick maintained his relentless attack, and there were other critical articles, mostly by academics, which effectively halted the momentum of Montessori education in America (Lillard, 1972: 8; Phillips, 1979: 16; Potts, 1980: 41). By 1919, E. P. Cubberley's definitive *Public Education in the United States*, 'repeated the gospel according to Kilpatrick that Montessori had been "rejected"' by 'most American educators' because of her erroneous psychology and her system's premature emphasis on formal learning' (Kramer, 1976: 232). Her star was on the wane and by the 1920s, references to her in American academic circles were 'infrequent' (Edmonson, 1963: 67). It does appear ironic that by 1925 Kilpatrick was arguing 'for more individualized curricula and expressing strong dissatisfaction with whole-class as opposed to individualized instruction' (Good, 1983: 1).

It was not until 1957 that a second phase of interest began for Montessori education in the USA. That year Nancy McCormack Rambusch had completed a course at the Sorbonne in Paris then traveled to London where she 'discovered' Montessori education and completed a course at St. Nicholas College, founded by Montessori in collaboration with Margaret Homfray and Phoebe Child after World War Two. On her return to the USA, Nancy Rambusch opened a 'pure' Montessori school in Whitby, Connecticut, in 1958. There, parents and educators renewed an interest in the Montessori Method. Part of their motivation was a desire to give their children a quicker start in the early years of their life. In 1962, Rambusch published her *Learning How to Learn* which explained the Montessori way to the American public. Even though the book was largely eulogistic, the parent body of the Association Montessori Internationale (AMI) in Amsterdam was not at all supportive of the book. For Rambusch, the Montessori Method was a 'point of departure not arrival' (Pines, 1966: 96) and she added easel painting, clay modeling, and educational toys as well as new mathematics and linguistics to the curriculum. Such modern embellishments did not please the European purists, and by 1963 Rambusch felt impelled to respond:

> The American Montessori Movement would be destroyed if it represented the fossilized outlook of these Europeans whose fidelity to Dr Montessori's memory is as unquestioned as is their innocence of American culture.
>
> (Pines, 1966: 97)

Rambusch was assisted by Mrs. Thomas Hopkins, a Montessori-trained teacher from England on her staff, who had taught in both England and France. She believed that European children were markedly different from American children, being more disciplined, much quieter in general, and with a discernible fear or respect for adults. Often, they would hold back, reluctant to make a decision until they were certain their proposed course of action was right and proper. Not so American children, she averred. They were much more independent and vital, and classrooms were rarely quiet. At Whitby, Hopkins learned that 'we must be more liberal than the Europeans' (ibid.). It was largely as a result of the Whitby experience that the American Montessori Association and the AMI went their separate ways. From 1958–63, Rambusch assisted in the establishment of more than 400 Montessori schools in the United States, and continued working for the rest of her life with teacher-training programs for the American Montessori Association, which she helped to found. In this work she was ever conscious of the role of the Montessori directress, always stressing that in a Montessori school the teacher's inactivity was 'a sign of success' (Rambusch, 1962: 92). An enthusiastic supporter of most of the Montessori Method, Rambusch was nonetheless of the opinion that the Movement had to move with the times, incorporating modern technology and the latest findings in child psychology that might supersede the findings of Montessori and make them obsolete. She ardently believed in the American model and a partnership between Princeton and the Ukraine was set up based on the American practice. The immediate goal was a model Montessori school along with a teacher-training institution in Kiev. Two Ukrainian teachers were to attend the teacher training in Princeton each year until all the Kiev teachers were fully accredited. Thereafter 'from this group of trained teachers and with the assistance of American trainers, leaders would emerge to become trainers in Ukraine' (Cusack, 1997: 1). Rambusch died in October 1994 while she was helping to develop a framework for the establishment of a Montessori school in the Ukraine.

Aline Wolf, mother of nine, was also a pioneer of Montessori education in the USA. Early in 1960 she heard and read about the school in Connecticut, admitting she had never heard of Montessori at college when she had taken a minor in education, nor had she been able to find the name in any educational journals. She visited Nancy Rambusch, who had been writing articles for parents and was creating a demand for Montessori education which could not be met because there was no teacher training in the country and no materials were manufactured or sold there. Aline Wolf started the third Montessori school in Altoona, Pennsylvania with help from Rambusch who found a Montessori-trained teacher from Sweden (AMI and St Nicholas trained) along with an elementary teacher. Classes were set up in the living room and sun room of the Wolf house in 1961. There was a demand for teacher training and when the parents of Altoona realized St Nicholas offered a correspondence course, six parents enrolled in 1964. They were to attend a two-week course in London before beginning their studies and when Aline Wolf thought it would be easier to have someone come from London, she wrote to St Nicholas with her suggestion and Margaret Homfray and Phoebe Child themselves accepted. Aline was given the names and addresses of all the St Nicholas students in the USA and was asked to write to them with information about the forthcoming course. Sixty students from as far away as Alaska and California attended that first St Nicholas course in the USA at Altoona. Today, Aline Wolf continues to write and lecture throughout the world. At her address to the final St Nicholas diploma ceremony in London in 1999 she declared: 'Without the St Nicholas course, Montessori education would not have spread throughout the world' (Wolf, 1999: 5).

Paula Polk Lillard found out about Montessori education in 1961 when a friend, who was determined her children would have a Montessori education, lent her *Maria Montessori: Her Life and Work* by E. M. Standing. Lillard admitted she had never heard of Montessori while majoring in education at Smith College and she was not impressed with Standing's book, especially Montessori's descriptions of the children in her schools. 'They seemed unrealistic to me,' she later wrote: 'I had been a public school teacher, and I could not reconcile her accounts of children's behavior with my own experience' (Lillard, 1972: vii). When William Hopple, assistant headmaster of Cincinnati Country Day School, the private school that two of her children attended, visited Nancy Rambusch's school at Whitby, he was so impressed with what he saw that he planned to open a Montessori class for children aged three to six years. Lillard had another look at Montessori education and when the class began, she accepted the post of assistant to Hilda Rothschild who had trained under Montessori in France and had taught there before World War Two. She fled to the USA when the Germans invaded France. Lillard notes, 'What followed in the days ahead was beyond my imagination or expectation' (ibid.: viii). The special respect that Hilda Rothschild showed toward children impressed Lillard from the start and she became deeply involved in Montessori education. In 1964, she met Helen Parkhurst who was visiting Cincinnati to see her friend Mary Johnson with whom she had traveled to Rome in 1913 to learn about Montessori education. Parkhurst visited the classroom where Lillard was working and was impressed. Lillard has continued her work and writing about Montessori education.

Since the revival of interest in Montessori education in the second half of the twentieth century, there has been much speculation about that early American decline in Montessori education. One critic, C. E. Morgan, described Montessori's overall contribution to education as totally lacking in 'cultivation and analysis of higher thought processes and feeling' (Potts, 1980: 41). Another, E. D. Evans (1971), claimed that Montessori had nothing new to offer but in her defense she had never claimed to have invented anything new. In her own words, 'Had I wished to pass as an inventor, I should have been shown up' (ibid.: 37). Moreover, she acknowledged many sources throughout her writings. Hunt (1964) attributed the initial and spectacular 'explosion' of interest in America in 1909–13 to a growing body of trendy educational reformers:

> Reports of Montessori's success in the Houses of Children made her pedagogic methods look to many of the most progressive-minded like the way to a new day, or like the most rapid route yet uncovered to fundamental reform.
>
> (Hunt in Montessori, 1964: xviii)

Hunt was constrained to add:

> Many of these progressive-minded people who visited Montessori or became interested in her work had, like Alexander Graham Bell, tremendous prestige; some of them, like McClure, controlled major sources of mass communication; others, like Dorothy Canfield Fisher (1913) and Ellen Yale Stevens (1913) had facile pens. They got the news out fast, and they spread it wide.

Another factor contributing to the decline in the US could well have been attributed to Montessori's insistence on strict adherence to the exact presentation of materials. There were indeed altercations with some of her followers on the issue, but Montessori might well have had a valid case according to Kramer who pointed out that 'while it is hard to take seriously today some purists' insistence on the necessity of using the identical materials in exactly the same way that Montessori used them in 1907, what is impressive is how these materials have stood the test of time' (Kramer, 1976: 209). What is undeniable is that those who follow the original process as described by Montessori obtain the same successful results. Children do become normalized and their skills develop, just as they did in the first four Children's

Houses. Moreover, those original self-corrective teaching materials are still identical to her originals. For teachers wishing to train and use the materials in the first phase, there was an element of commercialism in Montessori's insistence on certifying all her teachers, and controlling the sale of her didactic materials has been raised as a contributing factor in her loss of favor in those early years (ibid.: 230). Both of these factors 'helped to put her outside the pale of the dominant educational world in the United States, although in such countries as England, Holland, Spain and Italy – wherever Montessori methods were adopted by the official school establishment – it was a different story' (ibid.). Others who purported to find slight flaws in Montessori's overall philosophy or who quibbled with parts of her methodology were substantially in support during the flush of her re-discovery. Hunt (1964) drew attention to the universal fact of life about a child's capacity to learn at his stage of development and a child of tender years is capable of advanced learning in the skills of writing and reading. Goodlad depicted her as the author of 'the first truly systematic attempt to educate children under six years' (Goodlad et al., 1973: 34), while Samuel Braun (1974: 127) described her as 'a woman of remarkable sensitivity.'

Individuals promoting Montessori education have established organizations to satisfy the need for Montessori teachers. In 1971, Helen K. Billings established the Montessori Institute of America (MIA) based in Kansan City, Missouri, and soon afterwards Tim Seldin, with long experience running a Montessori school in Silver Spring, Maryland, became president of the Montessori Foundation and chairman of the International Montessori Council (IMC). In 1976, Lee Havis began the National Center for Montessori Education (NCME). In 1979, that became the International Montessori Association (IMS) also run by Havis. Another meriting mention is David Kahn, executive director of the North American Montessori Teachers' Association and founding program director of the celebrated Hershey Montessori Farm School which follows Montessori's *Erdkinder* principles at its campus at Huntsberg, Ohio. Kahn delivered a paper on the Montessori *Erdkinder* at the Twenty-fifth International Congress in Sydney in 2005 (Kahn: 2005).

18 The British Isles

It was 1919 before Montessori visited the British Isles to give a training course. Before she reached London *The Times Educational Supplement*, 30 October 1919 reported that Mrs. Hutchinson and her assistants had been applying Montessori principles and methods for several years. They had also established the first advanced classes in England for children to eleven years. Montessori and Anna Maccheroni visited these classes on their 1919 visit (*Communications*, 1975: 18). It is beyond dispute that she and her students exerted a profound influence within the British Isles. Her ideas were liberally absorbed into the English infant school from the earliest days, as exemplified by the experience of Susan Isaacs. According to Silberman (1973), in the early 1920s, Isaacs had opened an experimental school in Cambridge, The Malting House, where Montessori was invited to visit and conduct lectures. He claimed the school was 'a precursor to the post-World War One informal infant school' (ibid.: 179). Like Montessori, Isaacs regarded children as the living aim of education and her observations were the source of her writings on child development and learning. She had 'a profound influence, direct and indirect on the development of informal education in England' (ibid.). Many of Montessori's ideas were incorporated into the public school system throughout the British Isles in curriculum and standard materials issued by local authorities and town councils. Glasgow's Education Department adopted many Montessori principles and curriculum.

In 1921, Montessori had a large number of students attend her diploma training course in London. Edward M. Standing attended and became a lifelong associate of Montessori, arranging lectures, collaborating and translating her works, and her official biographer. There was a great interest in Montessori education and demand for trained teachers was high. Claude Claremont, 'a well known figure in the Montessori world from before 1913, when he followed a Montessori course for the first time' (*Communications*, 1974), attended some lectures. He was head of the Science and Mathematics Department at St George's School, then at St Christopher's School, London until 1925 (Kramer, 1976: 271). When he became principal of Montessori teacher training, courses were held in his large home, Studio

House, Hampstead. He worked closely with Philip and Tacey, manu-
facturers of Montessori materials in England from 1913–39 (*Montessori International*, issue 63, 2002). He staunchly supported and promoted the Montessori movement until his death in Los Angeles in
1967. Lawson and Silver (1973) noted that established private schools
throughout Britain also adopted Montessori education. The famous
co-educational Bedales, founded in 1904 by J. H. Badley, offered students from five years a whole range of creative activities as well as
'headwork.' An important feature of this school was the school parliament. Badley and his staff 'were to become enthusiastic supporters
of the Montessori approach to children and education ... and in
many respects it was the parent of the progressive school movement
in England' (Lawson and Silver, 1973: 356). The King Alfred and
Bryanston schools also followed Bedales with the objective of 'whole-
ness and a large measure of self-disciplined activity and learning,' but
it should be noted that they were also influenced in the 1920s by the
Dalton Plan (ibid.: 399). Both programs enabled children to control
their own studies. The Dalton Plan, devised by Helen Parkhust (a
Montessori protégée of 1913), found wide support in many primary
(or elementary) schools in the 1920s in America, Great Britain, and
Australia. A. S. Neill, an iconic figure in twentieth-century education,
who opened his school, Summerhill, in 1921 to provide education free
of authoritarian figures, saw Montessori as 'one of the big four along
with Rousseau, Pestalozzi and Froebel' (Neill, 1962: ii). Significant
changes were seen in open classrooms being constructed especially
in infant schools from the 1930s. Sir Alec Clegg, education officer of
West Riding, Yorkshire, widely acknowledged as one of the greats of
British education, was concerned with those children suffering from
social and educational deprivation which lingered still in some areas
in England into the 1950s, and he was involved with the implementation of the recommendations in the Plowden Report which tackled
this problem in the 1960s. He was regarded as one of the leaders of
the quiet revolution that has transformed British primary education
since World War Two (Silberman, 1973: 65–84). The views espoused
about Open Classroom education and the recommendations of the
Plowden Report supported Montessori education, although the name
Montessori is not mentioned. It was reported about this time by the

Association Montessori International magazine that Gypsy Hill Council, London, had built a permanent school on a caravan site for the children of that area. They were described in the Plowden Report as being 'the most educationally deprived group in the country' and the nursery group was to be based on Montessori methods (*Communications*, 1969: 3). When Sir Alec was invited to speak at a conference in Washington in 1971 on 'the revolution in British schools,' he was asked if he had statistics to show the achievements of students in these 'informal' schools, which confirms that schools in the US were continuing to 'measure' children using classroom tests and examinations. Sir Alec produced a folio of samples of each children's work, adding 'all these are by-products; the children are the products' (Silberman, 1973: 65) then he described what he had observed in one of the English schools:

> The quality of teaching is completely upsetting the national norms ... there is a dramatic change in the children's behaviour, and how this has come about I cannot readily explain. One thing I know is that the changes in our schools are affecting the human spirit just as much as they are affecting the human mind.
>
> (ibid.: 83)

He also confirmed that there were no intelligence test results, reading techniques, or history syllabuses, but it was 'the way children took part day to day in the classroom and how they behave towards one another that was important' (ibid.: 73). In retrospect it sounded very like a Montessori answer from the classrooms of those first Children's Houses of 1907.

In 1952, after Montessori's death, Mario Montessori founded an AMI teacher-training center in London, which he named The Maria Montessori Training Organization. The organization offered full-time courses only, because Mario disagreed with St Nicholas offering part-time courses as well as correspondence courses. The St Nicholas Montessori College established in London has played a considerable role in the promotion of both Montessori education and teacher training from 1947. Founded by Montessori in collaboration with Margaret Homfray and Phoebe Child, St. Nicholas grew with two important offshoots: one, the Montessori World Educational Institute (MWEI) born in 1980 with huge input by Margaret Homfray and co-founder Dr. Robert Bloget and based in California; the other, the London Montessori Centre, founded by Leslie Briton in the 1980s. St Nicholas and the London Montessori Centre united in 2000 to become the Montessori Centre Internationale. At present all the Montessori colleges in the UK have united to have Montessori qualifications recognized and to negotiate with the government over their new qualification frameworks (*Montessori International*, issue 63, 2002).

19 India

According to A. M. Joosten, a Dutchman who assisted Mario Montessori with teacher training in India for many years, there are two phases of Montessori education in India: before Montessori came to India in 1939 and after her ten years residence in India. He points out that delegates from India had attended every International Teacher Training including Rome in 1913. Mahatma Gandhi had visited the Montessori schools in Rome, subsequently promoting Montessori education in his homeland. Montessori and Gandhi had also met in London, sharing their common views as 'apostles of peace, champions of equality in the dignity of all men and human activity, dedicating themselves to the development of the human being as an individual and builder of society' (Joosten, 1969: 21). Both believed in nonviolence and the sacred, inviolable rights of all men. When Montessori arrived in India in 1939 to conduct the international conference, Gandhi sent a message of welcome to her and, when she was interned, he expressed profound sympathy and regret for the restrictions imposed on her. During her internment she met Rabinranath Tagore, Zakir Husain, S. Radhakrishnan, Vijayalakshimi Pandit, and Saraladevi Sarabbai who came to listen and learn about Montessori education. She gave many courses and while thousands of followers from all social backgrounds attended, their children, the future citizens, all mixed together (Joosten, 1955: 7–11). She returned to Europe at the end of the war in 1945 and traveled back to India at the end of 1948 for the planned opening of a Montessori university, but she was caught up in an enormous upheaval of huge numbers of people who were journeying north to the newly created Pakistan (Potts, 1980: 40). Montessori returned to the Netherlands and Amsterdam where Mario married and settled. In 1952, the Central Ministry of Education recognized the Montessori Diploma awarded by AMI. In 1977, it was reported that thirty-three teacher-training courses had been conducted since 1949, each attended by 150–80 students with many led by Mario Montessori. The Montessori materials used were manufactured locally (Joosten, 1955: 12). Courses had been held in Gwailior, Bombay, Delhi, Hyderabad, Jharia, Calcutta, Varanasi, Ranchi, and Bangalore.

20 Australia

Dr Montessori never visited Australaisia. Credit for introducing the fundamentals of the Montessori Method to Australia belongs partly to Peter Board (1858–1945), director of education in New South Wales from 1905–22, who took an active interest in Montessori education as early as 1909. Board had created the Sydney Teachers' College at Blackfriars Demonstration School with Alexander Mackie as inaugural principal, and Miss Martha Margaret Mildred Simpson (1865–1948) as first infants' mistress, soon afterwards first lecturer in infants method. Simpson deserves major credit for introducing Montessori education to Australia and New Zealand. In 1912, she was asked to report on *The Montessori Method*. 'Though it contains no new educational principles, it undoubtedly gives new and novel interpretations of familiar educational thought' she told the Department in July 1912:

> The Montessori apparatus commends itself at once to every Kindergarten because of its simplicity and close association with the everyday life of the child. The thoughtful teacher will see in it, too, an instrument whereby the child will be led to see and correct his own mistakes.

Simpson offered the NSW Department her opinion that Italy 'must be very much behind modern educational thought in the matter of method' since many of the ideas presented by Montessori as new and original were 'already well understood and practised in Australian Kindergartens.' As proof, she argued that 'no Kindergarten would think of doing for the child anything he could possibly do for himself.' She noted the established kindergarteners had movable furniture and they cared for the room (dusting, tidying, arranging flowers, and watering ferns and pot plants). In Froebelian kindergartens each child was allowed 'every liberty to do right, but no licence to do wrong,' and the only punishment was isolation. Courtesy and right behavior were taught by means of games and real experiences, children 'were taught to move easily and gracefully, to be respectful and considerate to all but afraid of no one.' There were musical activities, games, and physical exercises, and Montessori's 'Games of Silence' were 'identical with the Kindergarten *quiet time.'* Simpson claimed that her kindergarten was already 'fully alive' to the all-important matter of sensory perceptions emphasized by Montessori – as shown in her nature rambles and frequent handling of objects.

There were a number of features in Montessori education which Miss Simpson conceded to be in advance of Australian methods, including the fuller liberty, the well-planned didactic material precisely designed to 'lead the child to educate himself,' and the direct method of teaching using the three-period lesson. 'Even our best teachers talk far too much,' Miss Simpson frankly admitted to the Department, the lesson being 'buried under such a mass of verbiage that the child loses sight of it.' Montessori's emphasis on the sparing use of words appealed to Simpson as a 'wholesome corrective.' The methods of reading and writing 'would of themselves stamp the Montessori Method as far in advance of anything of a similar kind yet introduced into our schools,' she admitted with unfeigned admiration: 'I am of the opinion that the Montessori Method in these two subjects will bring about a revolution in the teaching of reading and writing in our schools.' The immense value of the sense of touch using sandpaper letters was for Simpson, 'the greatest thing' in the Montessori Method. 'Every teacher knows the tedious drudgery of teaching children to read and write – sugar coat it as we may the drudgery (to the teacher at any rate) remains,' she reported:

To get over this as the children in the Montessori Schools get over it sounds like a fairy tale. We may not accomplish such miracles, owing to the difficulties of our language, but if the experiments now being carried out at Blackfriars do not deceive me, I think the results if not so magical as those of Italy will be sufficiently marvellous to warrant the introduction of the Montessori Method of reading and writing into all schools.

The chief defect Simpson found was the 'limited appeal to the heart and imagination,' a criticism largely negated by Simpson's own spirited defense of Montessori:

This failure on the part of Dr Montessori to recognise the importance of the child's emotional nature and vivid imagination is all the more surprising when we realise that her whole book is the intensely emotional appeal of a wise, far-seeing, large-hearted woman for a better condition of things for this and future generations of little children.

Simpson enthusiastically recommended that the Montessori Method and materials be introduced in the schools of New South Wales but only after being introduced to teachers by experienced instructors. She also recommended that one or more experienced teachers be dispatched to Rome to study the working of the Montessori schools and infant education generally, such teachers to be 'well versed in the latest methods of teaching young children' with 'an open and unprejudiced mind toward the new education, together with a sufficient knowledge of our system to compare, adjust and adapt.' The ideal person to send would be someone with 'a sufficiently wide knowledge and mature judgement to know what to accept and what to reject.' Intended or not, the specifications Simpson drafted appeared to fit with remarkable closeness to Simpson herself. For several months she had been trialing Montessori ideas and her work was attracting interest (O'Donnell, 1996).

Peter Board convinced the NSW Minister for Education to send Simpson to observe and report on the new ideas and by December 1912, she traveled to Rome, with the backing of the NSW educational hierarchy. On 23 January 1913, she disembarked at Naples to join the other eighty delegates attending the first International Training Course offered by Montessori in Rome. Simpson resided in Montessori's own home for some months, her understanding of the total philosophy and methodology enhanced by absorption of some of the infectious spirit transmitted by the esteemed Dottoressa who took pains to congratulate Simpson for 'the first and most complete experiment of her system outside Italy.' Simpson's subsequent report of 1914 'recommended the adoption of Montessori methods, while insisting that the schools should also retain their Froebelian emphasis' (Crane and Walker, 1957: 204). As the record shows, Blackfriars became the model for the rest of Australasia. Queensland, Victoria, South Australia, Western Australia, Tasmania, and New Zealand all keenly studied the Blackfriars' experiment, some actually recruiting Simpson-trained staff in order to implement their own versions of Montessori education in action.

One of the participants at that first course offered by Maria Montessori in January 1913 was one of her closest friends, Anna Maccheroni, who has documented valuable first-hand recollections of the occasion in her book *A True Romance: Dr Maria Montessori as I Knew Her* (1947). The course was held at Via Principessa Clotilde, the lecture room containing a corner alcove which provided the platform for the Dottoressa. Participants were from all over the world, even at this early stage of the Movement: the Transvaal, India, the United Kingdom, America, and Queen Margherita of Holland for one lecture. 'Two young ladies from Australia, who had sold their house in order to come, had obtained with their children the same results as Dr Montessori had described in her book,' Maccheroni recalled: 'Later the head of the Board of Education in Sydney came to ask Dr Montessori to go there to direct the whole organization of the schools.' Maccheroni also furnished her own personal discovery of the efficacy of the Montessori way with inner discipline, especially in regard to a large class she was then teaching in Via Trionfale. 'My children were about forty in number, all under six,' she wrote:

How well I remember the noise of the first days! It was not really disorder, it was only that the children could not walk without making a noise, could not utter a word unless with a very loud voice. Every morning I did a few exercises, such as walking very quietly, talking very softly, running on tiptoes. The children did all these things very well. During the exercises the children could talk softly, could put down a wooden box on the table without noise etc. But as soon as they went to fetch some object and began to work, they were as noisy as ever. One day, they walked, talked, moved about, with hardly any noise. They had gained control over their muscles and their movement. It was what Dr Montessori calls 'an explosion'.

(Maccheroni, 1947)

In Sydney, Miss Simpson was echoing identical sentiments. 'Children burst into writing of their own accord and without any formal teaching,' she reported officially to the NSW Department of Public Instruction in her *Report on the Montessori Methods of Education* in 1914. Within six months North Newtown Infants opened and had the added advantage of obtaining ready supplies of Montessori didactic materials from the NSW Department's own workshop. That source of supply equipped all other NSW infants' schools throughout the state (O'Donnell, 1996). Another Montessori school at Fort Street Infants was under Miss Banks who had trained in kindergarten methods under Professor Hoffmann and Professor Wollmer, both pupils of Froebel. Miss Banks was adamant that Froebel himself 'would have been the first to welcome Dr Montessori's furtherance of his work' (Longmore and Davidson, 1915). World War One boosted Montessori education, the Germanic connections of Froebel discrediting the traditional kindergarten methodology but only for that dark period of war when Froebel came back into vogue and Montessori's stocks declined (Petersen in Turney, 1983: 244). For Miss Simpson, there was an unbroken connection with the Montessori Method. In 1917, she was promoted to Inspector of Infants' Schools, the state's first woman inspector and ardently advanced Montessori ideas until her retirement in 1930. She died in 1948, by which time Montessori education was in danger of becoming a relic of the past.

In mainland states of Australia, a similar pattern of government interest occurred, the phenomenon not surprising given the monopoly held over education by state departments of education, all, without exception, derived their interest in and knowledge of

Montessori education from the work of Miss Simpson in Sydney. In 1914, just prior to the outbreak of World War One, the Queensland Department of Public Instruction dispatched three of its senior officers to Blackfriars to observe and report on the system being carried out in that school. On returning to Brisbane they enthusiastically recommended that Montessorian methods be incorporated into the Queensland system. Their report was published in the official *Education Office Gazette* (October–December 1914), all Queensland teachers being informed of the 'apostolic spirit' permeating Blackfriars where the staff devoted themselves to the work of education and found delight therein:

> Under such control, it is hard to conceive how any system could possibly fail. The outward and visible signs of careful selection of teachers, skilful training and special adaptability are manifest at once to the experienced eye – the gentle voice, most excellent to be desired amongst teachers, the silent and graceful movement, the sympathetic address, the cultivated enunciation, the unwavering patience, the self-control, and above all the devotion.

One Queenslander, Miss Harriet Emily Barton, had attended Montessori's first International Training Class in Rome in 1913 at her own expense. She had been assistant mistress of the Maryborough Grammar School but little is known about her work. It is of enormous interest that Montessori remembered the Queenslander sufficiently well four years after the 1913 course to cite her as an exemplar of her Method. At the opening of another Children's House, Montessori made special reference to her:

> Another most significant fact is related by Miss Barton, an Australian teacher: Among her pupils was a little girl who had not yet developed articulate speech, and only gave utterance to inarticulate sounds; her parents had her examined by a doctor to find out if she were normal; the doctor declared the child to be perfectly normal, and considered that though she had not as yet developed speech, she would do so in time. This child became interested in the solid insets, and amused herself for a long time taking the cylinders out of the cavities and putting them back in their places; and after repeating

the work with intense interest, she ran to the teacher saying: 'Come and see!'

(Montessori, 1916)

In July 1912, a departmental official from the state of Victoria journeyed north to Sydney to see for himself the new methods but interest was to be short-lived in Victoria.

The South Australian experience with Montessori is unique because there was a distinct spirit of harmony between the State Department of Public Instruction and the Kindergarten Union. R. C. Petersen (Turney, 1983: 254) has drawn attention to an important ingredient in the South Australian equation: 'the particularly animating role played by the greatest of Australian kindergartners, Lillian de Lissa' (1885–1967) who had attended Sydney Kindergarten Teachers' College from 1903 to 1904 when the Chicago-trained Francis Newton was principal. De Lissa became director of the first Adelaide kindergarten in 1906, principal of the Adelaide Kindergarten Training College in 1907 and general director of the South Australian Kindergarten Union (Jones in Turney, 1983: 127). She enthusiastically embraced Montessori practices and principles and completed Montessori's International Course in 1914. As Helen Jones makes clear, de Lissa amalgamated Montessorian ingredients into her Froebelian origins but gradually discarded the Froebelian equipment in favor of Montessori materials. She left Adelaide in 1917 to take up headship of Gypsy Hill Training College in England where she remained until 1947. One of her students at Gypsy Hill, E. M. Fearnside, was later to emigrate to South Australia to re-ignite the Montessori flame. In February 1917, Miss Lydia Longmore was promoted to school inspector, virtually controlling infants' schools for the next seventeen years. In the course of those duties, she inspired scores of South Australian teachers to incorporate Montessori principles into their daily work. Her name is perpetuated in the Longmore Medal awarded to the top graduating student from the de Lissa Institute of Montessori Education. By 1926, the Superintendent of Primary Education formally commented that 'greatly advanced work is being done in the Infant schools' (Tresize in Turney, 1983: 7), the results largely attributable to the Montessori Method. On a visit to South Australia that year, Miss Simpson commented that what she had seen of state schools was 'a delight':

> The tone, excellent standard of merit and attitude of teachers and children towards work, has not been excelled in my opinion in any part of the world. The general level of excellence in Infant work is outstanding and Australia should be proud of this. It is all most inspiring and fills me with enthusiasm.
>
> (Tresize in Turney, 1983: 7)

Colin Thiele, eminent South Australian author and educator, has recounted in *Grains of Mustard Seed,* a timeless example of mindless opposition from lawgivers and other influential people to educational innovation. The following exchange over Montessori education took place in the South Australian Parliament in 1915 during a debate on Montessori education:

> The Hon. A. H. Peake: Do not let us lose our heads over a fad like this.
> The Treasurer: It is no fad.
> The Hon. A. H. Peake: It is.
> The Treasurer: It is firmly established all over the world.
> The Hon. A. H. Peake: It is by no means established all over the world.
> The Treasurer: It is too firmly established to be regarded as a fad.
>
> (Thiele, 1975: 128)

One Montessori school in Adelaide opened in 1919 under Miss Hilda Ramsay Smith, daughter of Dr. William Ramsay Smith (1859–1937). He had migrated to South Australia from Scotland in 1896 to accept the post of physician to the Royal Adelaide Hospital. Naturalist, anthropologist, and civil servant as well as physician, Ramsay Smith encouraged Hilda, one of his four daughters, to open her own Montessori school in Glen Osmond in Adelaide. The school was close to the home of Nancy Cato who became an early pupil and later one of Australia's best-known novelists. Miss Cato has furnished invaluable information about this little-known school. 'I was interested to hear that the Montessori movement is active again,' she wrote in July 1996 when she was aged 79:

> I had an excellent education, staying at Miss Ramsay's till I was eight, and skipping kindergarten class at P.G.C. The school was opened and ran for about ten or twelve years, in Glen Osmond. It had been running for at least two years before I joined in 1921, just after my fourth birthday in March. Most of the pupils walked up the hill to Portrush Road in the morning, passing our gate, and crossing the busy road to the entrance of the school, which was held in a very modern pre-fab building on stilts, with shutters all round instead of windows. It was painted pale green and in spring was surrounded with a covering of Sweet Peas.
>
> (Personal letter to Dan O'Donnell from Nancy Cato, July 1996)

There is little doubt that Montessori education exerted an enduring influence on Nancy Cato, both Miss Ramsay and her father being remembered with gratitude. 'I am always grateful to Dr Ramsay Smith for insisting that my left-handedness should not be corrected,' she acknowledged, certain that it had been his inquiring medical mind which had rejected out of hand the then prevalent notion in educational bureaucracies that left-handed children should be rigidly converted to right-handedness. 'I feel sure he would have helped his unmarried daughter, Hilda Ramsay Smith, to set up her kindergarten,' she speculated,

> and may have helped with the design – a perfectly square room with blackboards and pictures on the walls, banks of toy cupboards low down and with no doors to open – they were covered with hangings of natural coarse linen on which we were encouraged to embroider, with large needles and bright yellow and purple wool, a design of butterflies. Whenever I smell Clag paste, I recall the teaching device of pasting a roneoed sentence to the matching picture. I loved this lesson, so perhaps I had a natural feeling for words.

Cato also remembered with clarity the creative and educational toys, the free play which encouraged the imagination, and the plentiful books: 'I cried on the first morning when I was sent to Kindy. By the second afternoon, I cried because I had to go home.'

In Western Australia a surge of interest in Montessori was aroused in 1913 with the arrival of Miss Simpson on her return home to Sydney from Rome. In 1914, the principal of the Perth Teachers' Training College plus a senior departmental inspector was dispatched to Blackfriars. Both fell under the sway of what they saw – the 'unorthodox arrangement of classes and furniture, a plan which in itself betokened freedom' (Petersen in Turney, 1983: 246) and the choices made by the children in the absence of constraints. A member of Miss Simpson's staff was employed as a lecturer in Infants Method at the Perth Teachers' College and Montessori methods taught to young trainees.

Tasmania also had a direct connection with Miss Simpson of Blackfriars. At the beginning of 1912, the Tasmanian Department of Public Instruction dispatched one of its kindergarten teachers to Blackfriars to absorb the new ideas, at the same time recruiting a member of Miss Simpson's staff to work in Tasmanian schools. In September 1912, Simpson traveled south to 'inspect the progress of infant education' and to advise and help. By mid-1917, the system was being practiced for some of the school day. With the coming of the Dalton Plan to Tasmania and the rest of Australia in 1922, enthusiasm for Montessori appeared to wane, and by 1923, Tasmania was already in a post-Montessori era.

21 New Zealand

Two months after Simpson presented her preliminary review of Anne E. George's translation of Montessori's *Il Metodo*, Wellington's *New Zealand Herald* on 10 September 1912 published a report on the Blackfriars experiment, citing Australian opinion that Montessori would revolutionize early primary training as well as kindergarten (Miltich-Conway and Openshaw, 1988: 190). Keen interest was immediately shown by Sir James Allen (New Zealand Minister for Education) and George Hogben (New Zealand Inspector-General). Simpson and Sir James had met at the end of 1912 when they journeyed overseas together on the same vessel, both continuing to Rome to meet the

Dottoressa and to see her Children's Houses. Sir James altered his formal itinerary to the Imperial Defence Conference in London to 'see Montessori's work at first hand' (ibid.). According to Petersen (1968: 237) he rapidly became 'a convert to Montessori.' On his return to New Zealand in 1913, he dispatched George D. Braik, the Chief Inspector of Schools to Blackfriars School (Braik, 1913: 4; Miltich-Conway and Openshaw, 1988: 191). Braik was clearly impressed. 'Our school work would be improved if our kindergarten and first preparatory classes were to receive some teaching in accordance with Montessori principles,' he wrote: 'I recommend that in all schools the teachers be encouraged to adopt the methods of the system in so far as they aid the teaching of the primary subjects.'

When Simpson produced her definitive 1914 Report, New Zealand's Inspector-General immediately ordered 5,000 copies for distribution throughout the profession in New Zealand (Braik, 1913: 6) and by the end of 1916, the Montessori system was being trialed throughout New Zealand, including all training colleges for teachers. With the introduction of the Dalton Plan in 1922, interest in Montessori waned and it was to be another half-century before the second stage of Montessori was to build on these earlier foundations.

22 The Second Phase in Australasia

The second phase in Australasia was in post-World War Two when awareness of Montessori was re-ignited. One obvious stimulus came with the successive waves of modern migration from Europe, with tiny, independent schools slowly and steadily attracting the notice of parents and teachers.

The first Montessori establishment on the east coast of Australia was the Children's House at West Lindfield in Sydney, NSW, in 1974 by the newly established Sydney Montessori Society. By the end of 1977, other Montessori Pre-Schools had opened in Sydney with interest being shown in Wagga Wagga, Yass, and in Canberra, Australian Capital Territory (ACT) particularly after the visit that year of Margaret Homfray, co-founder of St. Nicholas College, London. With the growth of Children's Houses came an increasing need for trained staff. Qualified teachers were recruited from Ireland, the US, and the Netherlands but it was clear that local training was an urgent need. At the inaugural meeting of the Riverina Montessori Association on 16 July 1979, Beth Alcorn (elected secretary) outlined the contents of the Montessori World Educational Institute (MWEI, California) co-founded by Margaret Homfray, Phoebe Child, and Robert Bloget, which offered a correspondence course from Atascadero, California, the only MWEI course available in Australia. When Beth moved to Perth in Western Australia soon afterwards, she continued her passionate work for Montessori education as Australasian co-ordinator for MWEI (Australia) Incorporated. In that capacity she made regular lecturing and training visits to every Australian state and New Zealand.

In Victoria, a notable contributor was Jean Kalker who had trained under Montessori in prewar Amsterdam and had worked for one term with the Dottoressa and Ada Montessori-Pierson (Mario's wife) in the Laren Montessori Experimental Kindergarten. When she migrated to Australia in March 1951, she continued to promote Montessori education (O'Donnell, 1996). In 1976, as a direct consequence of her work, the Victorian government granted Montessori kindergartens the identical subsidy allowed for state pre-school centers. Waverley Montessori Pre-School, Melbourne, opened in 1974 and the Melbourne Montessori Kindergarten was formed. Caulfield Montessori School and Plenty Valley Montessori School opened in 1976. In January 1996, Plenty Valley Montessori hosted a ten-day workshop conducted by Helen Wheatley, Montessori consultant, tutor and examiner from London for MWEI and a former principal of St Nicholas College, London. The workshop was well attended by Montessorians from every part of Australasia. Wilma Carter, experienced state teacher and lecturer at the Burwood campus of Victoria Teachers' College attended the Workshop. In 1987, she became a co-ordinator of MWEI and organized workshops for budding Montessorians, often with respected lecturers from farther afield. In January 1994, the Victorian Directorate of School Education advised Wilma Carter that three-year-trained primary teachers who had completed the MWEI Associate Diploma of Montessori Education, 'would be regarded as four-year-trained primary teachers' by the Victorian

Department of Education. It was a landmark in Montessori education in Australia.

In Queensland during the years 1975–2005, steady growth in the movement also occurred. The initial stimulus came from a handful of dedicated Brisbane enthusiasts including Elsie Richter, Sylvia Middleton, Cathie Hazzard, and Jan Luff. By 1982, there were Montessori pre-schools at Auchenflower, Chapel Hill, and St Lucia, and that year the first primary school opened at Fig Tree Pocket in Brisbane headed by Georgiana Poulter who had trained under Margaret Homfray in Adelaide. A Montessori workshop was led by Dr. Vickie Midgley (née Matthews), a highly regarded Montessorian from MWEI (California) in 1986. She was a trained secondary teacher from California State College (Los Angeles) and a graduate of the St Nicholas Training Centre in London. Another Queensland pioneer was Mignon Weber. Before migrating to Australia, Mignon had qualified as a Montessori teacher in Trincomalee, Sri Lanka, where she opened her own pre-school in 1974. Her AMI Diploma bears the personal signature of Mario Montessori. Mignon later taught at Montessori schools in South Carolina, USA (1979), and in Brisbane where she opened her long-running Montessori pre-school in Arana Hills in 1987, assisted by Carol Callaghan. There were other pioneers, too. Carmel Ellis (St Nicholas trained) set up her pre-school in Indooroopilly in 1986 assisted by Sharon Hepburn. Gloria Bainbrigge established her center at Rochedale in 1992 and Glenda Sawtell opened Harmony Children's Houses at Caboolture in 1987 and Buderim in 1993, followed by primary schools at both campuses and in 2005 a secondary top at Buderim. There has been an interesting recent development of Montessori education and the church with the first Catechesis of the Good Shepherd Australian training course conducted in 1995 by Linda Kaiel. Among the attendees were Anne Delsorte and Mary Hare who started the Atrium that year in Brisbane. The center has flourished under their guidance with Atria spreading throughout Australasia and parts of Asia. Anne traveled to Rome where she met Sofia Cavalletti and Gianna Gobbi. She was invited to speak about the impact of the first ten years of the Catechesis of the Good Shepherd at the Montessori Congress in Sydney, 2005. One other Montessori school in Queensland meriting special note is the Mapoon Montessori

School in a remote portion of Western Cape York Peninsula. It was funded by a generous bequest by Bob Masterman, originally from Holland, who, at the age of 86, was struck by the plight of the Aborigines whose tribal ways had been dislocated in 1963. Masterman set up a trust fund of $2.7 million to build a Montessori school specifically for the indigenes. His interest in Montessori had been excited by his daughter, Ardyn, a trained Montessorian. Less than a year after his first visit to Mappoon in 1990, Bob Masterman died, but his school is prospering. His daughter Ardyn Masterman addressed the Montessori Congress in Sydney in 2005.

Montessori education in South Australia burst into life in about 1963 with the work of Emma M. Fearnside. Already ardently Montessorian following her teacher training at Gypsy Hill Teachers' College, England, under Lillian de Lissa, in April 1977, she was responsible for bringing Mrs. Gool Minwalla, director of Montessori Education in Pakistan, to Adelaide for a series of lectures and workshops. Mrs. Minwalla had worked in close co-operation with Mario Montessori in Pakistan and was personally responsible for the training of hundreds of teachers in the Montessori Method. Fearnside also helped to bring Margaret Homfray to Adelaide in 1980 and again in 1984 to conduct workshops. Margaret Cronin long-standing co-ordinator and chairperson of MWEI in South Australia was the directress at two independent Montessori primary schools. Cynthia Morris completed Montessori credentials at the St Nicholas Centre and under Margaret Homfray in Adelaide. Cynthia, a friend of both Miss Homfray and Phoebe Child, won the Lydia Longmore Memorial Award in 1980, a prize named after one of South Australia's first Montessorians. Another is Nita Maloney who taught at the Para Hills Montessori School from 1986 and has long been active with MWEI (SA). In 1981, the Alberton Montessori School opened with an exciting development in Montessori education in Australia since it involved direct co-operation between individual parents and the State Department of Education, the latter agreeing to cover the cost of teachers' salaries. A similar spirit of co-operation occurred in 1992 when the northern suburbs of Adelaide also benefited from the State's enlightened policies. The acceptance by the S.A. Department that such a class could operate within their mainstream system offered enormous hope to parents elsewhere, simply by making Montessori education more easily attainable and affordable.

In Western Australia, a similar postwar revival occurred in Montessori education. The first Montessori school to open in the second phase was Mrs. Duyker-De-Vries's school at Kingsley, the longest-surviving Montessori school in Australasia. Opened in 1962, it predates others in the West by a decade or more, and is actually one of the most spectacular success stories in the total Australasian experience. Willemien Duyker-de-Vries, who migrated to Australia a decade earlier, had gained her Montessori Diploma in Holland in 1939 under Maria and Mario. Before migrating to Australia in 1952, Mrs. Duyker gained valuable practical experience at a school she set up in her home and at the Pallas Athene Montessori School in Amersfoort. The catalyst for her Perth school occurred in 1959 when she adopted a three-month-old Aboriginal boy and it was for his education that she was inspired to commence her own Montessori school, first in her own home in Scarborough and from 1962 on a five-acre property on Robertson Road, Struan Heights in Wanneroo. That humble start has seen impressive growth from a modest pre-school to a primary school (1965) and in 1972 to a secondary top. It was the first Montessori high school in Australia and in 1994, it was fully accredited as a senior secondary high school offering courses of International Baccalaureate standard. Such has been Willemien Duyker's impact in the Wanneroo District that the Wanneroo Shire Council passed a Special Resolution in 1982 altering the name of Robertson Road to Montessori Place in honor of the institution that was bringing credit to the community. In June 1994, a training course for teachers devised by Mrs. Duyker was approved by the Western Australian Government. It was over a decade before the second Montessori pre-school opened in Perth. By June 1993, there were thirteen schools – six pre-primary, six primary, and one secondary. There was a need for teachers to be trained locally and a branch of the Montessori World Educational Institute was opened in Perth after Margaret Homfray's visit to Australia in 1984. Beth Alcorn was the first Australasian co-ordinator of MWEI (Australia) Incorporated. Julie Spencer now holds that position, her husband Lawrence as long-serving chairman of the board, with Bernadette Hendry as administrator.

The Northern Territory was slowest of all states to embrace the Montessori philosophy, obtaining its first center only in 1990. Its roots go back to 1982 when a small group of parents sought to form the Darwin Montessori Playgroup. That later grew into the Darwin Montessori Society. In 1988, Vickie Matthews conducted workshops and public lectures which the Department of Education agreed to fund. It was an indication of the growing respectability of Montessori in Australia's North. In 1989, there were moves to extend Montessori ideas and practices into the primary area. Much heart was derived from the acceptance by Margaret Muirhead, wife of the administrator of the Northern Territory who had started her school life at the Wilderness School in Adelaide, which was Montessori-based (O'Donnell, 1996).

The second phase of the Montessori Movement in New Zealand took firm root with the visit of Margaret Homfray and Phoebe Child in Christchurch in January 1977. It was an outstanding success and both returned the following year for workshops in Auckland and Christchurch. While the Montessori philosophy had never been totally extirpated, the work of Binda Goldsbrough stands out in post-World War Two years. Binda was born in 1912 on a farm at Aperfield in England. Her parents had been deeply impressed after reading *The Montessori Method*, published in English that year. They passed on their ardent belief in the educational merits of the 'Method' to their daughter and in 1931, Binda attended Montessori's International Course in London, gaining her Montessori Diploma at the age of nineteen and subsequently teaching in Montessori establishments in England. In 1938 and again in 1946, she had been appointed assistant demonstrator at Montessori's International Courses in London. In 1951, she migrated to New Zealand and was soon heading two small Montessori schools on the east coast. As principal of a school for the physically disabled, she remained in charge for seventeen years and utilized Montessori ideas and materials to great advantage. In retirement she began to pursue vigorously Montessori teacher training, persuading Homfray and Child when she was on holidays in England that they should visit New Zealand. Their historic visits in 1977 and 1978 are now part of the Montessori story. Goldsbrough, as author of the four-volume *The Aperfield Montessori Course, 1991–1994*, was awarded an MBE for her work with handicapped children.

In 1974–75, Elizabeth Hainstock visited New Zealand to set up the New Plymouth Montessori School. Other Montessori schools that were established include the Henderson Montessori Pre-School in Auckland (1977) and the Beehive Montessori School at Gisborne (1977). In January 1979, Lena Wikramaratne, director of the Montessori Education Center in Palo Alto, California and an AMI trainer, visited New Zealand. Wa Ora Montessori School at Lower Hutt (1988) became a state-integrated school in 1993. The Arthur Street Montessori Primary at Dunedin (1993) is of special importance in the history of Montessori in both Australia and New Zealand insofar as it points the way to the future: a marriage of state and private education in the interest of parents and children. Pam Shand was the teacher entrusted with the vital work. Subsequently, schools have been established at Ashburton (1994), Balclutha (1994), and Blenheim (1994).

One feature of the Montessori movement in Australasia (shared with other countries) is the absence of a central authoritative body able to fuse the eminently respectable but fragmented Montessori bodies into a cohesive whole. In 1974, a Sydney Montessori Association was formed by a handful of enthusiasts and by 1979, this had grown into the New South Wales Montessori Association (NSWMA), comprising seven Montessori schools operating in Sydney and the Blue Mountains. A notable feat by NSWMA in 1983 was the establishment of the Sydney Montessori Teachers' College (renamed the Montessori Teachers' College of Australia, or MTCA). The College offered a one-year full-time AMI Pre-Primary Teaching Diploma, with plans for a primary teacher course. Patricia Hilson played a large part in the founding of the College. With a long history of service to the Montessori movement in England, Western Australia, and the ACT, she served the MTCA successively as administrator (1983–84), deputy principal (1986), and principal and director of training (1990–93). Notwithstanding the quality of staff and courses, nor the commitment of the Montessorians associated with the College, the MTCA closed in October 1994. By 1988, NSWMA became the Montessori Association of Australia (MAA), its fundamental aim being to foster the growth of Montessori education. In 1995, MAA portrayed itself as the national umbrella organization for Montessori education in Australia (*Montessori of Australia Magazine*, issue 2, 1995). Each year membership has grown and it has organized a conference, with most states taking a turn as host. In July 1995, delegates from all over Australia attended the conference in Sydney. Keynote speaker for the occasion was Dr. Silvana Montanaro, a director of training for the AMI at Bergamo, Italy. In August 1996, the keynote speaker was Kay Baker, the primary director of the AMI Institute in Washington, DC. Other well-attended conferences have been held across the nation, culminating in the very successful AMI International Congress held in Sydney in 2005. At present, in multicultural Australia, there are moves toward having qualifications from different national and international Montessori organizations formalized and accredited.

Part 4

The Relevance of Montessori
Education Today

A century after the initial explosion of Montessori education onto the world stage, its relevance at the beginning of the twenty-first century remains undimmed. The sheer evidence of Montessori's significant presence on every continent today strongly suggests that not only is her method of enduring educational value but also that mainstream education could well take on board at least some of the ingredients in her program. As noted previously, she began with the work of her predecessors Itard, Séguin, and Sergi and it is useful in an examination of her relevance to re-visit them since they also offer solutions to the timeless riddle of how children learn best. In this regard, it is well to bear in mind the reminder of Walker that 'writing about the past is concerned very much with the issues of the present in mind' and of Hamilton stating 'history about a person or a period can continue to be written because the questions are always changing' (Walker and Hamilton, 1992). In the case of Montessori, it is also important for parents and teachers to bear in mind that she was not simply a teacher/researcher but a dedicated pediatrician concerned with the spiritual, physical, emotional, and psychological health of children as well as their intellectual growth. From Itard and Séguin she derived the basic mechanics of working with children in need. 'I followed Séguin's book, and also derived much help from the remarkable experiments of Itard,' she told the world in 1909 (Montessori, 1964: 36). She recognized childhood as a special period of life, realizing development could not be rushed but that each stage was dependent on what had been learned during the previous stage. From Sergi she absorbed a crusading fervor that elevated her work to a mission concerned with civilization and mankind, inspired by his 'principles of a new civilization based upon education' (ibid.: 2). The benefits accruing from the injection of Sergi's elevated vision of education (as opposed to mere inculcation of the 3Rs on a daily basis) are incalculable. On the question of relevance, it has to be emphasized that the influences of Itard and Séguin are eminently apparent today in every Children's House around the world in the unobtrusive observation of the children and how the didactic materials are introduced to each child individually. Sergi's crusading fervor is less obvious, and varies from individual directress to directress. Nonetheless, the Montessori philosophy always embraces each child as a citizen of the future, encouraged from his very first years to play an active role in his own destiny and to live in harmony with others. The Montessori dream that the hope of mankind lies in today's children is still worthy of consideration.

23 The Place of Freedom

A basic tenet in Montessori education – perhaps the most important of all her principles – is 'the liberty of the pupils in their spontaneous manifestations' (Montessori, 1964: 80). In 1948, after forty years, Montessori regarded children as still being 'oppressed' (Montessori, 1975: 51) just as they had been throughout history, which was basically concerned with the study of adults and children were hardly mentioned except for references to punishments. They had no voice to protest and had suffered 'a history of injustices' which 'were not taught as part of history in any grade' (ibid.). She pointed out that 'the Rights of Man' drawn up after the French Revolution included the right of everyone to be able to read and write. The burden fell to the child who was 'condemned to a life-sentence because for the whole of his child life he was sent to prison' (ibid.: 52). She questioned what happened to the spirit of each child sentenced to a state of immobility and silence all day in school, his status worse than adults in jail. Children's physical health was at risk because lack of movement meant muscles became deformed and children developed humpbacks. She called for radical change. She allowed free children to move about, choose activities, work at individual desks with movable chairs made to suit different heights of children. Research by Leon Straker (cited in Cole, 1999) has found that children are especially vulnerable to physical disorders caused by inappropriate furniture. Research by school principals in Queensland (Australia) indicates that the school-room boom in computer education has not been accompanied with suitable ergonomic furniture. An American study has shown that the introduction of adjustable computer furniture has led to significant improvement in children's posture. Some published data suggest that the very use of computers in schools could result in poor health for a whole generation of children.

In 1907, any suggestion of liberating children and allowing them to move about in a stress-free environment, choosing and working with didactic material was new. Today freedom to move is found in most early childhood rooms. Montessori recognized that all natural move-ments had to be controlled by the child's will and not the teacher's imposed will and she wanted to develop the child's capacity to foster that independence. She observed that by giving each child the oppor-tunity to move about and exercise his own will within the prepared environment, he became self-disciplined, independent, and master of himself. She had discovered the connection between freedom and self-discipline describing it as 'two faces of the same medal, the plain side being freedom, and the chiselled side discipline' (Montessori, 1967: 258). For Montessori, justice in the classroom was 'to ensure that every child shall make the best of himself' by giving 'every human being the help he needs to bring about his fullest spiritual stature' (ibid.). Of major concern to her was the mental treatment of children in schools in 1907 which depressed each child's spirit (Montessori, 1964: 20) and accordingly she provided conditions within the Chil-dren's House environment which produced healthy, happy children. It was in this stress-free environment that she supplied the means for happy children to learn to write and read spontaneously. The spe-cial spiritual conditions within the environment produced dramatic results: spontaneous writing by the children at four years. It was this minor miracle that convinced Montessori to give up everything and devote her life to education and according to Mario Montessori, her son, 'the realization of the part spirituality played overwhelmed his mother.' She gave up a brilliant career as a doctor and a lecturer at Rome University. She gave up her position among the socialists and her standing among the feminists. She even left her family to devote her life 'to nourishing the inner spirit of the child' (Bennett, 1984: 41–51). She saw happiness, which could not be measured, as 'a key to life.' James McConvill (2006) averred 'the study of happiness is now a science' reporting that 'happiness psychologist Tim Kasser (2006) reviewed the results of a range of studies of human happiness' in his book *The High Price of Materialism*. He 'names the psychological needs for greater human happiness' as being: safety, security, competence, efficacy, self-esteem, connectedness (closeness with others), and autonomy (freedom to be self-directed). The role of a Montessori directress has been to provide for all these psychological needs since the first Children's House opened in 1907.

On the other hand, Montessori warned that she had observed that when children found themselves in classrooms where every error was corrected, and they were punished or rewarded, or not allowed to move or talk or help each other in class, they became depressed. When neither recognized nor treated as human beings over a number of years, they felt humiliated, disgraced, guilty, as though they had committed crimes, and so 'brotherhood was not born' (Montessori, 1967: 240). They were disciplined, and reduced to immobility and silence for no apparent purpose (Montessori, 1964: 26), many children experiencing similar depressing conditions at home. Montessori warned what happened to children growing under such conditions. These 'unloved, abandoned, forgotten children organized themselves into gangs in rebellion against authority and adult made regulations' (Montessori, 1967: 235). She forewarned what could happen in adolescence if children had lived daily for years in such an atmosphere where 'rivalry, emulation, ambition have been encouraged through education' (ibid.: 242). If adolescents 'were treated as babies, with petty threats of bad marks on which their future depends, quite suddenly they become very sensitive to rudeness and humiliations that they had previously suffered with patient indifference' (Montessori, 1973: 101). Those who grew up in such an oppressive atmosphere could not hope to become 'good' citizens simply because the teacher preached goodness when 'no preparation has been made for the life of the spirit; goodness came from reciprocal helpfulness' (Montessori, 1967: 242). Often adolescents experienced bitter, rebellious feelings which gave rise to amoral characteristics, sometimes criminality (ibid.: 101). Worse still, oppressed children with depressed spirits, emotions in turmoil, no prospects, and loss of hope, turned to self-abuse. Tragically, the highest percentage of suicides reported in Australia today is by fourteen-year-old adolescents.

At present there are those, such as Colin Lankshear and Michele Knobel, who ardently espouse the cause of Critical Literacy in order to emancipate all oppressed people, including children in the classroom and they see it as 'a universal avocation' (Muspratt et al., 1997: 151). Such views are not inimical to Montessori's original advocacy of the emancipation of the children of the world from the strictures of traditional education. Indeed, postmodernists who have concentrated on oppression of minority groups and those who favor Critical Literacy to open the eyes of children and adults in order to create a just society both demonstrate the ongoing relevance of the very point made by Montessori in her *Il Metodo* (1909). Ramon A. Serrano, an academic from a working-class background has maintained, like Montessori, that 'school oppression leads to gang formations' (Edelsky, 1999: 226) and that the path to freedom for these oppressed children is through education and graduation (ibid.: 232). Serrano's viewpoint has been strongly supported by Paul Willis who pointed out that in the current climate of globalization those who have only 'their manual labour power to live by or sell' will soon discover that there is a global over-supply of labor (de Castell et al., 1989: 139). One hundred years after Montessori put into practice her hitherto unknown notions of freedom of the child, Willis made the telling point that at the end of the twentieth century 'no one really imagines any more that schools are about emancipation for the working class' (ibid.). On the question of the relevance today of that principle of freedom, it is worth noting that Carole Edelsky appeared to mirror the words of Montessori one century later: 'Modern educators need to analyse, not just complain about or to feel oppressed by our own actions' (Edelsky, 1999: 145). Moreover, she urged her readers to transform themselves, their classrooms, and schools to effect the change (ibid.: 315). Children, she pointed out, need freedom and responsibility, both of which are 'often withheld in schools' (ibid.: 336) something which Montessori gave to young three-year-old children.

In extreme cases of oppression, tragedies such as the shootings of twenty-four students at Springfield High, Oregon in May 1998 by a fifteen-year-old boy, shocked everyone. Less than a year later the massacre of twelve students at Columbine High School, Colorado, in April 1999, by two boys aged seventeen and eighteen was seen to be due to poor relationships between some teachers, some senior boy athletes, and these two boys. The killers saw themselves as having been treated unjustly. They had grown in an atmosphere of rivalry and competition receiving negative messages from teachers and peers alike. An American psychologist, Dr. James Garbarino, stated at the time, 'Most boys who kill do so because of a history of troubled relationships with parents, peers and the community and they feel justified in punishing those who have hurt them.' His report continued, 'parents should get to know their children's friends and school environment'. But Dr. Garbarino predicted that 'it is inevitable that massacres will continue to happen because the conditions that produce them remain largely unchanged' (*The Australian*, June, 1999). This happened more than ninety years after Montessori began writing about providing correct social conditions which could avoid such tragedies and other criminal behavior.

At the beginning of the twentieth century 'Pedagogy must join medicine ... was the thought of the time' (Montessori, 1964: 31) and an attempt has been made above to show how effectively Montessori was able to marry the two. Through liberty and freeing the spirit, children's mental health and physical health improved. She maintained that education was about life and living but pointed out how 'education (traditional) does not take into account life itself' (Montessori, 1967: 9). Montessori education has always been concerned with the development of the whole child. The concept of Health Promoting Schools in Australia today specifies that 'health is created and lived by people within the settings of their everyday life; where they learn, work, play and love' (World Health Organization, 1986). Health Promoting Schools today seek much that can be found in Montessori environments. A recent study conducted by the British Government's Home Office recommended 'that children as young as three years should be targeted as potential criminals' from evidence of nursery school bullying or family history. It reported that children who were not under control by three years were four times as likely to commit a violent offence. It found that eighty-five per cent of prison inmates had been school bullies who did not suffer from low self-esteem but acted as gang leaders. It was suggested that if 'potential criminals were spotted early enough, better results could be achieved by "soft measures" such as improving their reading, language and social skills' (Daly and Stack, 2005). Much research is done today into the psychosocial development of children which involves both medicine and education. Ongoing research into Educational Resilience was reported by Dr. Alison van Haeringen in Queensland in 2003. 'Work on resilience in the psychosocial domain and the prevention of criminality will be built upon to investigate educational and learning outcomes,' she wrote. Resilience 'injects hope and optimism into the dispiriting story of risk and adversity' and has arisen from 'the observation that even among the most disadvantaged children, some do well.' Questions she asked included: 'What makes people strong?' and 'Can we intervene to change life paths?' The research looked at the family and social factors affecting child development, the importance of early intervention to create better pathways and outcomes for children at risk. It explored the factors which occur during early childhood and the intellectual ability of children at five and fourteen years. Such investigations show a clear union of education and medicine working together to solve present-day problems. Some answers to this problem may be found within Montessori education.

A greater focus on the need for freedom and equality in schools began in the 1970s. Divorkin saw justice in schools in the manner Montessori applied it. He made a distinction between treating people equally and treating them as equals, asserting that

> When we treat people equally everyone gets the same regardless of need. When we treat people as equals, the claims of each are equally considered whether or not this leads to unequal treatment. Most people agree that the needy should get more.
>
> (Corson, 1993: 30)

In practice, Montessori did treat children as equals giving each child the help needed to succeed. It was Farganis (1975) with a deep interest in Critical Social Science, who called for emancipation of all concerned in schools but the problem of how to establish that emancipation remains unresolved in his model (Carr and Kemmis, 1994). Montessori education has shown for virtually a century how children can be freed at the same time as they are guided into making sound decisions which are right and just for the whole group. There is continuing debate about the place of freedom. Soohoo (1993) has pointed out that somehow 'educators have forgotten the important connection between teachers and students' and teachers 'need to find out ways to continually seek out their silent voices.' Brian Street emphasized the fundamental importance of literacy 'to free children from oppression and ignorance' (Street, 1995: 1). Advocates of whole-language methodologies such as Kenneth Goodman, approached freedom from a different perspective from Montessori, but also sought to 'free the minds and creative energies of pupils for the greatest gains in their intellectual, physical and social development' (Courts, 1997: 110). Edelsky also calls for 'critiquing systems of domination – in order to increase democracy and promote justice and equality ... by making whole language critical' (Edelsky, 1999: 19). These viewpoints appear to be very close to Montessori's of 1907 when she freed the minds and creative energies of children. In Montessori education, children from three years experience democracy, justice, and equity firsthand in their everyday environments.

Today, there is support for Montessori's views on freedom as worthy of attention, with the timeless issue of justice for children being as valid today as it was in her lifetime. Children's mental freedom and social rights were recognized by Montessori but as she noted thirty years after *Il Metodo*, there was 'no recognition of the rights of children in history ... the word education was synonymous with punishment ... and there was no one to defend them' (Montessori, 1978: 236). It was in 1951 that she took the issue to the world with her UNESCO paper entitled 'The Rights of the Child.' That was no feeble gesture of protest by a misguided zealot, as is tellingly indicated by the continuing relevance of her demand. It is worthy of note that the eminent public figure Hillary Rodham Clinton, herself a Montessori mother, continues to call for the rights of children. On the broader education front, today, there is also an unanswerable need for emancipating the child from the shackles of oppression, exploitation, brow-beating, sex abuse, slave labor, and atrocities of war.

24 Observation of Free Children

One of the enduring lessons of the Montessori experience is the crucial importance of observing free children as individuals as opposed to treating all as identical. While lip-service is paid to the much-vaunted mantras of individual differences and individual tuition, the reality is that many systems provide a blanket, one-size-fits-all approach. In one of the poorest districts in Rome in 1907, Montessori closely observed the children, aged three years to seven years, minutely noting their natural tendencies. As a consequence, she shed many time-honored pedagogical theories and practices to establish a genuinely individualized learning program in which the child himself had a significant input. Even though it ran counter to the prevailing educational theories of the day, the Montessori Method has stood the test of time. It was not until the 1970s that observation of children in classrooms began to be acceptable. Montessori's grandson presented a paper in Dublin addressing his grandmother's 'careful, patient and systematic observations of children' (Montessori Jr., 1972: 22) over a period of forty years. It was Montessori who told the world, 'At most, I have been the children's interpreter, through observation' (Montessori, 1961: 4). Today, observation of children is a respected tool for classroom research.

High among Montessori's priorities was the timing of intervention by the directress. It is one critical aspect of the teacher's role and in her first Children's House an overriding concern was to avoid snuffing out of existence 'spontaneous action,' or the very spirit of life itself (Montessori, 1964: 87). Timing was of critical importance in introducing the didactic materials to the children. There is little that is controversial in the concept, other educators identifying it as 'readiness.' Montessori's distinguished follower, Jean Piaget, also emphasized the importance of introducing a piece of material to a child at the exact psychological moment. Duckworth (1979) found 'applying' Piaget difficult since it was her experience that teachers intervened too early for the child to grasp the skill or master the intricacies of the concept, or too late after the child had already learned how to perform the task. The well-known reading-researcher Kenneth Goodman has written of what he called 'teachable moments.' For him, such key times in the learning process were 'best for metacognition,' or, as he put it, 'knowing what you know and how you know it' (Goodman, 1986: 53). In his studies in the United States, he carefully analyzed errors, or miscues, and his work was replicated in New Zealand by Professor Marie Clay; both studies enhancing the understanding of learning to read. Miscues are seen as providing insights into how the learner thinks about reading, and provide teachers with information to deal with errors or problems on the spot. Although not all educators are in agreement about the definition of 'spontaneous action' or timing of 'teachable moments,' there is continuing debate about the concept raised by Montessori. At the source, lies the importance of the Montessori principle of observation.

Unlike Montessori, leading, influential psychologists at the end of the nineteenth century did not work with children. They were informed by research on animal behavior using rewards and punishments (Clarke-Stewart et al., 1985: 11). Montessori was completely out of step with the eminent Pavlov (1849–1936) and his theory of conditioning, favoring instead a stress-free environment with no rewards and no punishments. The emphasis on extrinsic rewards is still influential in the thinking of many teachers and parents today. Punishments are still common in schools (often psychological), although corporal punishment has been banned by law in many countries. Donaldson (1978) has argued against external rewards, while Kohn (1993) was able to show that students were punished rather than rewarded when they received external rewards. Edelsky (1999: 62) has discussed at length the 'unjust reward system in schools.' Montessori children in 1907 were free and did not require rewards or punishments because they taught themselves through their inner spontaneous urge not through the external means of prizes and punishments. If a child disrupted others at work, he was treated with gentleness and respect. He was offered a chair where he could observe all the children working in harmony and when his nervous system was calm, he was invited to rejoin the group without his spirit being suppressed.

Montessori did not see the need for tests or examinations. Her careful, detailed notes of each child's development made from direct observations meant there was no need for formal testing because she already knew what each child could do. Moreover, the elimination of tests and examinations helped to further reduce stress in the prepared environment. Children were accordingly more relaxed and their mental health was enhanced, as Montessori attended to the spirit of each child. 'The *bad marks* with which teachers weigh up the work of girls and boys is like measuring lifeless objects with a balance,' she wrote: 'measured like inanimate matter, not judged as a product of life' (Montessori, 1973: 100). As Montessori had shown from 1907 onwards, there were other ways of measuring growth, including continuous assessment, especially by close observation. The controversy has continued. In her well-known article 'Kid watching: an alternative to testing,' Yetta Goodman (1987) concurred with Montessori in the view that observation was an alternative to psychological testing. The reward system in today's schools, which depends on examinations and competition, could be seen as unjust, leading to frustration, unhappiness, and anger in students. Edelsky has queried the impact of examinations and testing. 'What is happening in these students' lives that make them so angry?' she asked in more recent times (Edelsky, 1999: 291). In the 1930s, Montessori (1967) showed how competition, tests, and exams provoked anger in students while continuous assessment of work done by students through observation without rewards and punishments, helped promote co-operation among children as anger disappeared. More than eighty years have elapsed since Montessori first raised such matters.

Montessori was opposed to Intelligence Tests such as those compiled by Binet (Binet and Simon, 1905, cited in Galloway, 1976) who claimed he was measuring intelligence, which he defined as being a general ability to learn, to reason, to grasp concepts, and to deal with abstractions. Montessori countered in 1916 that 'the tests can neither measure anything nor give an approximate idea of intellectual level of intelligence according to age and whether response was due to intrinsic activity or individual action on the environment' (Montessori, 1969: 111). She had already demonstrated with children found in asylums (1898–1900) 'that children's intelligence could be raised' (Hunt in Montessori, 1964: xv) if the child experienced the correct conditions for learning. To Montessori, the child was seen as one whole personality and could not be divided into parts. She did not see how a number could measure a child's development and by 1907, she was certain that human intelligence could not be tested with any accuracy at all, and that tests told nothing of a child's personality. All they could reveal is how a child performed on a particular test on a particular day. Support for Montessori's stance against IQ tests was slow in coming but as Lohmann scarifyingly points out, Skeels and Dye had, in the 1930s, 'virtually proved the malleability of the intelligence and the unreliability of IQ scores with regard to the environmental experience ... and [they] were pilloried by the academic establishment' (Lohmann, 1988: 7). Until very recent decades, support for IQ testing has been global in extent but some signs of a re-assessment began in the early 1970s when cracks began to appear in the notion of infallible IQs and it was reported that it was becoming increasingly apparent that a child's learning could not be determined wholly by his *mental age* but it could be assessed more accurately from a determination of sensory development (Evans, 1971: 63). Later, Weber (1984) and Silin (1990) suggested that childhood educators were relying more and more exclusively on knowledge derived from studies of child development. Yet, IQ testing continues to this day.

It is a century since Montessori's views on IQ and testing first appeared, but it was not just testing that concerned her. There was also what she perceived as a dearth of top-level studies into children and their psyches. In 1946, having just been released from her exile in India and already in her seventy-sixth year, Montessori wrote about the urgent need for deeper studies into this neglected area:

More research and more investigations were needed to discover the mysteries and the hidden powers of the children ... the energies and powers embodied in a tiny little child are more powerful than the newly discovered energy of the atomic bomb.

(Montessori, 1963: 72)

In relatively recent times, Howard Gardner (1983) has identified multiple intelligences – linguistic, logical, mathematical, spatial, musical, interpersonal, and intra-personal. More recently he has added naturalist (exploring nature) and also spiritual intelligence (Schiller, 2000). It is important to note that spiritual development was the very first consideration in Montessori education and, always, all things in nature (as well as nurture) were included. To her, it was the interaction of all the intelligences identified by Gardner (including naturalist and spiritual) which combined to make each child's personality and it was the child's personality that Montessori sought to develop in her holistic approach to education. When she spoke to a child, it was the child as a person or a unique personality. It is also important to note that Howard Gardner (1983) found intelligence tests to be 'limited not only in competences that they examine but in the ways that they examine them' (Courts, 1997: 101). This is a striking confirmation of Montessori's views.

Toward the end of her life, Montessori's vision of future education was noted in the preface of *From Childhood to Adolescence* (1958):

> My vision for the future is no longer of people taking exams and proceeding on that certification from secondary school to University, but of individuals passing from one stage of independence to a higher, by means of their own activity, through their own effort of will, which constitutes the inner evolution of the individual.
>
> (Montessori, 1973: xiv)

In this first decade of the twenty-first century, when the Western tradition of compartmentalized education from infants through primary to secondary and tertiary components is being challenged, Montessori's vision of the future may have arrived. Some postmodernists are challenging assessment procedures by putting forward proposals similar to those proposed by Montessori. In Australia, for example, Education Queensland is at present examining the possibility of introducing 'seamless education' from pre-school through to university graduation. In these 'new times' when the Western canon is being challenged, a re-examination of Montessori education could be in order.

25 Child Development

Maria Montessori ranks among the pioneers of child development, her theories based solidly on the immutable laws of nature. To her, the prepared environment was 'a plan for allowing children to develop according to natural laws' (Montessori, 1966: 81). In 1914 she wrote, 'The laws of development are there, they have to be observed, ascertained and followed,' (Montessori, 1963: 21) and just as the universe worked according to the laws of nature, with regular cycles for all things in the cosmos, so did the growth of a child (Montessori, 1967: 19). By the 1930s, Montessori's observations were still not considered by educators to be scientific. She recognized the newborn as a psychic embryo with a psychic life before birth (Montessori, 1967) but immediately after birth care of his 'mental life' was neglected (see Part 1). Increasing weight is being given today to the notion first raised by Montessori of the importance of the prenatal and post-natal care up to three years when she claimed the child possessed an unconscious absorbent mind which 'is indeed a marvellous gift to humanity' (Montessori, 1961: 28). It was she who coined the phrase 'absorbent mind' to describe those first years when the newborn absorbed impressions from the environment naturally which laid the foundation for his subsequent 'marvellous progress' (Montessori, 1967: 24). While the phrase helped to explain how children learned language from the environment, she cautioned that exactly how the child's mind worked remained 'one of nature's secrets' (Montessori, 1965: 34). Today, the term 'absorbent mind' is found in many texts dealing with early development.

One of the most important discoveries made by Montessori, through her observations, was 'the sensitive periods.' From the first hours of birth the child's mind remained in 'a sensitive period,' a term first used by de Vries for plant growth and adopted by Montessori and applied to periods of development in children. Physically the child was incomplete at birth and 'motor nerves are not yet provided with their covering of myelin that enables them to transmit the brain's orders' (Montessori, 1967: 72). She advised parents in the 1930s that the newborn must be allowed to move for motor nerves to develop in order to obey the brain, warning that if a child was unable to move, the connections between the brain and the nerves remained incomplete and died (Montessori, 1967). Continued observations showed her that every child passed through sensitive periods at approximately the same age when 'children were endowed with special psychic powers' (Montessori, 1966: 2). She defined the sensitive periods as 'a predisposition to a period of growth and transient in nature, occurring for a few weeks, months or years, when a child, guided from within, had an insatiable desire to acquire a skill' (Montessori, 1978: 35). Physical development (e.g. walking and talking) and cognitive development (e.g. writing and reading) had sensitive periods. It was the child who knew when it was time to learn and that learning was entirely spontaneous. A skill missed during a sensitive period could be learned later but only with much effort on the part of the child (Montessori, 1978). Montessori stressed that parents should know about the sensitive periods and their order of occurrence otherwise 'one cannot understand the construction of the psyche of the child' (Montessori, 1963: 21). In recent times, Berk used the term 'sensitive period' and defined it as 'a time span that is optimal for certain capacities to emerge and in which the individual is especially responsive to the environmental influences' (Berk, 1996: 27). She provided neurological evidence about the importance of the sensitive periods from birth when a baby 'is born with its full complement of neurons . . . and connecting nerve fibres grow at an astonishing rate. Connecting synapses frequently used survive while those seldom used die off.' Armstrong (1999) cited a more recent study of research into brain development in which it was discovered that tens of thousands of nerve connections that exist in the newborn infant's mind die if not used in the first months. Findings correspond with Montessori's writings about myelination in 1938 where she explained the importance of repetition of movement from birth, warning parents about swaddling clothes, failure to interact with the newborn, and placing the child alone in a nursery. Some of her recommendations for newborns are now seen in practice in some hospitals. She pronounced the infant to be 'an unknown being who does not arouse awe and imagination for what he is able to do to create himself' (Montessori, 1975: 49). She urged mothers to help the essential development of the newborn by placing the child where he could see and hear everything in the environment. There could be no direct adult influence because 'the child created himself through his own unconscious efforts and by nature's inner urge' (Montessori, 1967: 24). In the early 1930s, it was commonly thought that a new-born had no psychic life but to Montessori 'the chief characteristic of a human babe is intelligence' (Montessori, 1963: 31). For continuity of development, Montessori advised parents that home and school should provide similar, stress-free living conditions.

As a pioneer of linguistics, Montessori, in 1909, pointed out that language was absorbed and perfected by the infant who passed through two distinct periods in the development of articulate language. By the 1930s, she noted the whole process of learning to speak was internal and perceived by Montessori as 'the mechanics of articulate language' (Montessori, 1967: 313–15), all hidden from observation. These complex preparations made by the child before he could begin to speak his mother tongue were absorbed from the environment. She recorded minute details of the mechanisms of articulate language noting that each child passed through four distinct stages of spoken language: separate sounds, syllables, a word, and syntax (ibid.: 139). It was not taught but was natural, spontaneous, and universal, following the laws of nature (ibid.: 111). In the 1970s, the field of linguistics caught the attention of researchers. Britton's (1970) research findings closely matched Montessori's observations. He stressed that the environment played a large part in the child learning to talk but it was the child who learned. Several linguists, including Chomsky, Katz, and Postal suggested that 'in beginning to learn language the child relies on an innate component of basic linguistic skill which is present in the brain' (Roberts, 1974: 4). These linguists did not acknowledge the significant work and effort on the child's part to master the mechanics of articulation. Lock (1978) regarded language learning as 'a process of guided reinvention' by showing the importance of significant others in the learning process, a view which concurred with Montessori. Montessori's early observations and findings about the very early developmental stages of learning the mother tongue match the findings of later research done by M. A. K. Halliday (1975) in England and Australia and Gordon Wells (1981) in England and Canada. Clare Painter (1985) in Australia has drawn attention to the fact that a number of psychologists had become interested in neonatal and infant behavior, a new field of infant psychology. Their method was to observe spontaneous behaviors in natural settings rather than data contrived from experimental situations. It was the identical method Montessori had followed eight decades earlier. Painter noted that some of these psychologists were particularly interested in vocal behavior of young children and have 'greatly contributed to our understanding of the pre-linguistic child' (ibid.: 6). In the processing of developing language, the child unconsciously internalizes the sound system, learns morphological rules, and masters most of the principal syntactic structures of the mother tongue even with no formal education (ibid.: 42). Painter's record of their findings closely matched those of Montessori more than fifty years earlier. Gee (1996) has noted that a child 'acquires' language with his unconscious mind, which agreed with Montessori. She viewed the acquisition of language as being universal, a natural process following the laws of nature, but it was a 'secret of childhood,' and the mystery of 'how each child sets about his inner building is a secret he will not reveal' (Montessori, 1978: 210). Moreover, latter-day psychologists also argue that every child follows the laws of nature which are universal, with Edelsky pointing out that there is 'substantial evidence for the universality of psychological processes in oral language' (Edelsky, 1999: 17). Montessori saw all development as being both psychological and social, maintaining that development was the same for every child and any differences within races arose from nurture, not nature.

Montessori had discovered that 'free' children taught themselves successfully, working with her practical life and sensorial materials without fear of punishment. She found there was no need for rewards; instead, success brought children an 'inner' reward, the sheer joy of succeeding. In this, she was completely out of step with her contemporaries who continued working on connectionists' theories informed by research on animals. Their classical conditioning theory was introduced by Ivan Pavlov (1849–1936) whose research recorded responses made by dogs to a stimulus. In the US, John Watson (1878–1956) continued this work applying classical conditioning to children, especially on his adopted son who was conditioned to fear a toy rabbit he had loved. The method was extreme but his research was to prove that children could be controlled by external means. Edwin Guthrie (1896–1959) researched the practical applications of principles of learning following the stimulus/response theory, his fundamental conclusion being that what we do is what we learn (Guthrie, 1952: 23). Edward Thorndike (1874–1949) showed in his research that when children's correct responses were rewarded, they learned, while incorrect responses and behavior were punished. His findings, published in *Principles of Teaching Based upon Psychology* (Thorndike, 1913), were not inimical to those of his contemporary Montessori. In 1924, a strong stance was taken by Vygotsky (1896–1934) 'against Pavlov's dominating theory of conditioning reflexes and he called for the recognition of man's conscious behaviour' (Wertsch, 1985: 8). Vygotsky, a psychologist, was 'the darling of the intellectual community' (Lohmann, 1988: 4). Lohmann suggests Vygotsky may have been aware of *The Montessori Method*, translated into Russian in 1912 when a Montessori classroom was set up in the Tsar's palace in St Petersburg for the royal children. Certainly the position Vygotsky took in his stance against Pavlov in 1924 matched that taken earlier by Montessori in 1907, as did the fact they both agreed on the importance of human consciousness. In a more recent article, Margaret Loeffler states that 'Montessori and Vygotsky admired each other's work' and that 'it is interesting to see the increasing influence of their ideas on current child development theories and practices' (Loeffler, 2002: 9). First published in 1934 and in English in 1986, Vygotsky's theories are popular today and several similarities to Montessori can be drawn. In the 1930s, it was B. F. Skinner (1904–90) in the USA who exerted a major influence on children's learning. His theory of operant-conditioning emphasized the importance of reinforcement by rewards and punishments, as a result of his research done on rats. Connectionists were concerned with learning where children were perceived as passive non-thinkers being stimulated from the outside. The method was whole-class teaching and every student was working on the same task at the same time and given the same amount of time to complete work. Children were expected to learn by rote. This view of learning had a dominant impact on education especially in the primary school years and it remained in many teachers' colleges until the 1950s and beyond. Reinforcement style of teaching/learning can still be found in schools. Children continue to be threatened with punishments and expulsion from school. These theories and practices are demonstrably in conflict with Montessorian ideas about free children in a supportive classroom environment. To quote Montessori, she and her directresses 'refrain from inciting reactions depending on the will of the experimenter ... offering free chosen activity by children' (Montessori, 1972: vii). The principle of free choice remains extremely important in Montessori education since that is dependent on the will of the child.

One of the special features of Montessori education in 1907 was individualized learning, a subject of major relevance across the whole education spectrum today and to Montessori it was critically important. In 1909, she noted the aim of education to be 'to provide the conditions favourable to a person's entire individuality' (Montessori, 1964: 104). When she addressed the group attending the teacher-training course in India in 1942, she told them that her method was the first to introduce the concept of individual learning 'developed upon systematic individual work ... its basis individual interest.' The problem for the teacher in individualized learning lay in organizing her/his classroom to allow each student the time he required. This is possible in Montessori education because there are no timetables. Directresses understand child development and realize the need for children to work to an 'inner' timetable, at their own rate to satisfy that 'inner' need. Directresses also understand that there are 'sensitive periods' when 'bursts' of development occur and therefore lock-step work is entirely unsuitable and they are able to follow the development of each child by providing free-choice activities. The children are in multi-age groups and work with those in the same developmental period spanning three years. Montessori showed how practical such an arrangement was by describing how a mother of six children copes better than a mother of twins (Montessori, 1967: 205). Children of different ages can help each other. A child of five years can explain things to a child of three years because 'the mind of a five year old is closer to the mind of a three year old' (ibid.: 206).

Education policies today specify individualized programs for learners in multi-age classrooms, often referred to as 'vertical grouping,' to improve outcomes of learning. Class sizes have been reduced to help in this matter but implementation has been elusive. In 1992, Peterson suggested teachers should 'follow the child' (as Itard and Montessori had done) because when you 'join in their march, the programme goes where they are going' and he urged teachers 'to try to take the child's lead' (Edelsky, 1999: 118, 150) rather than the children following the teacher's program. Peterson does not explain exactly how this has to be done, unlike Montessori who demonstrated how it was possible in practice with forty or more local children from the area where she was presenting her workshops. Skinner, after thirty years of research, finally designed an individualized program of learning, graded into such small learning steps that all students always succeeded but children could not miss a step. He described this process of programming knowledge and skills as the construction of carefully arranged sequences which led to objectives (Skinner, 1963: 169). Forms of programmed learning continue to be used for individual learning to this day. About this time, John Carroll attributed learning to the attitude of the child along with the quality of instruction and he believed that if a child was allowed all the time he required to complete a task, he would be successful (Carroll, 1963: 725). Mastery learning, an instructional approach by Benjamin Bloom was developed from the theories of John Carroll. The problem for the teacher in mastery learning lay in organizing the classroom to allow each student the time he required. Montessori always allowed children as much time as they required to complete self-chosen tasks by organizing blocks of three hours of uninterrupted work cycles. During these work cycles she observed children's learning was not linear but appeared suddenly, in an explosive manner. There could be no timetables because children work to an inner timetable at their own rate, to satisfy an inner need.

The reception approach to learning had David Ausubel as its spokesperson. Children were presented with the content to be learned and did not need to discover on their own, which 'is unduly time-consuming and unnecessary for most school learning.' The task of the teacher was to organize instruction so 'the content will be received by the learner in a form that can be incorporated easily with previous learning' (Galloway, 1976: 4). There was the discovery approach supported by Jerome Bruner which helped learners 'get the feel of how scientists go about their work.' The method engaged students in discussions and the use of concrete materials, which causes learners to gain insights into the processes of knowledge 'the stuff of which real and lasting learning is made' (ibid.). Evidence of both the reception approach and the discovery approach are found in the Montessori approach. The brief three-period lessons presented the new content only when children were prepared with prerequisites using the Montessori materials. Having young children work with didactic materials as though they were scientists making discoveries was often criticized.

Robert Gagné listed five requirements which caused learning to occur: clear objectives, prerequisites, attention to the task, knowledge of results along with time to complete their work. It was Donald Broadbent (1958) who produced one of the earliest models of information processing, which he described as a theory of attention to explain what happened during listening tasks. It subsequently exerted an influence on the fields of cognitive psychology and cognitive development and by the 1970s, a consensus was emerging from the findings of behaviorists, learning theorists, cognitive psychologists, developmentalists, and researchers of information processing. Information processing has been described as beginning in the learner's senses followed by application to a task. If the learner had the opportunity to practice and repeat an experience, the new information was learned and stored in long-term memory (LTM) (Gage and Berliner, 1979; Clarke-Stewart et al., 1985). After more than two decades of research, an interactive-model of information processing had evolved which considered the interaction among the activities of the learner, the characteristics of the learner, the nature of the materials to be learned, and the qualities of the task by which the learner was assessed (Browne et al., 1983). The interactive information-processing model in 1983 was more closely matched to Montessori education than the stimulus/response model of behaviorist psychology put forth by researchers in 1907 when the *Casa dei Bambini* opened. In a sense, all of these educators were catching up with the ideas Montessori had been propagating over half a century earlier about what goes on inside children's minds, how they learn and how they remember.

On Montessori education, Galloway (1976: 412) points out:

It is hard to understand how an instructional approach based on a philosophy that subsumes so many of the key ideas of the world's outstanding theorists of development, learning and education could have gone relatively unnoticed, particularly in the United States and Canada for a period of nearly fifty years. Yet, from the time her first book *The Montessori Method,* was published in 1912 until the 1960s there were only a few places in the world where the Montessori method and materials were being used.

Montessori recognized the child 'as her fellow human being' (Mario Montessori, Dublin Conference, 1977) but it was only when the new field of humanistic psychology evolved in the 1960s that psychologists began to examine children as human beings and not as objects. It was described by Jarrett as 'a school of psychology that sets itself up against all other psychology,' which he listed as being mechanical psychology, natural psychology, S-R psychology, behavioristic to operant conditioning psychology, and other schools that were based on a rigorous scientific, experimental, quantitative approach (Jarrett, 1972: 106). Advocates of humanistic approaches to education hold the belief that the learner should take more responsibility for determining what is to be learned and become more self-directing and independent. The new discipline of humanistic psychology brought a new vocabulary with such terms as 'psychological education,' 'affection,' 'humanistic,' 'personalogical,' 'eupschian,' and 'syoetic' to describe the major thrust of this new discipline (Borton, 1970: 135). In spite of the jargon, it was a personal approach to psychology (Kong, 1970: 135). Norman Gronlund described humanistic psychology as the study of the whole person, including all the qualities that explained a child's uniqueness, not just part of him. It included his emotions, his personality, his reactions with others and alone, his behavior under stress and at play, the person himself as he actually was, not as he probably was according to a traditional psychological stereotype. How to empathize was important, a crucial ingredient in understanding one's fellow man. The 'affective domain' became paramount rather than the coldly dispassionate intellectual 'cognitive area' (Gronlund,

1970: 18). Kong concluded that humanistic psychology was relevant to education. It had been relevant to Montessori education since its inception. Carl Weinberg defined humanistic psychology as 'the application of principles of humanistic psychology to education' explaining how 'it shies away from experiments which involves treating persons as so many numbers' (Weinberg, 1972: 116). When applied to learning 'it assumes that learning is more than we can measure' and by specifying in advance 'what has to be learned, the student may be diverted from real progress that could occur as he chooses his own learning goals' (ibid.: 115). Arthur Combs defined humanistic education as being concerned with success and failure, with interactions between pupils, with their emotions of trust, respect, and freedom. It was about self-realization. The individual had to grow and develop as a free, thinking, acting person. The aim of humanistic education was to produce persons who possessed deep feelings for others, fostered a bond of trust which led to respect for each other (Combs, 1967: 89–91). Combs summed up: 'we can live with a bad reader but a Bigot is a danger to everyone' (ibid.: 91).

Montessori education has been concerned with humanistic principles which Montessori applied from 1907. She provided the correct classroom climate for humanistic learning to take place daily. The long-term outcome was a youth prepared to adapt to any environment and take his place as a contributing member of society. The humanistic teacher has been described by Dillon as 'a giver, who gave respect, empathy, affection, kindness, encouragement, freedom, friendship, confidence, security and help'. She did not have disciplinary problems because she was liked and loved. The children in her care achieved so much and although it was impossible to measure the change, it could be observed. Joe Hiderich used 'lover' to describe a humanistic teacher (Dillon, 1971: 135). Humanistic education meant 'a change in the teacher's status from superior to the student to equal with the student ... the choice of subject matter is considered to be a student's right' (Gage and Berliner, 1979: 559). Shelley Phillips (1980: 10) found that 'surprisingly few people genuinely regard young children as being of the human species and as persons one can take seriously as suffering hurt and damage to feelings.' Some teachers in the 1980s, she thought, 'were clutching at a new style of teaching described as authoritative which sought a balance between the duties and rights of teachers and the duties and rights of children' (ibid.: 11). She even suggested that the findings of her study 'were exactly what Montessori had considered to be the responsible way of treating children but now went under the new name of "authoritative". Teachers who used the "authoritative" approach were quite unconscious that the ghost of Montessori hangs over them' (ibid.: 14). Humanistic psychology and the humanistic teacher closely resembled what Montessori education had practiced since 1907. It was possible that the psychologists advocating a humanistic approach were not aware of Montessori's work, but if they did know about her humane, personalized approach, they failed to acknowledge her.

26 The Environment

It was observation of children's natural tendencies as they worked with self-chosen activities that, Montessori maintained, led her to providing a suitable psychological and physical environment. It had been prescribed by the children themselves. She saw the first task of education as being 'to furnish an environment which will permit and aid the child the functions given to him by nature' (Montessori, 1961: 34). The special environment for psychic and physical development was to be 'a living room' where children lived and worked together harmoniously (Montessori, 1978). A carefully prepared environment satisfies children's love of activity by containing objects they can move, use, and put back. The attraction leads to inexhaustible and prolonged activity (Montessori, 1967: 123). It is prepared to arouse interest and 'engage the child's whole personality' (ibid.: 188). Above all, children learn to respect the environment, the materials, their teacher, and their fellow students. In a lecture, Montessori gave reasons why only one piece of each material was placed in the environment, recounting an observation that when a directress put more than one set of any material into the classroom, discipline slackened and when reduced to one set, discipline returned. She reminded the audience that 'the whole of our school is based upon the manifestations given by the children' (Montessori Lecture, India, 1942). Only one piece of each material is found within the environment since Montessori had stressed that it was wrong to think that children with many materials and generous help from an adult were the best developed mentally and noted how 'a confused multitude of things raises more chaos in the mind and oppresses the child with discouragement' while one piece of each material 'enables the child to reduce his mind to order' (Montessori, 1967: 124). The hand was connected to the mind and her materials involve careful manipulation of the fingers working together. The hand was guided by the mind and when actions, made by the co-ordination of the fingers, were observed, they revealed thought. In recent times, Professor Earl Owen, a pioneer of microsurgery, was able to show scans of how a man, with his severed hand reconnected to his arm, had to learn the co-ordinated movements of the thumb and forefinger acting together which activated forty per cent of the brain. All ten fingers working together activated the whole brain (Owen, 2001).

Today, Montessori directresses worldwide prepare the environment for children with self-teaching Montessori materials providing a variety of activities which help them develop the foundations of a healthy education by following their own interests. Aesthetics within the environment are important since everything has to be beautiful to attract children and nurture the spirit. The 'humanistic' directress is considered to be part of the environment and her beautiful appearance is the first step to gain the child's confidence and respect along with the spiritual qualities of beauty of inner self, speech, graceful actions, courteous manners, and a sensitive, sympathetic nature. Montessori suggested one picture should adorn each school, that of Raphael's *Madonna della Seggiola,* which to her captured motherhood best. Beauty comes through simplicity, order, and hygienically spotless presentation of the room and Montessori materials. Objects are in natural wood or light, harmonious colors to avoid over-stimulation. Montessori noted how each child 'obeys any object which at that moment corresponds with his most acute needs for action as certain flowers attract insects' (Montessori, 1967: 122). This suggests that each child has a limited choice because he is always guided by nature. Children's reactions while using the materials are closely observed and those materials which interest and attract the child 'into doing voluntarily and repeatedly an exercise chosen by himself' (ibid.: 120) are regularly included as part of her prepared environment.

Over the years there have been mixed responses by educators to the importance Montessori attached to the physical environment (materials) and the psychological conditions. There seems to be confusion among some educators as to the purpose of Montessori materials. It should be noted that Montessori stressed again in 1939 that the directress should present new materials 'when the child has exhausted all possibilities of those he has been using' (ibid.: 256). Margaret Drummond, a Scottish teacher, praised the Montessori materials, which she saw involved children learning 'by experiment and thought' (Drummond, 1947: 8). She experimented herself producing valuable materials for learning mathematics for children of five to twelve years using Montessori principles. In the 1960s, Beth Stubbs claimed that Australian pre-schools had materials 'richer in variety' than those offered by Montessori education (Stubbs, 1966: 25). A. M. Gillet, a respected French Montessorian, expressed some concern at a conference in Italy in 1969. She had found experienced Montessori teachers added materials to Montessori materials to show every single step and she feared 'this excessive increase in material would lead to sclerosis of the intelligence and kill the child's sense of observation and imagination.' She reminded the audience of Montessori's recommendation 'keep the material limited' and so stimulate the imagination. Relationships between 'things' have to be discovered by the child outside the classroom as he becomes conscious that everything in the world is interrelated (Gillet, 1969). Emmy Louise Widmer in the USA was under the impression that 'experimentation, exploration and improvisation with materials were not permitted' (Widmer, 1970: 57). Mario Montessori announced in 1975 that research still continued 'with the preparation and production of eventual Montessori material' (Grazzini, 1975: 170). These materials for algebra and geometry were being devised from Montessori's notes twenty-three years after her death. Beryl Edmonds visited a Montessori environment in the Northern Territory, Australia, and noted, 'there is not enough material and its use is too limiting for a child's resourcefulness' (Edmonds, 1976: 3). In contrast to Montessori environments where children think while manipulating materials, Donaldson (1978) noted that in many traditional classrooms children are often 'engaged in disembedded thinking' which depends wholly on language (abstract thinking). She illustrated how language used by Piaget in his research confused children's thinking. For Cambourne (1984) the importance of the environment is crucial because it can lead to a humane, just society in which children can engender useful ideas. According to Wood (1994), there are four key factors in creating an environment – its physical features, the materials available, the overall organization, and the climate (or emotional atmosphere set by the teacher). Gee has argued that the right environment leads directly to well-behaved, productive children and ultimately a humane, just society (Gee, 1996). Another educator, McClay, has recently argued that the climate in a classroom should be relaxed where children feel secure, can interact easily with each other and staff (McClay, 1996). For Lankshear and colleagues (1997) the environment should be 'enchanting.' Montessori environments have always met these criteria since 1907, though some educators still see that the creation of an appropriate environment as being 'one of the most neglected aspects of school' (Blenkin and Kelly, 1996: 1).

27 Multiple Literacies

From the time of the first Children's House in 1907, there has always been a focus on social graces and basic courtesies within the children's learning environment, even while they were working with materials. Socially acceptable behavior was encouraged in children from the earliest age in all Children's Houses. Today, social practices including grace and courtesy have been renamed 'social literacies' because, as Castells explains, the meaning of literacy has been expanded (Castells et al., 1999: 98). Gee and colleagues (1996) suggest that literacy is 'much more than being able to follow words across a page' (Christie and Mission, 1998: 174). There are multiple literacies (Cope and Kalantzis, 2000) including 'discourses' (Gee, 1996) in which participants learn how to act and when and how to speak. According to some educators, 'situated' literacies focus on social and cultural interactions while literacy practices link the activities of reading and writing experienced in daily life with the social situations in which they are embedded (Barton et al., 2000). To Street, literacy embraces social contexts in which literacy occurs – general daily behavior, including writing and reading, being regarded by some educators as social practices 'concerned with social literacies' (Street, 1995: 2). Further, these writers claim that an understanding of all 'literacies' is important for living harmoniously within multicultural societies and Australian classrooms since we all belong to many societies (Gee, 1996: 21). Montessori education embraces 'multiple literacies' close to the literacy events and practices described by Street and others.

Barton and Hamilton see literacies as being 'situated literacies' with a focus 'on social and cultural interactions' (Barton et al., 2000: 10). Literacy is seen as a social practice (Morgan in Christie and Mission, 1998: 129), a historical practice, a material practice, a political practice (ibid.: 129–31), and viewed as critical social practice (Muspratt et al., 1997: 228; Luke, 1997: 10; Gee, 1996: 124). Multiple literacies to be considered (Barton et al., 2000: 7; Street, 1995: 106) include: film literacy, academic literacy, workplace literacy, home literacy, computer literacy (Barton et al., 2000: 10) as well as school literacy, community literacy (forms, letters and so on), photographs, diaries, peer literacy, neighborhood literacy (Street, 1995: 110–18).

An overriding aim of Montessori education has been the inculcation of respect for all cultures and religions (Montessori, 1932). In every Montessori environment throughout the world, practical life materials can be found matching the culture of the child. Each child learns the social graces and courtesies of the culture in which he lives either through acquisition (daily living) or through direct teaching. Sensorial materials, based on those used by Itard and Séguin, are used to enhance the child's social literacies, help him make intelligent observations within his environment, and enable him to teach himself. In Montessori's view, refinement of the senses was a basic element of all learning, and it is clear that other educators today concur in that view. De Castell and colleagues, for example, have noted that 'Montessori introduced children to sensory training and learning materials which engaged their attention and when children are engaged by something their learning is prodigious' (de Castell et al.,

1986: 45). In this regard, it is well to remember that Montessori saw each as a 'universal child,' bringing the fruits of his enlightenment to the world at large. New multiple literacies, including social literacies, situated literacies, and multicultural literacies, can be found within the framework of Montessori education.

28 Beginning Writing

In the 1970s Don Holdaway noted that parents were deeply concerned with only one aspect of schooling: 'Teach my children to read and you can do anything else that you like with them' (Holdaway, 1979: 25). His succinct depiction of the experience was similar to Montessori's experience more than seventy years before. Baker and Freebody observed that 'learning to read was the most central objective of early schooling' (Baker and Freebody, 1989: xv).

Departments of Education everywhere administer tests to standardize reading skills early. Most parents today do expect their children to learn to read and write early but, more and more, parents are being asked to prepare their children for reading before they enter school. Montessori demonstrated in 1907 how children began first to write and then to read words spontaneously at four years. She believed that a child must be prepared, needed to be shown exactly how to do a task before being obliged to execute and practice it. To her, articulate language was directly connected to writing and reading and she designed sensory materials – metal insets, sandpaper letters, and a movable alphabet to help the spontaneous development of both. Children were prepared for writing and reading using these materials. In her 1907 study, four-year-old children were helped to become aware of the sounds in words and their position in them – beginning, end, and middle – when they were introduced to sounds using the sandpaper letters (see Part 1). These children went on to recognize the letters of the movable alphabet and to match them to sounds said by the directress before composing words. Montessori describes in full what happened when a little boy of two and a half years was left with her for a moment by his mother. Some children were playing free games on the terrace at the time and Montessori was putting letters of the movable alphabet 'back in their respective compartments' as the little child watched. When she had finished, the child took one of the letters in his hand which 'chanced to be f, (and) at that moment children running in single file, passed us and, seeing the letter, called out in chorus the corresponding sound and passed on' (Montessori 1964: 278). The child put back f and took r. The children passing called out 'r, r, r!' As the child continued to hold up letters the children 'cried out the sound' (ibid.). Montessori wished 'to observe how long he would persist without becoming tired and he kept it up for *three quarters of an hour!*' He had held up f several times 'and had received from his public the same response.' Now 'he took the letter again, showing it to me and saying "f, f, f!"' Montessori concluded 'that from out the great confusion of sounds which he had heard, the long letter had made a great impression upon him' (ibid.: 279). A child of two and a half years could match a movable letter with the sound it represented.

When first composing words with the movable alphabet, Montessori explains how exactly it was done in 1907:

> We pronounce any word, taking care only that the child understands separately the letters of which it is composed. He composes the new word, placing one after the other, the signs corresponding to the sounds.
>
> (Montessori, 1964: 283)

Some children, she noted, require a great deal of practice at this stage of the process, others do not. She describes her observations of an Italian child as he works with the letters of the movable alphabet for the first time by himself. He sits looking at the box of letters 'moving his lips almost imperceptibly, and taking one by one the necessary letters, rarely committing an error in spelling. The movement in the lips reveals the fact that he repeats to himself an infinite number of times the words whose sounds he is translating into signs' (ibid.). An Italian child could compose any word which was clearly pronounced and 'at first we dictate to him only those words which are well known, since we wish his compositions to result in an idea' (ibid.). Finally, he spontaneously rereads the word many times, 'repeating its sounds in a thoughtful, contemplative way' (ibid.). When he finishes composing and reads the word, he puts away all the letters which is 'the habit of order we try to establish in all our work' (ibid.: 284). The exercises are used 'to fix the image of the graphic signs corresponding to the sounds of the words' (ibid.). The letters of the movable alphabet are tangible objects representing sounds spoken by the directress and heard by the child. Montessori notes, 'One day a little boy four years old, running alone about the terrace, was heard to repeat many times, "to make Zaira, I must have z-a-i-r-a"' (ibid.: 286). Further she notes that:

> This child *has never written* but he has mastered all the acts necessary to writing. The child who, when taking dictation not only knows how to compose the word, but instantly embraces in his thought its composition as a whole, will be able to write, since he knows how to write, with his eyes closed, the movements necessary to produce these letters, and since he manages almost unconsciously the instrument of writing.
>
> (ibid.: 286)

He had prepared himself and would explode into writing in his own time and 'this is, indeed the marvellous reaction which has come from my experiment with normal children' (ibid.).

Today there are varying views about phonological awareness, phonemic awareness, and segmentation with some commentators viewing these as being the same; others viewing them as being different. All refer to an awareness of sounds in words. All agree that children need to be aware of the relationship between spoken sounds and written letters but there is no agreement about how or when this should be done. In Montessori education today, directresses who introduce children to concrete materials (materialized abstraction), that is, the sandpaper letters and the movable alphabet, as described in *The Montessori Method* in 1907, observe the same successful results Montessori observed.

The Montessori approach, described as a phonic approach, is by explicit, direct teaching using the three-period lesson to introduce the links between sounds and letters to each child individually before he writes and reads. It differs from abstract non-phonic approaches which expect children to cultivate an awareness of sounds and their link to letters while they learn to read and write. Unfortunately, many common English words do not conform to one-to-one correspondence between sound and letter. Montessori suggested English-speaking children should begin composing phonetically regular words (phonetic words in Montessori education) so they met with success in spelling. Non-phonetically regular words (non-phonetic words) were presented to English-speaking children as soon as they were successful in composing phonetically regular words with more than three letters. Activities were designed to focus the child's attention on combinations of two or more letters (phonograms) which made one sound in English. There was a green box containing pictures and words for every phonogram and the letters forming the phonogram were displayed on the lid. The procedure of how to discover the sound the phonogram made was guided by the directress once to each child. Using the pictures only and saying the name of the object shown on each, the child was to recognize the common sound in each word. That sound was the phonogram represented by letters on the lid. The child continued alone choosing from any of the forty-two green boxes for phonogram work. The repeated activity helped children's spelling move closer toward conventional English spelling. Montessori education has had this material in place since 1916. Later, the same boxes of pictures and cards are used for reading with the focus on the word cards.

Phonemic awareness means hearing sound/s in language. It was the 1980s before Bissex (1980: 119) stressed that 'when children are making passage from language heard to language seen, awareness of sounds is a key concept.' Linguists Bradley and Bryant (1983), Henderson (1986, in Yaden and Templeton, 1988), and Lundberg (1988) emphasize the need for children to develop 'meta-linguistic' orientation to speech and language for spelling, writing, and reading. Spelling is the tool of the writer and a poor speller resorts to guessing just as a poor reader must guess (Rivalland, 1985: 21, 23). Downing observed that many children of three to seven years fail to distinguish sounds and letters and 'are cognitively confused' (Hall, 1987: 60). Lunberg saw the necessity to deliberately draw each child's attention to 'a word,' to the phonemic properties of speech and sometimes this could be done effectively 'if drawn out of context, beyond meaning' (Lundberg, 1988). Marilyn Adams maintains that youngsters 'must develop a ready knowledge of spelling in order to become confident, able readers' (Adams, 1991: 207). Galbraith makes it clear that, 'Essentially, children beginning reading or writing must know word awareness (a word is a unit of speech) and phonemic awareness (to segment words into phonemic elements)' and children need direct teaching for the development of phonemic awareness emphasizing that 'it is not sufficient for phonemic awareness skills to be embedded in a rhyming story in the hope that the child will somehow pick up phonemic awareness' (Galbraith, 1991: 15, 16). Williams points out that phonemic awareness is about awareness of sounds in the speech stream, while listening involves 'how to listen and what to listen for' (1995, cited in Clay, 1998: 56). Ong speaks of the 'vocalic alphabet, which is a breakthrough representing sound graphically,' while 'writing is representation of sounds' (Street, 1995: 154) which echoes Montessori's sentiments and practice.

Phonemic awareness and segmentation have been studied by many researchers. Yopp and Singer point out that kindergarten children are neither consciously aware of words in sentences nor that 'words can be segmented into phonemes.' Their article discusses how children in the US after one year at school (at six or seven years) are asked to hear a sound in the middle, the beginning, and at the end of a word as teachers see this 'as being essential for reading progress' (Yopp and Singer, 1994: 382). Education psychologists describe segmenting words into phonemes by young children as being a complex process. Baynham (1995) points out the difficulty of segmenting 'bat.' The consonants /b/ and /t/ are distinct sounds but /ə/ is known as a minimal *schwa* vowel sound, or an indistinct vowel sound, common to some English dialects. So much depends on the correct enunciation of letter sounds for vowels by the teacher. Indistinct vowels can be the cause of spelling errors (Emmitt et al., 1996: 133). Burns et al. (1999: 220) state, 'pre-schoolers rarely pay attention to the smallest meaningful segments (phonemes) of words . . . gaining awareness of phonemes is an advanced aspect of phonological awareness' and children need to understand that there are three phonemes in the spoken word *mud* and three letters stand for these phonemes. The main point is that children come to understand the connection between the sounds they hear in the spoken word and the letter/s they select. Edwards points out that a child 'getting to the stage of understanding that letters are relevant involves a massive learning process' (cited in Fields and Spranger, 2000). Identifying sounds in words is still considered by some researchers to be essential for learning to read. Montessori children learn this skill in connection with beginning handwriting using sandpaper letters and composing words using the movable alphabet at four years.

The study of linguistics now includes meta-linguistics defined as the analysis of speech and language in terms of its structure (sentences, words, phonemes, syntax, and pragmatics). These 'orientations' require the individual to be able to view language and speech as an object when everyday use of language is communication, centered around meanings, not structure. Researchers continue to be aware of the difficulties some children experience in becoming aware of sounds in speech, as well as representing sound graphically. The difficulties children experience today show that 'recognition of letters evolves slowly in young children' and, as they are 'trying to hear phonemes they are trying at the same time to distinguish between letters that look the same to him' (Clay, 1998: 51, 73). By four years of age Montessori children are confident and can identify the letters of the movable alphabet. Kale and Luke point out that there is a broad consensus among linguists and psychologists that children need 'to learn how to manipulate language to facilitate the development of more complex cognitive processes' (Riordan, 1997: 116). Montessori children can physically manipulate language as they work with concrete materials (named materialized abstraction by Montessori) and they do make the connection between sounds heard and shapes they see or touch. There is no confusion. Sandpaper letters offer children 'a scaffold' during each individual short three-period lesson. Phonemic awareness allows Montessori children to teach themselves as they continue to work with the Montessori materials. At the same time the children prepare themselves physically and psychologically to write every letter of the alphabet. They perfect their movements by practicing with the metal insets for control of a pencil and tracing the sandpaper letters for writing the graphic signs.

The pronunciation by every child of each sound (represented by a letter) had to be perfect, Montessori insisted in 1907. Defects were to be noted and immediately corrected. Caring for the development of pronunciation in this manner at an age when language was being established in children, eliminated the need for remedial work when children were older (Montessori, 1964: 325). Because there was a direct connection between spoken language and written language (spelling), Montessori attached great importance to the correction of speech defects as early as possible. Records were kept of each child's progress 'since pronunciation is a necessary part of learning graphic language' (ibid.: 279, 280). She introduced directresses to the practice of correcting speech defects (ibid.: 323). One of Montessori's students, Dr. Anne McAllister, became a leading authority in speech training at Jordanhill Teachers' College, Glasgow. Her books and methods were found in most English-speaking teacher-training colleges throughout the world during the 1950s and 1960s. Today the Department of Speech Therapy at the University of Strathclyde, Jordanhill Campus, is a leader in speech therapy in the UK (*Strathclyde People*, 1999).

In the first Children's House in 1907 Montessori observed how quickly handwriting was learned. The child traced a sandpaper letter several times before taking up the pen and writing the letter in ink and she noted, 'We begin to teach only those who show a desire for it' (Montessori, 1964: 293), explaining:

> Our children handwrite well from the moment in which they begin ... it is surprisingly simple and one of the easiest and most delightful of all the conquests made by the child due to the fact the minds and hands of our children are already prepared for writing.
>
> (Montessori, 1964: 294, 317)

She commented how written language was not a natural function of man – 'it adds itself to natural man' (ibid.) being supernatural, above nature, entirely man-made. It required 'new mechanisms' to be established permanently in the nervous system and these were far more simple than the internal movements required for a spoken word. The movements 'are performed by large muscles, all external, established by psycho-muscular mechanisms upon which we can directly act' (ibid.: 318). Without preparation, children were under 'immense strain when we set them to write directly without a previous motor education of the hand' (ibid.: 312). Montessori's observations of children in state schools at six and seven years 'were too often taught at an age when all the defects have been established and when the psychological sensitive period in which the muscular memory is ready, has been passed' (ibid.: 295). Goodman (1986: 48) observed that 'handwriting is laborious' for young children and required a great deal of physical co-ordination. Montessori also found this to be true if children were unprepared. They 'experienced all sorts of depressing feelings' because they produced 'imperfect and erroneous signs' (Montessori, 1964: 294). She found that if left till six years, children struggle to write because they were no longer interested in the sandpaper letters because they had passed that sensitive period, and now it would take them longer to co-ordinate their muscles. They would never be able to write as perfectly as they could have at four years (ibid.).

At an early stage, Montessori had the child 'write under dictation, which materially translates sounds into signs . . . always easy and pleasant for him to do, analogous to the development of the spoken language which is the motor translation of audible sounds' (ibid.: 267). It was 'a perfect parallel with spoken language since the motor action must correspond with heard speech' (ibid.: 317). Judith Rivalland shows how beginner spellers need to understand grapho-phonics and this is done by children 'encoding the symbols for all phonic units' (Rivalland, 1985: 25). The sounds need to be represented by one or more symbols and in the correct sequence (Clay, 1977; Chomsky 1971). Rivalland (1985: 25) suggests that the best way to do this is to have systematic daily practice at encoding by dictation. Montessori saw much value in dictation because it was an opportunity to see progress both in handwriting and in spelling.

When Read began researching creative writing in pre-schools in 1971, he found children creating spellings, especially in Montessori schools where writing was encouraged and creative spelling was accepted. He also reported that these Montessori children had solved the segmentation problem and possessed extended knowledge of letter names and standard spelling, and most had begun to read early (Read, 1975). In later research, it was noted that segmentation remained a problem in many state classrooms because it was not obvious to children how speech could be segmented and spellers 'must be able to perform specific analysis, and divide the stream of speech into units which are represented by alphabetic spelling' (Read et al., 1986: 107). Bissex (1980) and Gentry (1981) researched children's creative spelling and agreed that spelling was developmental. Research into inventive spelling when composing words by Lomax and McGee (1987, cited in Dahl et al., 1999) and Clarke (1988, cited in Dahl et al., 1999) found that experimentation led to better spelling and improved reading. More recent research by Bingham and colleagues (1995: 62) has found that 'children develop from inventive spellers to conventional spellers quite naturally' but Clay observed children in classrooms 'writing nonsense which no one could read and it was accepted by teachers as creative writing' when the main point for children to understand was that writing is used to communicate ideas to others (Clay, 1998: 89). Bear and Templeton (1998) report that beginner writers use the alphabetic principle representing sounds with letters and 'concentrate on consonants,' suggesting children cannot yet hear the vowel sounds in their inner speech. To this day researchers continue to try to discover ways of helping children learn the conventional spelling of English words. The managing director of Jolly Phonics Limited has produced and published *Jolly Phonics*, which he claims is 'used by forty per cent of Primary Schools in the UK and Canada' with successful results. In *Jolly Phonics* 'we use the Montessori colours for consonants and vowels and follow her coloured materials. Later in *Jolly Grammar* we use Montessori colours for parts of speech ... in a small way, it is another example of the influence of Montessori in education' (Jolly, 2002: 30).

Dictation is not found in curriculums today and the art of handwriting is no longer a priority since children can be introduced to computers at an early age in pre-schools and at home. In former times when writing was a vital form of human communication, it was imperative for an educated child to master the skill. Some ardently believe that handwriting is still indicative of an educated person. Spell-checks can be made with computers which tell the child privately to reconsider the spelling of a word without teacher intervention. With the emphasis for school-age children learning to express meaning through the written language and not on the mechanics, a young child using a computer is able to fully concentrate on expressing his thoughts without having to think about the formation of the shapes of letters. The computer is a modern movable alphabet. This means that today each child does not have the opportunity to develop the character traits which helped perfect his personality because in Montessori's view, 'handwriting teaches the child prudence to avoid errors, dignity to make him look ahead and guide him to perfection, and humility to make him strive to do better' (Montessori, 1964: 292). Much research has been done on spelling errors over the years while Montessori concentrated on what a child had accomplished. Errors served a purpose revealing areas where the directress could provide individualized lessons. In Montessori environments today, children in their sensitive period at four years, or earlier if a child shows an interest, learn to write. As Montessori noted, it took children about six weeks from when they were introduced to the sandpaper letters to being able to compose phonetically regular words in English with the movable letters. Clay (1998) and other current researchers suggest plastic magnetic letters are useful for children experiencing difficulties with phonemic awareness.

Technological literacy is seen as a major resource for teaching and learning (Mallett, 1999: 22; Luke, 1997: 6; Warger, 1990: 13). Solomon and Gardner warn that some computer programs for schools can become rote learning inside a box, worksheets in computers are dull and uninteresting, so teachers must choose programs with care (Solomon and Gardner, 1986: 121). Indeed Cycle One directresses with children three to six years, weigh up new innovations and judge whether or when to include some, one, or none into the environment because they recognize computer literacy is part of life and living today. Many children choose to communicate using the popular, swift, text messages which convey meaning by the use of a new 'short hand' code which completely disregards spelling rules, grammar, and punctuation.

29 Beginning Reading

Reading for interpretation 'stands in direct relation with writing and has no sounds; books are mute' (Montessori, 1974: 172). Silent reading from the beginning was advocated by Montessori in 1907 and she devised activities 'through which children might without effort, learn to read words mentally' (Montessori, 1964: 297). Children were to match word cards with toys and when they demonstrated they could read words silently, Montessori wrote: 'I do away entirely with the old fashioned primer' (ibid.). Being able to match word cards to objects or pictures was not considered to be reading by Montessori but she observed children generally demonstrated a keen interest in words at an early age. They practiced reading words mechanically which is 'closely allied to spoken language' (Montessori, 1974: 171) and so they prepare themselves for reading. The whole learning process depended on the development of the child's intelligence, judicious intervention by the directress, and the individual's mastery of the didactic materials. Between four and seven years Montessori observed, 'children are word lovers and understand words' (ibid.: 9) and all the early activites she made and used for word reading survive today and all are done silently. Montessori found children were 'greatly interested in *puzzling* out the alphabetic signs' written on the cards and 'children's minds were working like adults who pore over prehistoric inscriptions' (Montessori, 1978: 144). Fred Schonell, the educationist whose work on beginning reading was 'based on scientific, psychological research,' noted that beginner readers with young immature minds 'need opportunities and time to sort things out, to understand what they are doing' (Schonell, 1945: 6). The pioneering work of MacKinnon (1959) showed 'there had been a wealth of research indicating that children find great satisfaction in puzzling out words, the problems of interpreting print' (MacKinnon cited in Holdaway, 1979: 210). Working out puzzles and codes continues to bring great satisfaction to children and adults alike, and Montessori education allows a period of time for children to puzzle out words. It is a mechanical ability which needs to be practiced so words can be read quickly and automatically. Similarly, Adams argues that, 'automaticity is the key to the whole system' (Adams, 1991: 207) for beginner readers. After much practice, and fun, completing a wide variety of activities reading words, children read books spontaneously. Today Montessori children continue to do just that.

By 1912, Montessori saw a need for a great variety of books with 'pictures of reality, facts and situations' within the classroom (Montessori, 1974: 198). She had to make an appeal to authors to write for young children as no suitable published material was available for her beginner readers (ibid.: 196) and she was instrumental in encouraging writers to write factual, illustrated books for young children as well as biographies. She introduced the idea of classroom libraries. Today Montessori children of five years read logically, and by six years some children research subjects of their own choice. Mallett conducted some case studies with young children in England and discovered in one instance that they integrated 'first hand learning about snails' with information that they had read in books and they were 'found to be critical readers right from the beginning' (ibid.: 49). Montessori classroom libraries contain a wide variety of non-fiction books and videos to satisfy children's curiosity, their need to find out and discover. Today the world can be brought into the classroom by video, television, and computers, just as Montessori had wished it could be in 1916. She maintained the wonders of nature were more wonderful than any man-made fantasy. Knowing and writing about the wonders of the universe help children's creative, inventive, problem-solving minds develop.

In 1912, Montessori argued that oral reading 'is foreign to true reading and an impediment to the development of true reading' (Montessori, 1974: 172). It required the beginner reader to interpret two languages, articulate language and graphic language. It was far more difficult and complicated than speaking and reading separately because it involved expressing someone else's thoughts using symbols. Interpretation was an affair of intelligence while pronunciation was quite different (ibid.: 173–6). Oral reading was often conducted in a slow, monotonous voice as 'the child's eye reads word by word and meaning was lost because meaning comes from the entire sentence' (ibid.: 172). Sometimes when seeking meaning a child's eyes traversed the sentence as a whole but his tongue could not keep up with pronunciation (ibid.: 173). He was forced to stop to pronounce, or work out an unknown word, for his eyes and thoughts were moving more rapidly than his tongue could move. It was the 'eagerness of the child to learn that was cheated when he had to stop from working (thinking) because his tongue refused to act properly' (ibid.: 174). Reading aloud was a complex problem for all readers but especially beginner readers as 'it is a combination of reading and articulate expression. No wonder reading is one of the rocks on which the rudderless ship of elementary education inevitably runs aground' (ibid.: 176). This problem remains today for many children in elementary schools.

For decades there has been controversy as to which literacy programs should be adopted by schools to attain a high level of successful readers at an early age. Schonell commented in the early 1940s that some children will fail to learn to read in the infant school, but not because of laudable efforts on the part of teachers, who intervened too much requiring little of pupils. 'My only wish is that some teachers, especially in the early stages do a little less work' (Schonell, 1945: 6). Like Montessori, Schonell saw that too much intervention can hinder child development.

In 1980, Brian Cambourne and Peter Rousch claimed that researchers were looking for the best way to teach reading but teachers 'ignored what was going on in children's heads' paying little attention to the processes used by children. There was no technology for 'getting inside readers' heads' and the best way to observe intellectual processes was 'to analyse errors as they read print' (Cambourne and Rousch, 1980: 107). Brain research in the US with scanners which 'can get under the scalp and into brain tissues has discovered what triggers thought in one area of the brain dealing with language,' but they still have not been able to discover what and how the mind works, and perhaps never will (Schiller, 2000). That remains the secret of the child. The traditional view of literacy (being able to read and write) is rejected (Gee, 1996: 22). Today, learning to write and read are considered to be social activities where 'in the past, reading and writing were solitary' (Mallett, 1999: 15). Reading and writing no longer play the central role, and there is movement from focusing on the individual to a social and cultural situation perspective (Barton et al., 2000: 116; Gee, 1996: 24, 40). Surely reading silently cannot be considered a solitary activity because the reader shares the absent writer's thoughts, a main benefit of graphic writing, therefore, all reading is both psychological and social.

In 2000, fifteen literacy programs were evaluated by the Education Queensland Literacy Review Committee into ways of attaining successful readers. Among these was a phonics approach described as a new reading and language teaching method with new hope for hundreds of students and their parents. This new method teaches sounds, symbols, and rules of how to use symbols which unlock ninety-nine per cent of words they will meet in a lifetime. In state pre-schools, children are being introduced to phonics through oral games for sound/symbol associations. In a trial, improvements in reading have been shown in all children and they are enjoying the work which fits the curriculum in multi-age classrooms (Gearing, 2000). Montessori directresses today continue to introduce children to Montessori's insets, sandpaper letters, and a movable alphabet and they see the same successful results directresses have seen, since Montessori described her first experiment in 1907. Many research findings in language development today concur with Montessori's pioneering research and practices. The developmental stages of learning to talk compiled by Montessori have been confirmed. The developmental approach to writing used in Australian schools has similarities to Montessori's spontaneous developmental approach but it involves so much teacher intervention and input, rather than using didactic materials. Knowledge of segmentation and spelling rules have been found to help children move from their own inventive spelling closer to regular spelling and children who possess such skills are better prepared to read. Most importantly, present-day researchers agree that children must at some stage make a connection between spoken sounds and written letters and that learning to read is a long, complex journey.

30 Should Children be Normalized?

In the profession of teaching in which inattention and disciplinary procedures are of growing concern, the Montessori concept of 'normalization' is of enormous relevance today. Montessori, as noted previously, regarded most children of three years of age as possessing some form of 'deviant' behavior. That is, children whose true course of development had been blocked by adults. Obstacles to their spontaneous and natural growth had been caused by lack of freedom and the absence of appropriate stimuli, and the big danger in such deviations was that if untreated they would become fixed in the child's personality for life. She was insistent that all deviations could be cured, observing that as a child worked with a piece of didactic material, there was a discernible difference in his behavior. Each child became visibly calmer, more self-disciplined, and even more contented as he repeated an exercise over and over. To her, it was a sign that the nervous system was stabilizing, a sign of the development of conscious thought. It was the start of what she called 'normalization.' That self-disciplined, normalized child was to become the heart of Montessori education, what she termed her greatest discovery, 'a psychological phenomenon which had remained unobserved for thousands of years' and which she chanced upon only because she 'taught little and observed much' (Montessori, 1967: 326). When reports of countless other normalized children were received from every continent in the following thirty years, Montessori was impelled to comment:

> Normalization was repeated unfailingly in all schools with children belonging to different social classes, races and civilizations. It is the most important result of our whole work.
>
> (ibid.: 204)

Normalization, she said, was 'the child's contribution to society' (ibid.: 201). These potential citizens were at peace with themselves and with others, self-directed and self-contained. It is an observation still worthy of the attention of all who around the world run schools.

Montessori warned that there was danger to character development if deviations were not cured early. By the 1930s, she recorded her observations in *The Absorbent Mind* noting that, in general, children at three years of age with deviations fell into three categories (ibid.: 195–201). First, there were strong, rebellious children who fought back against adults. They sometimes had violent tantrums, were defiant, cruel, usually identified as 'bad'. Second, there were weak children who had given up the fight, were submissive, quiet, and often labeled 'good' except for some who lied. And third, there were 'bright' children who were highly imaginative, intelligent, possessed of good language skills, were restless with poor control of movements, had chosen not to fight and not to give in. Society had become so used to some of these abnormal behaviors that they applauded and valued the traits 'good' and 'bright' (See Part 2). Results of a longitudinal developmental research project into the health, development, and behavior of children also has much relevance in this discussion. It was originally begun and directed by Phil Silva in 1972 but reported by Avshalom Caspi in 1999. There is an interesting parallel between its observations about children's behavior and those of Montessori ninety years previously. The report found that children respond to the environment in which they find themselves living and that by three years it is possible to predict the types of adults they will become. In Silva's study, children of three years of age were tested in cognitive and motor tasks and classified in three categories as under-controlled, inhibited, and well adjusted. Fifteen years later, the under-controlled children were found to be reckless, careless, and partial to dangerous and exciting activities. Also they were found to enjoy causing discomfort to others. The inhibited students were found to be highly cautious and loathe to influence others. The well-adjusted children were found to be very much as they had been fifteen years earlier. In Silva's project, behavioral disorders in children were identified but no cure was offered. Montessori took decisive action which resulted in a transformation of all children into well-adjusted, 'normalized' citizens, which is a main aim in Montessori education today.

Inattention has never been a serious issue in the Children's Houses. It is sometimes claimed that children at the beginning of the twenty-first century are different from children at the beginning of the twentieth century but perhaps it is the lifestyle provided by adults which has changed. Children as young as five years are reported as being taught relaxation therapy to deal with stress (Amorsen, 2001). The thrust of Montessori education is that the basic nature of child development remains unchanged and it is universal. A stress-free environment can do much to normalize all children. Some local doctors and psychologists in Queensland today direct children suffering from Attention Deficit Disorder (ADD) to a Montessori environment and special needs children fit easily into Montessori environments. The didactic materials are eminently suitable for children classified as requiring special education. These children respond to the Montessori-prepared environment where they are left to choose something of interest, in their own time, armed with knowledge they have acquired incidentally through observation of others receiving three-period lessons. The materials attract slow developers who can be helped to learn to read and write successfully as Montessori had demonstrated with her special needs asylum children in 1898 in Rome. All children can benefit from a hands-on approach, especially if there is no threat of failure or punishment. Wendy Fidler (2004), a special needs consultant, explains in a series of articles how the Montessori-prepared environment can help children with special needs including children with dyslexia (and other vision difficulties), children with disorders on the autistic spectrum (autism, asperger syndrome, semantic pragmatic disorder) as well as dyspraxia (developmental co-ordination disorder). Montessori put her trust in children and in her materials to bring about 'normalization' as a natural development in all Montessori environments.

In every state in Australia, mobility of attention is endemic today with some 11.2 per cent of 520,000 Australian children reported as suffering from some form of mental illness being treated for attention deficit hyperactive disorder (ADHD). Of that large cohort of over half a million children, some 40 per cent are treated for anxiety, aggression, and poor social interaction (from the National Survey of Mental Health, Canberra, 2001). It has also been estimated that Australian doctors prescribe 50 million tablets a year simply to calm children down (Duffy, 2001). The director of South Brisbane Child and Youth Mental Health Service reports that children's mental health has been neglected over years and has led to an increase in anxiety, depression, and hyperactivity disorders. A high percentage of children and adolescents receive medication (Beech, 2001). Professor Barry Nurcombe, child/adolescent psychologist at the University of Queensland, has warned that there is 'potential for even greater problems if children are not treated early on, including suicide, substance abuse and criminal behaviour' (Hart, 2001). The dire predictions bring to mind similar warnings sounded by Montessori more than three decades earlier: 'Any child who is not protected with a view to his normal formation will later avenge himself on society by means of the adult who is formed by him' (Montessori, 1967: 71).

Some teachers, administrators, and doctors continue to treat behavioral disorders, mental deficiencies, and emotional disorders with medication, physical exercises, and outside professional counseling as first steps to 'normalization' when far less invasive educational procedures such as advocated by Montessori in her safe, supportive Children's Houses could well prove more successful. Her Children's Houses certainly appeared to contain 'a system of mental treatment that was very logical and superior to that of the established state schools' (Montessori, 1964: 20). Of significance is the quality of tributes to Montessori from some of her medical peers. One was Dr. Crichton Miller who reported 'that doctors of medicine and professors of psychology were saying her work would eventually make the nerve specialists superfluous and if the Montessori method was established in all schools, alms-houses would need to be established for psychologists' (Kramer, 1976: 264). In Montessori's own words:

> I was made to realise that certain conditions which fulfilled psychic needs had eventually also influence upon the physical body ... health and happiness were closely linked and the time came when doctors recommended our *Case dei Bambini* as a sort of health resort.
>
> (Montessori Lecture, London, 1933)

Children attending a Children's House with behavioral problems have them identified early. There is an observable transformation in a child's behavior in a stress-free environment when he concentrates on a piece of didactic material of his own choice. This is the beginning of normalization. Normalization remains the Montessori child's 'contribution to society' (Montessori, 1967: 201).

31 Developmentally Appropriate Curriculum

In Montessori education, each child follows his own agenda, with no set curriculum or timetable to follow and in Montessori's words, 'each child knows what he needs to help him construct himself' (Montessori, 1967: 223) and only the child is able to choose the material to match that need and further 'such awareness of one's needs and ability to act on them is part of being an autonomous individual' (Montessori, 1969: 71). While Montessori education since 1907 has been based on the observations of each child's development with activities matched to that stage of development and the interest of each child, the curriculum was accordingly based on development. Soon she extended the curriculum for children three to six years because 'small children are able to do things far above expected capacity' (Montessori, 1966: 108, 109). By 1912, history, geography, science, art, and music were introduced to young children, Montessori stressing always 'we must enlarge the syllabus and by doing so we enlarge the mind' (Montessori Course, London, 1946). In 1948, she noted that a young child accepted everything 'if put in an acceptable manner, suited to the child's psychology' (Montessori, 1961: 28).

When Bruner proposed the 'spiral curriculum' and presented 'the bold hypothesis, that any subject can be taught to any child at any stage of development' (Bruner, 1960: 33), Mario Montessori challenged him by stating the idea had been bold when his mother started experimenting with it sixty years before and 'startled the world with the obtained results' (Montessori Jr., 1974: 19). It was not until 1975 that the concept reached a wider audience. In that year, Stenhouse put forward the notion that 'emergent curriculum must be grounded in classroom practice.' He further advanced that the principal sources were 'the psychology of learning, study of child development, social psychology and sociology of learning' (Stenhouse, 1975: 25). It approaches close to the Montessorian theory. A year later MacDonald and Walker approached even closer with their query: 'Why start with theory, rather than action?' (MacDonald and Walker, 1976: 4). The idea of beginning with practice sounded radical to researchers and curriculum developers in the 1970s yet Montessori had done just that successfully, seventy years before.

The place of storytelling in the Montessori curriculum, especially the 'Great Stories,' is of continuing relevance in the Montessori experience. For Egan and Nadaner (1988), the centrality of stories in the early years was important because storytelling always captured the attention of children. Advocates of whole language also use stories in their curriculum including fantasy. Edelsky (1999: 22, 25, 26) stresses that the whole-language teachers 'should be tuned into the interests of students ... curriculum should be grounded in students' lives ... and teachers and students should be partners creating the menu' to be studied. These sentiments repeat Montessori. It is clear that Steiner education introduced everything in the curriculum through long stories to gain attention and aid the memory to remember number facts and spelling. Teachers know there is something about listening to stories that fascinates children and stories continue to remain supreme as a source of language and learning (Mallett, 1999).

In England, Geva Blenkin and Vic Kelly (1996) were working with researchers and teachers at Goldsmith's College of London University on a new form of early childhood education which aimed at being developmentally appropriate and required a developmentally appropriate curriculum. They saw 'education as development,' their work based on a neo-Piagetian theory which had taken years to develop. Many aspects of that theory confirm basic tenets of Montessori education, a fact that should not surprise since Piaget was a student of Montessori. The work of Blenkin and Kelly has been to match the developmental stage of each child appropriately with tasks. It is Montessori education revisited. Today there is still a gap between Montessori and Piaget; Montessori began with practice and Piaget began with a theory. Another fundamental difference is that Montessori's approach is educational and Piaget's is psychological. Kieran Egan has pointed out a radical difference between the two. Any educational program, he cautions 'must be informed by the polis the child is being prepared to inhabit or change, and the end product must be a recognisable person (educational theory) rather than a set of skills (psychological theory)' (Egan, 1983: 115–16). It was certainly the real world that Montessori's program was preparing her children for, along with the skills of adaptability.

32 The Directress

Today, a directress respects every child in her care. Respect ranks as the most desired human quality of the many she must possess to put Montessori principles into practice. Anyone who chooses to become a directress has to grasp first the need to empower children from the earliest age. To observe children requires planning large blocks of uninterrupted time so children can follow their individual interests. Montessori observed how 'interrupted cycles of activity affects the conditions of the inner mind' (Montessori, 1961: 82). Interruptions could lead a child to 'a lack of self-confidence, perseverance or being unable to finish what he had started' (ibid.: 93). Each Montessori child may choose what interests him from the wide curriculum and the directress shares a wide knowledge 'to satisfy children's mental hunger, unlike a non-Montessori teacher who is limited by the syllabus – prescribing just so much of every subject to be imparted within a set time' (ibid.: 8). She finds herself challenged 'in knowing how to meet unexpected claims on the part of her pupils, on having to teach then and there, things she never intended to teach' (Montessori, 1966: 41). It means 'following the child,' a form of respect, and not following a timetable (ibid.: 103). Montessori took the directive 'Follow the Child' from Itard and there has been one method in Montessori education from birth to adulthood: follow the psychic needs of the child. Each is prepared to become an independent learner and inevitably all become lifelong learners following their own interests. The directress provides the correct social conditions for the development of the whole child where 'repression is avoided' (Montessori, 1961: 92) and where normalized children 'naturally develop a sense of community and solve their problems peacefully' (Montessori, 1967: 205) which Montessori found was not possible with fewer than forty children within the classroom. Respect and trust grow between student and directress, which can partly be attributed to the short three-period lessons which must be demonstrated exactly. Long sessions give the directress the opportunity to work with every child individually several times every day uninterrupted. She learns much from each child during these short experimental experiences discovering whether the child is relaxed, happy, anxious, timid, confident, willing to co-operate, along with details about length of attention span, focus, and concentration on the materials and other details about development and personality.

The short three-period lesson is used by Montessori directresses today and could be characterized as proleptic instruction, a term introduced by Stone and Wersch (1984) where prolepsis refers to the assumption that a learner's competence is true before it is so. During proleptic instruction the teacher (or teacher and learner) performs a task. The form of communication during the performance requires the learner to construct his own interpretation of the teacher's unstated instructional message (Forman, 1989) which strongly resembles the format of a three-period lesson. By contrast there is currently an emphasis in mainstream education on teachers being explicit to children about what they are teaching (Clay, 1998), but, according to Montessori, too many words confuse the mind and children teach themselves. Mountain (2000) suggests that teachers should try mini-lessons and spend a minute a day, teaching words to each child individually. He further suggests that in just a minute, instruction can be individualized and personalized, which is exactly what is done in three-period lessons. In the present view of theorists and researchers, the new multi-literacies do not recognize learning as an individual's ability to be 'done in the head,' but consider learning to be of an 'inherent social character embedded in social practices' (Lankshear et al., 1997: 2). A three-period lesson could be considered to be 'a secondary discourse' described by Gee as 'a process that involves conscious knowledge' (Gee, 1996: 138) or as being 'explicit focusing and instruction through the interaction with a person or an experience that triggers conscious reflection' (Muspratt et al., 1997: 287). For Montessori in 1907, a three-period lesson required both a child's individual psychological ability and the interaction with a person and remains relevant today.

In 1907, Montessori found herself with a group of multi-aged children and discussed the advantages of a society of mixed-aged children. Forty or more children formed a mini-democratic society and 'added charm to social life because of the number of different types one meets' (Montessori, 1967: 226). She saw children experiencing community spirit as being normal because they could not suddenly acquire social skills as teenagers and to her it was important for children to experience and live under such social conditions in school and out of school to lead a happy life. Their adult companions at school and at home needed to be humane and to treat them as fellow human beings. There were critics of Montessori's multi-age grouping who purported to find relatively little evidence of young children learning together. Beryl Edmonds, for example, argued strongly that 'children work as individuals and have little to do with each other' (Edmonds, 1976: 4). To Montessori, every child was unique simply because the differing combination of genes meant 'every human being is different from every other' (Montessori, 1967: 38). Collective lessons were rare in Montessori education because they required children to remain still, listen, and watch the teacher (Montessori, 1964: 108), which did not encourage development. It was the learner who chose the individual approach, 'he educates himself' (ibid.: 173) and 'we found that individual activity is the one factor that stimulates and produces development and that is not more true for the little ones of preschool age than it is for the junior, the middle and upper school children' (Montessori, 1967: 8).

Montessori's ideas of what is now termed 'vertical integration' are meeting with broad acceptance. According to some, multi-age classrooms seem to be 'a strange concept' but they are 'one good way to provide the kind of education current theory suggests to respond to the changing and varied world in which today's children find themselves' (Bingham et al., 1995: 6). Bingham and colleagues (1995) point out that child-centered teaching 'is grounded in the theories of Piaget and Vygotsky who see each child as being on an individual developmental path,' each working to 'an internal time clock' (ibid.). Children follow their own interests, choosing from a wide curriculum called 'The Fascinating World' (ibid.: 74) and they work with concrete manipulative materials within an humane environment. Bingham and colleagues have also argued that research about child learning and development supports the theory that child-centered learning is basic to creating a productive learning environment and that active, concrete learning experiences are essential for young children, with development of the whole child a major aim. Other distinctive elements of the Montessori method also emerge from their recent findings, including the importance of physical health and well-being in the quality of learning, the enormous implications of the theory of multiple intelligences, and the critical need to assess each individual child by looking at his own progress, not by comparing him with others (Bingham et al., 1995: 10–12). Grant and colleagues (1995: 44) have also found advantages in multi-age grouping. They claim 'children develop good mental health when the needs of the whole child are met in a nurturing environment' and developmentally appropriate experiences are provided. They give points of contact where multi-age classroom teachers can find details about conferences and in-service teacher-training courses. Bingham and colleagues (1995), Grant and colleagues (1995), and Kasten and Lolli (1998) provide many practical experiences for children in multi-age classrooms which have taken twenty years to compile. They claim whole-language teachers today, 'enjoy flexibility' in their multi-age classrooms as they build trust, and discover more about the children they teach and their families (Edelsky, 1999: 38). All these 'latest' findings of the ancient profession were practiced by Montessori in her first multi-age classroom back in 1907. Wood (1994), Charbonneau and Reider (1995), and McClay (1996), who also have researched multi-age classrooms, made findings that closely matched those of Montessori. They aver that multi-age classrooms using a developmental model are best to prepare children for the twenty-first century.

Montessori proposed in 1907 that the role of directress included that of 'a scientist, a researcher, a psychologist, teaching little and observing much; directing the psychic activity of children and observing closely the length of time a stimulus held a child's attention' (Montessori 1964: 173).

She noted, 'teachers of the old school were prepared in principles of philosophy so immersed in theory that they remained forever in a field of theory, left standing without the door of real experimental science and that experience which makes real scientists' suggesting that teachers must be prepared 'in the method of the experimental

science' (ibid.: 7, 8). She stressed that training was 'especially necessary to those accustomed to the old domineering methods of the
common school [because of] the great distance between our methods and theirs' (ibid.: 88). Her observations were not considered to
be scientific, yet the experiments conducted by Montessori in the first
Children's Houses were examples of what is known today as 'action
research' which, according to Andres (1966: 317), 'is conducted on
the spot by interested individuals.' It is in relatively recent times that
teachers have been encouraged to be researchers within their own
classrooms. Research in classrooms had been the work of researchers,
usually from a university and it was 1994 when Carr and Kemmis suggested that teachers should become action researchers. Montessori
described in detail the many actions she took immediately after an
observation and reported the surprising results which led her to conduct more trials to confirm her findings. The same successful results
are reported today by directresses if the experiments are conducted
correctly. Montessori's work is what Lawrence Stenhouse (1975) and
Barry MacDonald (1975) describe as 'a curriculum research' because
it 'related to the needs of teachers who had the right to know, to be
informed' (Stenhouse, 1975: 121). The classroom as a laboratory was
a very new idea in 1907 and when Stenhouse proposed the idea of
the teacher as researcher he pointed out:

> Education ideas expressed in books are not easily taken into pos-
> session by teachers (yet) curricular specifications exposes them as
> testing teachers ... the idea is that of an educational science in
> which each classroom becomes a laboratory, each teacher a mem-
> ber of the scientific community.
>
> (Stenhouse, 1975: 142)

Harste and Short (1988) advanced an ethnographic inductive
methodology of research beginning with observation and progressing
to a theory or explanation of an observation. In *The Scientific Pedagogy
as Applied to Child Education in the Children's House* (1909), Montessori
reported her first experiments over a two-year period which is an
example of ethnography. In 1912 when it was renamed *The Montessori Method* and printed in twenty languages, it sold out in four days

and remains a best seller. Teachers were able to follow the 'method' from her ethnographic account. Montessori education was scientific pedagogy, advocated in 1907 and put into practice by Montessori and her teachers and others in many parts of the world who bought a copy of her findings. It began with observations of children and then practice not theory, therefore there are no 'gaps' and, as a result, it has continued to be put into practice to this day. Every individualized three-period lesson gives the directress the opportunity to be 'a researcher.' She receives immediate feedback as to whether the child has understood the lesson or not, by observing how the child works with the materials. Montessori's suggestion a century ago of how to assess children's development is relevant today. Continuous evaluation with anecdotal and qualitative notes was made of each child, since Montessori did not consider a number could measure a child's development. The element of the directress as a researcher has meant the Montessori approach has remained open-ended and environments can and have continued to include some modern innovations after trialing by following Montessori principles.

In a Montessori environment in 1907, children found themselves living in an atmosphere of love, respect, truth, and harmony. To Montessori, social and emotional development evolved together through social conditions and social relationships. The most powerful emotion, Montessori averred, was love and there were different levels of love. The first was the personal care and affection of a parent, the second was not personal, not material but was a spiritual relationship practiced by the teacher (Montessori, 1967: 283). Love united children and adults and this love was universal (Montessori, 1964: 13). Montessori was always aware of the reality of wars in her time and in the past, but she had a vision of a peaceful world that could become a reality, not a utopian vision. Children had shown that if the correct social conditions could be provided in school, they could live in harmony naturally. The new environment with the new teacher was a microcosm of 'a new world' to come. Through time, every community would become orderly and finally the whole of society leading to a world of peace. Reconstruction of the world was possible only through children and because love of children was universal. Love and the hope of it 'is part of life's heritage' (Montessori, 1967: 290).

Montessori observed that the universal love for children unified adults and, as a result, it was the children who could bring peace to the world (Montessori, 1997: 93).

---

33 Conclusion

A century ago the first Children's House opened on 6 January, 1907, and it is arguable that Montessori's approach to education is much closer to the theories advanced by twenty-first-century educators than the stimulus/response theories when she began her work. Montessori has been vindicated time and again by theories being put into practice over the past 50 years. It is worthy to note that during the last century many Montessori principles and materials have been integrated into mainstream early childhood education without acknowledgment, while several important Montessori principles and practices from 1907 remain unique to Montessori education. These include children being treated with respect as unique individuals with individual needs; providing children with opportunities to prepare themselves for the next stage of development; observing free children displaying mastery and understanding of the learning process; considering all children as they pass through developmental stages including the sensitive periods when children learn best leading them to write and read spontaneously at four years; creating a stress-free environment with activities which engage children in higher-order thinking; giving children help to construct knowledge through short three-period lessons; using didactic materials to learn; having children responsible for their own learning and empowering them to choose their own subject areas and follow their own interest at their own pace, unthreatened by competition; acknowledging that children have rights and responsibilities from the earliest age and that they are in the process of learning to become contributing members of their democratic classroom; recognizing social relationships, with active encouragement of social harmony during work and play; fostering social literacies through example, along with lessons in specific social graces; and being concerned about the mental health of each child, nurturing the spirit at each stage of development by providing therapeutic conditions for quality living in order to produce happy, normalized children. By the age of 6, independent 'normal' children of healthy mind and body grow true to natural characteristics and should possess a good character, which is every child's birthright. These children are calm, self-controlled, willing, obedient, affectionate, cheerful, lively, and enjoy stillness. Montessori found 'this phenomenon recreated unfailingly in all our schools with children belonging to different social classes, races and civilizations.' This process of normalization, she averred, was 'the most important single result of our whole work' (Montessori, 1967: 185, 186), such children being able to relate to others, being prepared to adapt to an unknown, fast-changing technological world and competent to make a contribution to society in these new times.

Montessori education today, offers free children many opportunities and experiences. Social interactions lead them to be truthful, co-operative, friendly, kind, helpful, able to solve social problems confidently from three years of age. Freedom to move results in physical development through working with materials resulting in large muscle control, the refinement of small muscles, and moving with ease and grace. Children show an interest in everything found in the prepared environment, which encourages intellectual development. Their natural love of beauty in nature, orderliness and cleanliness of their environment helps aesthetic development and understanding of conservation. Emotionally, children's nervous systems become calm and rested when they concentrate and work with self-chosen activities. Spiritually, children possess inner happiness, contentment, and a love of life. The inherent human qualities nurtured in children are important in life; respect ranking as the most desired quality. Such qualities become part of each child's character in stress-free environments where they develop a well-balanced personality becoming cultured, refined, honorable, truthful, self-respecting adults, equipped to relate harmoniously with others and able to take a place in the wider community. This is made possible when parents and teachers work together, understand the stages of child development, and provide stress-free living environments. What stands out in Montessori schools is the behavior of students – while not quantifiable, it is observable in actions and words. Montessori education is well established with reports from schools worldwide showing this to be true. Montessori education is relevant today and will continue to be relevant because it is based on the 'needs' of each individual child.

The basic principles and materials remain as Montessori described in her writings. Contemporary studies in education appear to validate Montessori's theories and practices, much evidence being based on the observations of children. Current research, with its new interpretation of literacy learning (multiple literacies including socially situated literacies), appears to confirm the merits of Montessori practices. In Montessori environments, special importance is laid on living in harmony and respecting the rights of others. In that regard, Montessori education fits happily into the thesis of Gee and colleagues (1996) who wrote about critical social literacy as a millennium literacy. They argued that the literacies needed for the new millennium contain elements that have been practiced and refined for thousands of years as well as new elements for this 'post everything age.' The new elements require finding ways of being humane on just and reciprocal bases, and to be able to recognize and act on what is happening in society. Gee and colleagues claim that literacy is 'much more than being able to follow the words across a page' (cited in Christie and Mission, 1998). Intelligent people of any day or age aspire to lives of dignity and fulfillment for all and are prepared to collaborate in building it, but as these commentators warn, we need to be able to respond to 'distinctive conditions of lived in times' (ibid.: 175). Montessori seems to have anticipated these same conclusions at the beginning of the twentieth century.

Montessori educational practices are based on the dignity of man, the fundamental equality of all men. At its heart, Montessori philosophy embraced mental health in general, especially peace of mind, inner peace in each individual, peaceful homes, and above all, peaceful classrooms. All these Montessori saw as an indispensable preparation leading toward a peaceful world. In *Education and Peace* (1932), *Education for a New World* (1946), and other writings Montessori spoke of her vision for a new world, a better world in which education would be a catalyst and principal agent for global harmony, peace, and happiness. This New World would be realized not through adults but by way of children. There was a need for all humans to uplift themselves to the laws that govern (human) nature, she argued, and to re-connect to the laws of the universe which for millions of years had been a prerequisite for harmony among mankind (Lecture, late 1930s based on the fixed laws that govern the universe). Montessori envisaged a world where all people experienced social justice precisely as children do in Montessori schools. She spoke of the 'universal' child growing into a teenager able to make wise choices in a free, democratic world, with a work ethic and a positive attitude toward life and living. They would not be expected to self-abuse their bodies through alcohol, nicotine, or drugs. They would be sensitive to the feelings of others with a well-developed understanding of human justice. Each graduate would be a cultured young adult, fully prepared to adapt to an increasingly technological society, no matter where he found himself as a world citizen.

Montessori considered herself to be a world citizen. Her plan for New Education for a New World involved helping the development of each child's unique personality from his birth, enabling him to become literate and equipping him to adapt and care for the world in which he lived. Civilization, she felt, was at risk since while Man had developed material things he had in the process 'forgotten himself' (Montessori, 1996: 103–13). The implication was that Man's spiritual development had not kept up with development of technology, and little or no thought was given to the cosmic construction of one whole human society based on mutual help among men (ibid.: 103–13). 'Humanity was on the down' she declared categorically, 'and all efforts in education needed to be directed towards raising humanity to a higher level' (ibid.: 87–92). That particular idea of Montessori appears especially important today in a world where globalization and multiculturalism are realities. She always considered relationships to be the crux of education (Standing, 1957) and in today's unsettled global village it would appear that relationships among peoples of the world are increasingly vital for its very survival.

Montessori education works for every child from all the manifold cultures of the world auguring well for the future of mankind. It is based on the individual child, and it is as relevant today as it appeared to be a century ago in the slums of Rome. Montessori's confident declaration of 1914 that 'only the child reveals the laws of man's inner development' (Montessori, 1914: 183) merits closer attention by those involved with education today. The fundamental value of the Montessori method, based on the natural tendencies of children, lies in its origin – a thorough, clinical evaluation of the individual child.

Bibliography

Adams, M. (1990) *Beginning to Read: Thinking and Learning About Print.* Cambridge, MA: MIT Press.

Adams, M. (1991) 'A talk with Marilyn Adams.' *Language Arts*, 68, 206–12, March.

Ahlfeld, K. (1970) 'The Montessori revival.' *The Education Digest*, 35, April, in *Nation's Schools*, 85, January 1970, 75, 78, 80.

Anderson, M. (1929) 'The Montessori method.' *The New Era*, 10.

Anderson, R. H. and Pavan, B. N. (1993) *Nongradedness: Helping it to Happen.* Lancaster, PA: Technomic.

Andres, D. J. (1966) 'Action research.' *South Australian Education Gazette*, 4 May, 4.

Arieti, S. (1976) *Creativity: The Magic Synthesis.* New York: Basic Books.

Armorson, A. (2001) 'Add relaxation to school's three R's.' *North West News*, Brisbane, 20, 14, June.

Armstrong, K. (1999) 'Brain research in infants.' Paper presented at Montessori Annual Conference, Crest Hotel, Brisbane, September.

Ashton-Warner, S. (1975) *Summerhill: For and Against.* Sydney: Angus and Robertson.

Ausubel, D. (1985) 'Learning as constructing meaning.' In Entwistle, N. (ed.) *New Directions in Educational Psychology.* London: The Falmer Press.

Baker, D. and Freebody, P. (1989) *Children's First School Books.* Oxford: Basil Blackwell.

Balson, M. (1992) 'Development of responsibility in students: self-discipline.' *Montessori Magazine*, Winter.

Barton, D., Hamilton, M. and Ivanic, R. (2000) *Situated Literacies. Reading and Writing in Context.* London: Routledge.

Baynham, M. (1995) *Literacy Practices: Investigating Literacy in Social Contexts.* London: Longman.

Bear, D. R. and Templeton, S. (1998) 'Explanations in developmental spelling. Foundations for learning and teaching phonics, spelling and vocabulary.' *The Reading Teacher*, 52 (3), 222–42.

Beech, M. (2001) 'Mental health at risk.' *Courier-Mail*, Opinion, 21 September.

Bennett, J. G. (1984) *The Spiritual Hunger of the Modern Child*. Charles Town, WV: Claymont Communications.

Berk, L. E. (1996) *Infants, Children and Adolescents*. London: Allyn and Bacon.

Berliner, M. S. (1975) 'Reason, creativity and freedom in Montessori.' *The Educational Forum*, 40, 7–21, November.

Bero, F. E. (1983) 'Teaching the ineducable: the impact of sensationalist philosophy on educational thought and practice.' Paper presented at the annual meeting of the American Educational Research Association, 11–15 April. Montreal, Quebec, Canada (ERIC ED235 632).

Berryman, J. (1980) 'Montessori and religious education.' *Religious Education*, 75, 3, May–June.

Beyer, E. (1962) 'Let's look at Montessori.' *The Journal of Nursery Education*, Washington, November.

Biggs, J. (1989) 'Towards a model of school-based curriculum development and assessment using the SOLO Taxonomy.' *Australian Journal of Education*, 33 (2), 151–63.

Binet, A. and Simon, H. (1905) 'Application des methods novelles au diagnostic nouveau intellectual chez enfants normaux d'hospice et d'école primaire.' *L'Anne Psychologique*, 11, 245–66.

Bingham, A. A., Dorta, P., McClasleay, M. and O'Keefe, J. (1995) *Exploring the Multiage Classrooms*. York, Maine: Stenhouse.

Bissex, G. L. (1980) *Gnys at Work: A Child Learns to Write and Read*. Cambridge, MA: Harvard University Press.

Blachman, B. A. (1991) 'Early intervention for children's reading problems: clinical applications of the research in phonological awareness.' *Topics in Language Disorders*, 12 (1), 51–65, 5 November.

Blenkin, G. M. and Kelly, A. V. (eds) (1996) *Early Childhood Education: A Developmental Curriculum*. London: Paul Chapman.

Blishen, E. (ed.) (1973) *The School That I'd Like*. London: Penguin Books in collaboration with the *Observer*.

Bloget, R. (1979) *The Importance of the Development of the Senses*. California: Montessori World Educational Institute.

Bodrova, E. (1996) *Tools of the Mind: The Vygotskian Approach to Early Childhood Education*. New Jersey: Prentice Hall.

Borton, T. (1970) *Reach, Touch and Teach*. California: Dimensions.

Bowers, P. G. (1988) 'Naming speed and phonological awareness.' Paper presented at the Annual Meeting of the National Reading Conference 37. Tucson, AZ , 29 November–3 December.

Boyd, W. (1917) *From Locke to Montessori: A Cultural Account of the Montessori Point of View*. London: Harrap.

Boyd, W. (1921) *The History of Western Education*. London: Adam and Charles Black.

Bracegirdle, H. (1992) 'The use of play in occupational therapy for children: What is play?' *British Journal of Occupational Therapy*, 55 (3), 107–9.

Bradley, L. and Bryant, P. E. (1983) 'Categorizing sounds and learning to read – a causal connection.' *Nature*, 301, 419–21.

Braik, G. D. (1913) 'Notes on education in Australia and New Zealand with some recommendations.' Wanganui.

Brano, H. J. and Weich, K. (1989) 'Cognitive and social – emotional development of children in different pre-school environments.' *Psychological Reports*, 65 (2), 480–2.

Braun, S. J. (1974) *Nursery Education for Disadvantaged Children: An Historical Review*. Westington, DC: National Association for the Education of Young Children.

Brehony, K. (2000) 'Montessori, individual work and individuality in the elementary school classroom.' *History of Education*, 29 (2), 115–28.

Britton, J. (1970) *Language and Learning*. London: Penguin Books.

Broadbent, D. E. (1958) *Perception and Communication*. London: Pergamon Press.

Brown, A. L., Bransford, J. D., Ferrara, R. A. and Campione, J. C. (1983) 'Learning, remembering and understanding.' In Flavell,

J. H. and Markman, E. M. (eds) *Handbook of Child Psychology* (4th edn), Vol. 3 *Cognitive Development*. New York: Wiley, 420–94.

Bruce, T. (1984) 'A Froebelian looks at Montessori's work.' *Early Child Development and Care*, 4 (1–2), 75–83, February.

Bruck, M. and Trelman, R. (1990) 'Phonological awareness and spelling in normal children and dyslexic children: case of initial consonant clusters.' *Journal of Experimental Psychology*, 50 (1), 156–78, August.

Bruner, J. S. (1960) *The Process of Education*. New York: Vintage Books.

Bruner, J. S. (1984) 'Vygotsky's zone of proximal development: the hidden agenda.' In Rogoff, B. and Wertsch, J. V. (eds) *Children's Learning in the 'Zone of Proximal Development'*. San Francisco: Jossey-Bass.

Bryen, D. N. and Gerber, A. (1987) 'Metalinguistic abilities and reading: a focus on phonological awareness.' *Journal of Reading, Writing and Learning Disabilities International*, 3 (4), 35–67.

Buckler, A. M. (1924) 'Freedom for little children. A chat with parents.' Paper presented at The Montessori Fellowship, London, 1–8 September.

Burns, S., Griffin, P. and Snow, C. (eds) (1999) *Starting Out Right. A Guide to Promoting Children's Reading Success*. Washington, DC: National Research Council.

Butts, F. R. (1955) *A Cultural History of Western Education. Its Social and Intellectual Foundations*. New York: McGraw-Hill.

Byrne, B. and Fielding, B. R. (1991) 'Evaluation of a program to teach phonemic awareness to young children.' *Journal of Educational Psychology*, 83 (4), 451–5, December.

Calvert, P. (1986) 'Responses to guidelines for developmentally appropriate practice for young children in Montessori.' Paper presented at the Annual Meeting of the National Association of Young Children, Washington, DC. 13–16 November.

Cambourne, B. (1984) 'Language, learning and literacy. Another way of looking at language learning.' In Butler, A. and Turbill, J. (eds) *Towards a Reading Writing Classroom*. PETA, NSW: Roselle.

Cambourne, B. and Rousch, P. (1980) 'There's more to reading than meets the eye.' *Australian Journal of Reading*, 3 (2), 107–14, June.

Carr, D. (1969) 'Art in Montessori schools.' *Communications,* 2/3, Amsterdam: Association Montessori Internationale.

Carr, W. and Kemmis S. (1994) *Becoming Critical: Education, Knowledge and Action Research.* Geelong, Victoria: Deakin University Press.

Carroll, J. B. (1963) 'A model of learning.' *Teachers' College Record,* 64, 723–33.

Caspi, A. (1999) 'The child is the father of the man.' *Medical Research and Council News,* 80, Winter/Spring.

Castells, M., Felda, R. and Freire P. (1999) *Critical Education in the New Information Age.* New York: Rowman and Littlefield.

Cataloo, S. and Ellis, N. (1988) 'Interactions in the development of spelling, reading and phonological skills.' *Journal of Research in Reading,* 7 (2), 86–109.

Cato, N. (1996) Personal letter to Dan O'Donnell.

Catts, H. W. (1991) 'Facilitating phonological awareness: role of speech/language pathologists.' *Language, Speech and Hearing Services in Schools,* 22 (4), 196–203, October.

Cavalletti, S. and Gobbi, G. (1964) *Teaching Doctrine and Liturgy.* New York: Schocken Books.

Cavalletti, S. (1992) *The Religious Potential of the Child.* Chigago: Liturgy Training.

Cavalletti, S., Coulter, P., Gobbi, G. and Montanaro, S. Q. (1994) *The Good Shepherd and the Child: A Joyful Journey.* New York: Don Bosco Multimedia.

Chall, J. (1967) *Learning to Read. The Great Debate.* New York: McGraw Hill.

Chaney, C. (1991) 'Language development, metalinguistic skills and emergent literacy in three-year-old children.' Paper presented at the biennial meeting of the society for research in child development. Seattle, Washington, 18–20 April.

Charbonneau, M. P. and Reider, B. E. (1995) *The Integrated Elementary Classroom. A Developmental Model of Education for the Twenty-first Century.* Needham Heights, MA: Allyn and Bacon.

Chase, P. and Doan, J. (1994) *Full Circle: A New Look at Multiage Education.* Portsmouth, NH: Heinemann.

Chattin-McNichols, J. (1991) 'Montessori Teachers' Intervention: Preliminary findings from an international study.' Paper presented at the Annual Conference of the National Association for the Education of Young Children, Denver, 7–10 November (ERIC ED 341 499).

Chattin-McNichols, J. (1992) *The Montessori Controversy*. New York: Delmar.

Chomsky, C. (1971) 'Write first, read later.' *Childhood Education*, 47, 196–9, March.

Christie, F. and Mission, R. (1998) *Literacy and Schooling*. London: Routledge.

Clair, R. P. (1991) 'The effects of tactile stimulation and gross motor movement on cognitive learning: a test of Montessori's muscular movement theory in the college classroom.' Paper presented at the Annual Meeting of the Eastern Communication Association, Pittsburgh, PA, 25–8 April.

Claremont, C. (1974) 'Science of education.' *Communications*, 1/2, Amsterdam: Association Montessori Internationale.

Clarke-Stewart, A., Friedman, S. and Koch, K. (1985) *Child Development: A Topical Approach*. New York: John Wiley.

Clay, M. M. (1977) 'Literacy for life. Reading acquisition. Do you get what you plan for?' Third Australian Reading Conference, Melbourne Hilton, sponsored by Ashton Scholastic, 28–31 August.

Clay, M. M. (1991) *Becoming Literate: The Construction of Inner Control*. Auckland: Heinemann.

Clay, M. M. (1998) *By Different Paths to Common Outcomes*. York, Maine: Stenhouse.

Coe, E. J. (1991) 'Montessori education and its relevance to educational reform.' Paper presented at the Conference on the Future of Public Montessori programs, New York, 17–19 October.

Cohen, S. (1969) 'Priestess or pedagogue?' *The Teachers' College Record*, 71 (2), December.

Cohen, S. (1974) 'The Montessori movement in England 1911–1952.' *History of Education*, 3 (1), 51–67.

Cole, L. (1950) *A History of Education: Socrates to Montessori*. New York: Rinehart.

Cole, M. (1999) 'PC classroom poses health risk for pupils.' *Courier-Mail*, Education Report 3, 29 November.

Combs, A. W. (ed.) (1967) *Humanizing Education: The Person in the Process*. Washington, DC: Association for Supervision and Curriculum Development, National Education Association.

Cope, B. and Kalantzis, M. (2000) *Literacy Learning and the Design of Social Futures*. Melbourne: Macmillan.

Corson, D. (1993) *Language, Minority Education and Gender. Linking Social Justice and Power*. Toronto, Canada: Ontario Institute for Studies in Education.

Courts, P. L. (1997) *Multicultural Literacies: Dialect, Discourse and Diversity*. Studies in Postmodern Theory of Education. New York: Peter Lang.

Crane, A. R. and Walker, W. G. (1957) 'Peter Board: His contribution to the development of education in New South Wales.' Australian Council for Education Research, 196, 204, 299, 323.

Crane-Fisk, C. (1986) 'Foreign language instruction within a Montessori environment.' Paper presented to the 120th Annual Meeting of the American Council on the Teaching of Foreign Languages. Dallas, TX, 21–3 November (ERIC ED 280 278).

Currie, J. and Breadmore, J. (1983) 'Montessori and Krishnamutri: a comparison of their educational philosophies and schools in practice in the USA and India.' In *Comparative and International Studies and the Theory and Practice of Education*, Proceedings of the 11th Annual Conference of the Australian Comparative and International Education Society, Hamilton, New Zealand, 21–4 August (ERIC ED 265 260 UD 024 660).

Cusack, G. (1997) 'Ukraine forms a Montessori Association and opens first teacher training center.' *The Ukrainian Weekly*, 26 January, 4. LXV, 1–3.

Cushman, K. (1990) 'The whys and hows of the multi-age primary classroom.' *American Educator: The Professional Journal of the American Federation of Teachers*, 14(2), 28–32, 39, Summer (ERIC ED 412 628).

Dahl, K., Scharer, P. and Lawson, L. (1999) 'Phonics instruction and students achievement in whole language first grade classrooms.' *Reading Research Quarterly*, 34 (3), 312–41, July/August/September.

Daly, M. and Stack, J. (2005) 'Criminal mind starts developing at three years.' *Courier-Mail*, 14 June.

de Castell, S., Luke, A. and Egan, K. (1986) *Literacy, Society and Schooling*. New York: Cambridge University Press.

de Castell, S., Luke, A. and Luke, C. (1989) *Language, Authority and Criticism. Reading on the School Textbook*. London: The Falmer Press.

De Ford, J. and Harste, J. (1982) 'Child language research and curriculum.' *Language Arts*, 59 (6), 590–600, September.

DeLemos, M. M. (1971) 'Controversy in preschool education.' Australian Council for Educational Research. Occasional paper, 4 January.

D'Emidio-Caston, M. and Crocker, E. (1987) 'Montessori Education: a humanistic approach for the 1990s.' (ERIC ED 314 212).

De Vries, R. and Artin, G. (1988) 'Interpersonal relations in four-year-old Dyads from constructivist and Montessori programmes.' *Early Childhood Development and Care*, 33 (1), 11–27 April.

Dewey, J. (1964) *John Dewey's Impressions of Soviet Russia and the Revolutionary World, Mexico-China-Turkey, 1929*. New York: Teachers' College Columbia University.

Dillon, J. T. (1971) *Personal Teaching*. Ohio: Charles E. Merrill.

Donaldson, M. (1978) *Children's Minds*. Glasgow: Fontana/Collins.

Donaldson, M. (1993) *Human Minds: An Exploration*. London: Penguin Books.

Downing, J. and Oliver, P. (1973–74) 'The child's conception of a word.' *Reading Research Quarterly*, 9, 568–82.

Drummond, M. (1947) *Learning Arithmetic by the Montessori Method*. London: Harrap.

Duckworth, E. (1979) 'Either we're too early and they can't learn it or we're too late and they know it already: the dilema of "Applying Piaget".' *Harvard Educational Review*, 49 (3), 297–312.

Duffy, M. (2001) 'Report on Attention Deficit Hyperactive Disorder.' *Courier-Mail*, 6 April, 26.

Edelsky, C. (ed.) (1999) *Making Justice Our Project. Teachers Working Towards Critical Whole Language Practice*. Illinois: National Council of Teachers of English.

Edmonds, B. (1976) 'Comments on the Montessori philosophy and pre-school education in 1975.' *Developing Education*, Northern Territory, 4 (2), 3–9, August.

Edmonson, B. (1963) 'Let's do more than look – let's research Montessori.' *The Journal of Nursery Education*, November.

Egan, K. (1983) *Education and Psychology: Plato, Piaget and Scientific Psychology*. London: Methuen.

Egan, K. (1988) *Primary Understanding: Education in Early Childhood*. New York: Routledge.

Egan, K. and Nadaner, D. (1988) *Imagination and Education*. Milton Keynes: Open University Press.

Ehrl, L. C. (1994) 'Development of the ability to read words: update'. In Ruddell, R., Ruddell, M. and Singer, H. (eds) *Theoretical Processes in Reading* (4th edn). USA: International Reading Association Incorporated.

Elkind, D. (1968) 'Piaget and Montessori.' *The Education Digest*, 33, March. Also reported in *Harvard Educational Review*, 37, 535–45, Fall.

Elkind, D. (1980) 'The role of play in religious education.' *Religious Education*, 75 (3), May–June.

Ellis, N. and Cataloo S. (1990) 'The role of spelling in learning to read.' *Language and Education*, 4 (1), 28.

Ellyatt, W. (1999) 'Increasing interest in Reggio Emilia.' *Montessori Educational Magazine*, 9 (2), 23–5, 39, Winter.

Emmitt, M. (1996) *Positions on Literacy Theories and Practices*. Sydney: Australian Reading Association.

Emmitt, M., Pollock, J. and Limbrick, L. (1996) *An Introduction to Language and Learning*. Auckland, New Zealand: Oxford University Press.

Epstein, P. (1990) 'Are public schools ready for Montessori?' *Principal*, 69 (3), 20–2 May (ERIC ED 410 166).

Erikson, E. H. (1950) *Childhood and Society*. New York: W. W. Norton.

Evans, B. (1971) 'The Absorbent Mind.' *The Leader*, 4 (6), 61–3.

Evans, E. D. (1971) *Contemporary Influences in Early Childhood Education*. New York: Rinehart and Winston.

Fanning, K. (1994) 'Montessori history: Ireland. Famous names in the visitor's book.' *The International Montessori Journal*, 14, 15, 19 May.

Farganis, J. (1975) 'A preface to critical theory.' *Theory and Society*, 2 (4), 483–508.

Faulmann, J. (1980) 'Montessori and music in early childhood.' *Educational Digest*, 46, 60–2.

Fidler, W. (2004) 'Special needs children in Montessori environments. Dyslexia; The Autistic Spectrum; Dyspraxia.' A series of articles in *Montessori International*, issues 69, 70, 71, 72.

Fields, M. V. and Spangler, L. (2000) *Let's Begin Reading Right* (4th edn). New Jersey: Merrill.

Fisher, D. C (1913) *The Montessori Manual for Teachers and Parents.* Cambridgen, MA: W. E. Richardson.

Fisher, L. (1982) *Pioneers of Education in Western Australia.* Nedlands: University of W.A.

Fisher, R. (1992) *Early Literacy and the Teacher.* London: Hodder and Stoughton in Association with UK Reading Association.

Flynn, T. M. (1991) 'Development of social, personal and cognitive skills of preschool children in Montessori and traditional preschool programs.' *Early Child Development and Care*, 72, 117–24.

Forman, E. A. (1989) 'The role of interaction in the social construction of mathematical knowledge.' *International Journal of Educational Research*, 13, 55–70.

Forman, E. A. and Cazdan, C. B. (1994) 'Exploring Vygotskian perspectives in education: the cognitive value of peer interaction.' In Ruddell, R., Ruddell, M. and Singer, H. (eds) *Theoretical Models and Processes of Reading* (4th edn). USA: International Reading Association.

Frost, J. L. (1968) *Early Childhood Education Rediscovered* (Readings). New York: Holt, Rinehart, and Winston.

Frost, J. L. (1973) *Revisiting Early Childhood Education* (Readings). New York: Holt, Rinehart, and Winston.

Fynne, R. F. (1924) *Montessori and Her Inspirers.* New York: Longman.

Gage, N. L. and Berliner, D. C. (1979) *Educational Psychology.* Boston: Houghton Mifflin Company.

Gagné, R. (1965) *The Conditions of Learning.* London: Holt, Rinehart and Winston.

Galbraith, H. (1991) *Reasoning and Rhyming into Reading.* Ipswich Special Services Centre: Department of Education, Queensland.

Galloway, C. (1976) *Psychology for Learning and Teaching.* New York: McGraw-Hill.

Gardner, H. (1983) *Frames of Mind: The Theory of Multiple Intelligences.* New York: Basic Books.

Gardner, H. (2000) *Intelligence Reframed: Multiple Intelligences for the 21st Century.* New York: Basic.

Gattego, C. (1969) *Reading with Words in Colour.* Reading, UK: Educational Explorers.

Gearing A. (2000) 'Choosing a literacy method.' *Courier-Mail*, 29 August.

Gee, J. P. (1990) *Social Linguistics and Literacies: Ideology and Discourses.* New York: Falmer Press.

Gee, J. P. (1996) *Social Linguistics and Literacies.* London: Taylor and Francis.

Gee, J. P., Hull, G. and Lankshear, C. (1996) *The New Work Order: Behind the Language of the New Capitalism.* Sydney: Allen and Unwin.

Gentry, J. R. (1981) 'Learning to spell developmentally.' *The Reading Teacher*, 34, 4.

Gettman, D. (1987) *Basic Montessori: Learning Activities for Under-Fives.* London: Christopher Helm.

Gillespie, R. R. (1978) 'Australian Education: Ideas in Transition 1900–1914.' PhD Thesis, University of Sydney

Gillet, A. M. (1969) 'Introduction to biology. Montessori Conference, Bergamo, Italy.' *Communications*, (4), 1972. Amsterdam: Association Montessori Internationale.

Good, H. G. (1983) *A History of Western Education.* London: Charles Black.

Goodlad, J., Klein, M. F. and Novontey, J. M. (1973) *Early Schooling in the United States.* New York: McGraw-Hill.

Goodman, K. (1976) 'Reading; A psycholinguistic guessing game.' Paper given for American Educational Research Association, New York, February. Published in *Journal of the Reading Specialist*, May.

Goodman, K. (ed.) (1986) *A Multidisciplinary Approach to Language and to Reading: Some Projections in the Psycholinguistic Nature of the Reading Process.* Detroit: Wayne State University Press.

Goodman, K. (1994) 'Reading, writing and written texts: A transactional sociopsycholinguistic view.' In Ruddell, R., Ruddell, M. and Singer, H. (eds) *Theoretical Models and Processes of Reading* (4th edn). Newark, DE: International Reading Association in USA.

Goodman, Y. M. (1987) 'Kid watching: an alternative to testing.' *National Elementary Principal*, 57 (4), 41–5, June.

Goodman, Y. M. (1990) *Literacy Development: Psychogenesis and Pedagogical Implications*. Newark, DE: International Reading Association.

Goodman, Y. and Goodman, K. (1994) 'To err is human: Learning about language processes by analysing miscues.' In Ruddell, R., Ruddell, M. and Singer, H. (eds) *Theoretical Models and Processes of Reading* (4 edn). Newark, DE: International Reading Association in USA.

Grant, J., Johnson, B. and Richardson, I. (1995) *Multiage Questions and Answers. 101 Practical Answers to Your Most Pressing Questions*. Peterborough, NH: Crystal Springs.

Graves, D. (1982) *Donald Graves in Australia. Children want to write*. Ed. R. D. Walshe. London: Heinemann, 17–28.

Grazzini, C. (1975) 'The International Center for Montessori Studies Foundation.' *Communications*, (2) Amsterdam: Association Montessori Internationale.

Gronlund, N. E. (1970) *Stating Behavioral Objectives for Classroom Instruction*. New York: McMillan.

Grundy, S. and Kemmis, S. (1981) 'Educational Action Research in Australia. The state of the art (an overview).' Paper presented at the Annual Conference of the Australian Association for Research in Education, Adelaide, November.

Guthrie, E. R. (1952) *The Psychology of Learning*. New York: Harper.

Guynn, S. J. (1989) 'Evaluation of the Indianapolis Public Schools' Montessori Option (K-6) Pupil Progress Report.' Indianapolis Public Schools, Indianapolis, May (ERIC ED 318 548).

Hainstock, E. G. (1971) *Teaching Montessori in the Home: The School Years* (Plume). New York: New American Library.

Hall, N. (1987) *The Emergence of Literacy*. London: Hodder and Stoughton.

Halliday, M. A. K. (1975) *Learning How to Mean: Explorations in the Development of Language (Explorations in Language Study)*. London: Edward Arnold.

Hamilton, D. and Walker, R. (Speakers) (1992) 'Research in the Workplace.' (Cassette Recording No. M1254) EdD901 Professional Doctorate, Geelong, Victoria: Deakin University.

Hans, N. (1994) *Comparative Education: A Study of Educational Factors and Traditions.* London: Routledge and Kegan Paul.

Harste, J. C. and Short, K. G. (1988) 'What Educational Difference Does Your Theory of Language Make?' Paper presented at the International Reading Association World Congress, Queensland, Australia, 11–13 July, 1988. Also, at the 34th Annual Meeting of the International Reading Association. New Orleans, 30 April–4 May, 1989.

Hart, M. (2001) 'Kids on the edge.' Report from the National Survey of Mental Health and Wellbeing, Canberra. *Courier-Mail,* 14 March.

Holdaway, D. (1972) *Independence in Reading.* Auckland: Ashton Educational.

Holdaway, D. (1979) *The Foundations of Literacy.* New York: Ashton Scholastic.

Holman, H. (1925) *Séguin and His Philosophical Method of Education.* London: Adam Black.

Holmes, D. L. (1973) 'The independence of letter, word and meaning identification in reading.' In Smith, F. (ed.) *Understanding Reading.* New York: Holt, Rinehart and Winston.

Holt, J. (1974) *How Children Fail.* Manchester: Penguin Books.

Homfray, M. (1955) *Phonetic Word Lists and Lists of Words Containing the Main Phonograms.* Perth, Western Australia: Montessori World Educational Institute.

Homfray, M. and Child, P. (1985) *Children and Education.* California: Montessori World Educational Institute.

Hranitz, J. H. (1985) 'Montessori and brain research.' Paper presented at the Conference on Children. Palm Springs: Bloomsburg University.

Hunt, J. McV. (1961) 'Intelligence and Experience.' In Introduction to *The Montessori Method* (1964). New York: Ronald.

Hunt, J. McV. (1964) 'How children develop intellectually.' *Children,* 11 (3), 83–91.

Hurworth, E. (ed.) (1914) 'Report on Montessori Education at Blackfriars, NSW.' *Education Office Gazette* (Old Department of Public Instruction), October 445–7, November 483–6, December 533–5.

Itard, J. M. G. (1802) *The Wild Boy of Aveyron.* Translated by G. and M. Humphrey. New York: Appleton-Century, 1932.

Jarrett, J. L. (1972) *The Humanities and Humanistic Education*. Philippines: Addison-Wesley.

Jolly, C. (2002) 'Jolly phonics.' *Montessori International*, 63, 29–30, April/June.

Jones, H. (1975) 'The acceptable crusader Lillian de Lissa and preschool education in South Australia.' In Murray-Smith, S. (ed.) *Melbourne Studies in Education*. Melbourne: Melbourne University Press.

Jones, H. (1983) 'Lillian Daphne de Lissa.' *Australian Dictionary of Biography*, 8, 273–4.

Joosten, A. M. (1955) *The Montessori Movement in India*. Madras: Indian Montessori Training Courses.

Joosten, A. M. (1969) 'Gandhi and Maria Montessori.' *Communications*, 2/3, 21–3. Amsterdam: Association Montessori Internationale.

Joosten, A. M. (1973) 'Preface.' In Maria Montessori, *From Childhood to Adolescence*. New York: Schocken Books. First published in 1948.

Joosten, A. M. (1974) 'Errors and their corrections.' Indian Montessori Training Course. Amsterdam: Association Montessori Internationale.

Kahn, D. (ed.) (1990) *Implementing Montessori Education in the Public Sector*. Cleveland Heights, OH: North American Montessori Teachers' Association (ERIC ED 327 286).

Kahn, D. (ed.) (1995) *What is Montessori Preschool?* North American Teachers' Association in affiliation with Association Montessori Internationale.

Kahn, D. (2005) 'Montessori Erdkinder: The social evolution of the Little Community.' Paper presented at the 25th International Montessori Congress, Sydney.

Kaplan, P. S. (1991) *A Child's Odyssey*. New York: West Publishing.

Kasser, T. (2006) 'The high price of materialism in James McConvill "Measure up to science's happiness".' *Courier-Mail*, January, 3, 15.

Kasten, W. and Lolli, E. (1998) *Implementing Multiage Education: A Practical Guide*. Norwood, MA: Christopher-Gordon.

Katz, L. G. (1990) 'Questions about Montessori to-day.' Paper presented at a Symposium of the American Montessori Society, Arlington, VA, April.

Kilpatrick, W. H. (1914) *The Montessori System Examined.* Boston: Houghton Mifflin.

Kneller, G. F. (1951) 'Education In Italy.' In Moehlman, A. H. and Roucek, J. S. (eds) *Comparative Education.* New York: Holt, Rhinehart, and Winston.

Kohlberg, L. (1964) 'Development of moral character and moral ideology.' In Hoffman, L. W and Hoffman, M. L. (eds) *Review of Child Development Research*, Vol. 1. New York: Russell Sage Foundation.

Kohn, A. (1993) *Punished by Rewards.* New York: Houghton Mifflin.

Kong, S. L. (1970) *Humanistic Psychology and Humanized Teaching.* Toronto: Holt, Rinehart and Winston.

Kramer, R. (1976) *Maria Montessori: A Biography.* Oxford: Basil Blackwell.

Krogh, S. L. (1984) 'Preschool democracy – Ideas from Montessori.' *Social Studies*, 75 (4), 176–81, June/August (ERIC ED 303 480).

Kunesh, L. S. (1990) 'A historical review of early intervention.' *North Central Regional Laboratory.* Illinois: Elmhurst.

Lankshear, C., Gee, J., Knoble, M. and Searle, C. (1997) *Changing Literacies.* Philadelphia: Open University Press.

Lawson, J. and Silver, H. (1973) *A Social History of Education in England.* London: Metheun.

Lawson, M. D. (1974) 'Montessori: The Indian Years.' *Forum of Education*, 33 (1), 36–49.

Lenchner, O. (1990) 'Phonological awareness tasks as predictors of decoding ability – segmentation.' *Journal of Learning Disabilities*, 23 (4), 240–7, April.

Liebschner, J. (1992) *A Child's Work: Freedom and Guidance – Froebel Educational Theory and Practice.* Cambridge: The Lutterworth Press.

Lillard, P. P. (1972) *Montessori. A Modern Approach.* New York: Schocken Books.

Lillard, P. P. (1996) *Montessori Today. A Comprehensive Approach to Education from Birth to Adulthood.* New York: Schocken Books.

Lillig, T. (1998) *The Catechesis of the Good Shepherd in a Parish Setting.* Chicago: Catechesis of the Good Shepherd.

Literacy Report (2001) *Responding to Literacy Needs: Implications for Teacher Educators and Training Consultants. Working Party* (Introduction). Queensland: Board of Teacher Registration.

Lock, A. (ed.) (1978) *Action, Gesture and Symbol*. London: Academic.

Loeffler, M. (ed.) (1992) *Montessori in Contemporary American Culture*. Portsmouth, NH: Heinemann.

Loeffler, M. (2002) 'New perspectives on old ideas.' *Montessori International*, 64, 8–11, July/September.

Lohmann, R. T. (1988) 'A re-vision of Montessori: connections with Dewey, Piaget, and Vygotsky.' US Department of Education Educational Resources Information Centre (ERIC ED 304 210).

Longmore, L. and Davidson, J. I. (1915) 'Report of investigations of Montessori Methods.' 7 August, SA Department of Education Archives.

Luke, C. (1997) *Technological Literacy*. Melbourne: Research into Practice Series 4.

Lundberg, I. (1988) 'Effects of an extensive program for stimulating phonological awareness in preschool children.' *Reading Research Quarterly*, 23 (3), 263–8. Summer. Presented as a paper 'Are letters necessary in the development of phonological awareness?' at the 12th World Congress on Reading, International Reading Association, Australia, July.

Maccheroni, A. M. (1947) *A True Romance: Dr Maria Montessori as I Knew Her*. Edinburgh: Oliver and Boyd. First published in 1913.

Maccheroni, A. M. (1985) 'A true romance: Maria Montessori as I knew her.' *MWEI Newsletter* 2, September, in O'Donnell, 1996. First published in Edinburgh in 1947.

MacDonald, B. (1975) 'Evaluation and the control of education.' *Schools Council*. Also in Stenhouse, L. (1975) *An Introduction to Curriculum Research and Development*. London: Heinemann.

MacDonald, B. and Walker, R. (1976) *Changing the Curriculum*. Bath: The Pitman Press.

MacKinnon, A. R. (1959) *How DO Children Learn to Read?* Vancouver, Canada: Copp Clark.

McAllister, Anne (1999) *Strathclyde People*. Glasgow, Scotland: University of Strathclyde magazine.

McClay, J. L. (1996) *The Multiage Classroom*. Sydney: Hawker Brownlow Education.

McConvill, J. (2006) 'Measure up to science's happiness list. Report on Tim Kasser's "The High Price of Materialism".' *Courier-Mail*, 3 January.

McGrath, H. (1980) 'The Montessori method of education: an overview of research.' *Australian Journal of Early Childhood*, 5 (4), December.

Mallet, M. (1999) *Young Researchers. Informational Reading and Writing in the Early and Primary Years.* London: Routledge.

Mandelson, L. A., 'Alexander Mackie.' *Australian Dictionary of Biography*, 10, 311–12.

Mann, V. A. and Liberman, I. Y. (1984) 'Phonological awareness and verbal short term memory.' *Journal of Learning Disabilities*, 17 (10), 592–9, December.

Mann, V. A. (1987) 'Measuring phonological awareness through the invented spelling of Kindergarten children.' *Merrill Palmer Quarterly*, 33 (3), 365–91, July.

Martin J. R. (1985) *Factual Writing: Exploring and Challenging Social Reality.* Geelong, Victoria: Deakin University Press.

Martin, N. (1976) *Interaction in the Classroom.* London: Methuen.

Martin, R. D. (1991) 'Empowering teachers to break the basal habit.' Paper presented at the 36th Annual Meeting of the International Reading Association, Las Vegas, 6–10 May.

Mass, L. N. (1982) 'Developing concepts of literacy in young children.' *The Reading Teacher*, 670–5, March.

Merrill, J. B. (1909) 'New method in kindergarten education.' *Kindergarten Primary Magazine*, 106–7, 142–4, 211–12, 297–8.

Miller G. A. (1956) 'The magical number seven, plus-or-minus two. Some limits on our capacity for processing information.' *Psychological Review*, 63 (2), 81–97.

Miltich-Conway, B. and Openshaw, R. (1988) 'The Montessori Method in Wanganui Education Board District 1911–1924.' *New Zealand Journal of Education Studies*, 23, 2.

Mitchell, B. 'Martha Margaret, Mildred Simpson.' *Australian Dictionary of Biography*, 11, 612–13.

Montanaro, S. Q. (1990) *The Importance of the First Three Years of Life.* California: Nienhuis Montessori.

Montessori, Maria (1913) *Pedagogical Anthropology*. London: Heinemann.

Montessori, Maria (1929) *The Child in the Church. Catholic Liturgy from the Child's Point of View*. London: Sands. First published in Naples in 1922.

Montessori, Maria (1942) 'Reconstruction in education.' *The Theosophist*, February, Madras. First published 1913.

Montessori, Maria (1956) *The Child in the Family*. London: The Chaucer Press.

Montessori, Maria (1961) *To Educate the Human Potential*. Madras: Kalakshetra Publications. First published 1948.

Montessori, Maria (1963) *Education for a New World*. Madras: Kalakshetra Publications. First published 1946.

Montessori, Maria (1964) *The Montessori Method*. New York: Schocken Books. First published in 1909.

Montessori, Maria (1965) *Dr. Montessori's Own Handbook*. New York: Schocken Books. First published 1914.

Montessori, Maria (1966) *What You Should Know About Your Child*. Madras: Kalakshetra. First published 1948.

Montessori, Maria (1967) *The Absorbent Mind*. New York: Dell. First published 1949.

Montessori, Maria (1968) *The Child*. Adyar, Madras: The Theosophical Society, Vasata Press. First published 1941.

Montessori, Maria (1969) *Spontaneous Activity in Education. The Advanced Montessori Method*, Vol.1. New York: Schocken Books. First published 1916.

Montessori, Maria (1970) *Education and Peace*. Chicago: Regnery. First published 1932.

Montessori, Maria (1971) *Reconstrucion in Education*. Madras: Theosophical Publishing House. First published 1942.

Montessori, Maria (1972) *The Discovery of the Child*. Madras: Kalakshetra. First published 1929.

Montessori, Maria (1973) *From Childhood to Adolesence*. New York: Schocken Books. First published 1958.

Montessori, Maria (1974) *The Montessori Elementary Material. The Advanced Montessori Method*, Vol. 2. New York: Schocken Books. First published 1916.

Montessori, Maria (1975) *The Formation of Man*. Madras: Kalakshetra. First published 1948.

Montessori, Maria (1976) *The Child in the Family*. Translated by N. Rockmore Cirillo. London and Sydney: Pan Books. First published 1916.

Montessori, Maria (1977) *Reconstruction in Education*. Madras: The Theosophical Publishing House.

Montessori, Maria (1978) *The Secret of Childhood*. Hyderabad, India: Orient Longman. First published 1936.

Montessori, Maria (1980) *Childhood Education*. New York: Meridian. First published 1975.

Montessori, Maria (1996) *The Child, Society and the World*. Unpublished speeches and writings. Oxford: Clio Press. First published 1989.

Montessori, Maria (1997) *Basic Ideas of Montessori's Educational Theory*. Extracts from Maria Montessori's writings and teachings. Oxford: Clio Press. Originally compiled by P. Oswald and G. Schulz-Benesch. Translated by L. Salmon.

Montessori, Mario M. Jr. (1972) 'Voices from the past . . . and present.' *Communications*, 2–6. Association Montessori Internationale.

Montessori, Mario M. Jr. (1974) 'Montessori and the process of education.' *Communications*, 1–2. Association Montessori Internationale.

Montessori, Mario M. Jr. (1976) *Education for Human Development: Understanding Montessori*. New York: Schocken Books.

Montessori, R. (2005) *Educateurs sans Frontières*. Amsterdam: Nienhuis.

Mountain, L. (2000) *Early 3Rs*. New Jersey: Laurence Erlbaum.

Moyle, D. (1991) 'Methods of teaching reading.' *Education Today*, 41, 3.

Müller, T. and Schneider, R. (eds) (2002) *Montessori Teaching Materials 1913–1935. Furniture and Architecture*. Berlin: Prestel.

Murphy, M. and Goldner, R. P. (1976) 'Effects of teaching orientation on social interaction in nursery school.' *Journal of Educational Psychology*, 68 (6), 725–8.

Muspratt, S., Luke, A. and Freebody, P. (eds) (1997) *Constructing Critical Literacies. Teaching-learning Textual Practice*. New South Wales: Allen and Unwin.

Nasgaard, S. (1929) 'The Montessori Movement in Denmark.' *The New Era*, 10, 61–6.

Neill, A. S. (1962) *Summerhill*. Harmondsworth: Penguin Press.

Nichols, A. E. (1984) 'Montessori language lessons: The almost silent way.' *Minne TESOL Journal*, 4, 7–22, Fall (ERIC ED 275 179).

Nicholson, T. (1986) 'Reading is NOT a guessing game – The great debate revisited.' *Reading Psychology*, 7, 197–210.

Nunn, Sir P. (1920) *Education: Its Data and First Principles*. London: Edward Arnold Limited.

O'Donnell, D. (1996) *Montessori Education in Australia and New Zealand*. New South Wales: Fast Books.

O'Donnell, D. (2002) *Brisbane Montessori School*. Twentieth Anniversary History, 1982–2001. Brisbane, Australia: Clark and McKay.

Olson, M. W. (1990) 'Phonemic Awareness and Reading Achievement (Research into Practice).' *Reading Psychology*, 11 (2), 347–53.

O'Neill, W. F. (1969) *Selected Educational Heresies. Some Unorthodox Views Concerning the Nature and Purposes of Contemporary Education*. Glenview, IL: Scott, Foresman, and Company.

Orem, R. C. (1967) *Montessori for the Disadvantaged*. New York: G. P. Pitman's Sons.

Ornstein, A. C. (1977) *An Introduction to the Foundations of Education*. London: Rand McNally Education Series.

Owen, E. (2001) 'Microsurgical reflections first hand.' The University of Queensland Medical Society. E. S. Myers Memorial Lecture, Mayne Hall, University of Queensland, 27 August.

Owen, R. (1997) *The Story of Robert Owen (1771–1858)*. New Lanark, Scotland: Conservation Trust.

Painter, C. (1985) *Learning the Mother Tongue*. Geelong, Victoria: Deakin University.

Perryman, L. (ed.) (1966) *Montessori in Perspective*. Washington DC: National Association for the Education of Young Children.

Petersen, R. C. (1968) 'The Montessoriians – M. M. Simpson and Lillian de Lissa.' In C. Turney (ed.) (1972) *Pioneers of Australian Education*, 3, 240–68.

Petersen, R. C. (1971) 'Montessori in Australia.' *Education News*, 13.

Peterson, R. (1992) 'Life in a crowded place: making a learning community.' In Edelsky, C. (ed.) (1999) *Justice Our Project, Teachers Working Towards Critical Whole Language Practice*. Illinois: National Council of Teachers of English.

Phillips, S. (1977) 'Maria Montessori and contemporary cognitive psychology.' *British Journal of Teacher Education*, 3 (1), 55–8, January.

Phillips, S. (1980) 'New fashions in child rearing and education.' *New Horizons in Education*, 62, Autumn.

Piaget, J. (1974) *To Understand is to Invent*. New York: Viking Press.

Pickering, J. S. (1978) 'Successful applications of Montessori methods with children at risk.' *Learning Disabilities* (ERIC ED 343 659).

Piers, M. W. (1978) *Infanticide*. New York: W. W. Norton.

Pines, M. (1966) *Revolution in Learning*. Bristol: Penguin Press.

Polakow, V. (1992) *The Erosion of Childhood*. Chicago: University of Chicago Press, ch. 5.

Pollard, M. (1990) *Maria Montessori. The Italian Doctor who Revolutionized Education*. Milwaukee: Gareth Stevens Books.

Potts, A. (1980) 'Montessori – A progressive educator?' *The Forum of Education*, 39 (3), 26–34, September.

Powell, L. E. (1989) 'Active Learning: Positive Impact for Schools and Democratic Society.' Ohio (ERIC ED 303 702).

Prakasam, G. A. (1948) 'Foreword' of Montessori's *What You Should Know About Your Child*. Law Library, Colombo, Madras: Kalashetra.

Pratt, A. C. and Brady, S. (1988) 'Relations of phonological awareness to reading disability in children and adults.' *Journal of Educational Psychology*, 80 (3), 319–23, September.

Rambusch, N. (1962) *Learning How to Learn*. Baltimore, MD: Helican Press.

Rathbone, C., Bingham, A., Dorta, P., McClaskey, M. and O'Keefe, J. (1993) *Multiage Portraits, Teaching and Learning in Mixed-age Classrooms*. Peterborough, NH: Crystal Springs.

Raymont, T. (1937) *A History of the Education of Young Children*. London: Longman's Green.

Read, C. (1975) *Categorization of Speech Sounds in English*. Urbanana, IL: National Council of Teachers of English.

Read, C. (1988) 'Phonological awareness and adult reading.' Paper presented at IRA World Congress, July.

Read, C., Zhang Y., Nie, H. and Ding, B. (1986) 'The ability to manipulate speech sounds depends on knowing alphabetic writing.' *Cognition*, 24, 31–4.

Renwick, A. (1967) 'A modern impression of Montessori education.' *Australian Journal of Education*, 11.

Richardson, P. (1991) 'Language as personal resource and as social construct: Competing views of literacy pedagogy in Australia.' *Educational Review*, 43 (2), 171–90.

Rieben, L. and Perfetti, C. (1991) *Learning to Read. Basic Research and its Implications*. New Jersey: L. Erlbaum Associates.

Riordan, C. (1997) *Equality and Achievement: An Introduction to the Sociology of Education*. New York: Longman.

Rivalland, J. (1985) 'Teaching spelling: helping the developing speller.' *Australian Journal of Reading*, 8 (1), March.

Roberts, R. R. (1974) *English in Primary Schools*. London: Routledge and Kegan Paul.

Röhrs, H. (2000) *Prospects: Quality Review of Comparative Education*. Paris UNESCO: Bureau of Education, xxiv, 1/2, 1994.

Ruddell, M. R. (1994) 'Vocabulary knowledge and comprehension. A comprehension process view of complex literacy relationships.' In Ruddell R., Ruddell, M. and Singer, H. (eds) *Theoretical Models and Processes of Reading* (4th edn). Newark, DE: International Reading Association in USA.

Ruddell, R. B. (1977) 'Psycholinguistic models.' In Singer H. and Ruddell, R. (eds) *Theoretical Models and Processes of Reading* (2nd edn). Newark, DE: International Reading Association.

Salk, Dr. L. (1975) 'An interview.' *Communications*, 16. Association Montessori Internationale.

Schill, B. (1962) 'The Montessori System.' *Childhood Education*, December. Association for Childhood Education International.

Schiller, P. (2000) 'Key findings in brain research development: brain research applications.' One-day workshop, Creche and Kindergarten Association, Newmarket, Brisbane, 14 June.

Schneir, W. and Schneir, M. (1971) 'The joy of learning – in the open corridor.' *The New York Magazine*, 30–1, 72–97, 4 April.

Schonell, F. J. (1945) *The Psychology and Teaching of Reading* (3rd edn). Edinburgh: Oliver and Boyd.

Schonell, F. J., McLeod, J. and Cochrane R. G. (1962) *The Slow Learner: Segregation or Integration*. St. Lucia: University of Queensland Press.

Schulz-Benesch, G. (1997) *Basic Ideas of Montessori's Educational The-ory. Extracts from Maria Montessori's Writings and Teachings*. Oxford: Clio.

Séguin, E. (1866) *Traitement Moral, Hygiène des Idiots*. Paris: Bibliothèque d'éducation speciale, 1906.

Séguin, E. (1866) *Idiocy: and Its Treatment by the Physiological Method*. Albany: Columbia University Teachers' College Educational Reprints, 1907.

Seldin, T. and Epstein, P. (2003) *The Montessori Way – An Education for Life*. Florida: The Montessori Foundation.

Sherman, R. and Webb, R. (eds) (1988) *Qualitative Research in Education: Forms and Methods*. Lewes: Falmer Press.

Shore, M. (1995) 'Students as tutors in early childhood settings: The acquisition and transmission of problem solving skills.' Paper presentation at BP International Conference, London, England.

Short, S. (1985) 'Montessori education from the viewpoint of analytical psychology'. Paper presented at the Annual Seminar of the American Montessori Society 25th Conference, Washington, DC, 19–21 April (ERIC ED 260 796).

Silberman, C. E. (ed.) (1973) *The Open Classroom Reader*. New York: Vintage Books.

Silin, J. G. (1990) *Early Childhood Teacher Education*. New York: Teachers' College Press.

Simons, J. L. and Simons, F. A. (1984) 'Montessori and regular preschools: A comparison.' In Katz, L. G. (ed.) (forthcoming) *Current Topics in Early Childhood Education*. Norwood, NJ: Ablex Publishing (ERIC ED 247 031).

Simpson, M. M. (1912) 'Report on Montessori's "The Montessori Method".' In Turney, C. (ed.) (1975) *Sources in the History of Australian Education, 1788–1970*. Sydney: Angus and Robertson: pp. 145–9.

Simpson, M. M. (1914) 'Report on the Montessori Methods of Education.' Sydney: Government Printer.

Skinner, B. F. (1963) *Reflections on a Decade of Teaching Machines*. Teachers' College Record. New York: Columbia University.

Skinner, B.F. (1968) *The Technology of Teaching*. New York: Appleton-Century-Crofts.

Smith, F. (ed.) (1973) 'The great debate.' In Smith, F. (ed.) *Understanding Reading: Psycholinguistics and Reading*. New York: Holt, Rinehart and Winston.

Smith, F. (1984) 'Psycholinguistics and reading.' In Smith, F. (ed.) *Understanding Reading*. New York: Holt, Rinehart and Winston.

Smith, T. (1912) *The Montessori System*. New York and London: Harper Brothers.

Snowball, D. and Bolton, F. (1999) *Spelling K-8. Planning and Teaching*. York, Maine: Stenhouse.

Snyder, L. and Downey, D. M. (1991) 'The language – reading relationship in normal and reading-disabled children.' *Journal of Speech and Hearing Research*, 34 (1), 129–40, February.

Solomon, G. and Gardner, H. (1986) 'The computer as education: lessons from television research.' *Educational Research*, 15 (1), 13–19.

Soohoo, S. (1993) 'Students as partners in research and restructuring schools.' *The Educational Forum*, 57, 386–93.

Spodek, B. (1972) *Teaching in the Early Years*. Englewood Cliffs, NJ: Prentice-Hall.

Spodek, B. (1998) *Sociolinguistics*. Oxford: Oxford University Press.

Springer, J. (1999) *Listen to Us: The World of Working Children*. Sydney: Allen and Unwin.

Standing, E. M. (1957) *Maria Montessori: Her Life and Her Work*. London: Hollis and Carter.

Standing, E. M. (1966) *The Montessori Revolution in Education*. New York: Schocken Books.

Stenhouse, L. (1975) *An Introduction to Curriculum Research and Development*. London: Heinemann.

Stone, C. A. and Wretsch, J. V. (1984) 'The social-interactional analysis of learning disabilities remediation.' *Journal of Learning Disabilities*, 17, 194–9.

Stoops, J. A. (1987) 'Maria Montessori: an intellectual portrait.' Paper presented at the Convention of the American Montessori Society, Boston, MA, 30 October–1 November.

Street, B. (1995) *Social Literacies: Critical Approaches to Literacy in Development, Ethnography and Education*. London: Longman.

Stubbs, B. (1966) 'Montessori and her influence on our work today.' *Australian Pre-school Quarterly*, 6 May.

Sullivan, H. G. (1985) 'Maria Montessori: pioneer of a unique method of education.' *The Australian Women's Weekly*, 252, 253, March.

Sulzby, E. (1994) 'Children's emergent reading of favourite story books: a developmental study.' In Ruddell, R., Ruddell, M. and Singer, H. (eds) *Theoretical Models and Processes of Reading* (4th edn). Newark, DE: International Reading Association Incorporated.

Swank, L. K. and Catts, H. (1991) 'Phonological awareness.' Paper presented at the 36th Annual Meeting of the International Reading Association. Las Vegas, 6–10 May.

Tallal, P. (1980) 'Auditory temporal perception, phonics, and reading disabilities in children.' *Brain and Language*, 9, 182–98.

Taylor, J. C. and Evans, G. (1985) 'The architecture of human information processing: empirical evidence.' *Instructional Science*, 13, 347–59.

Teale, W. H. (1981) 'Learning how written words work.' *Australian Journal of Reading*, 4, 3, August.

Tharp, R. G. and Gallimore, R. (1988) 'Rousing minds to life: teaching, learning and schooling in social contexts.' Paper presented to Educational Research Association, Montreal, Canada, April.

Thiele, C. (1975) *Grains of Mustard Seed*. South Australia: Department of Education.

Thorn, M. E. (1951) 'Dr Montessori in the home.' Paper presented at the International Montessori Congress, London. Montessori Trust (Scotland) Edinburgh: The Darien Press Ltd.

Thorndike, E. L. (1898) 'Animal intelligence.' *Psychological Review Monograph Supplement*, 2, 8.

Thorndike, E. L. (1906) *Principles of Teaching Based on Psychology*. New York: Seiler.

Thorndike, E. L. (1913) *Educational Psychology*. New York: Columbia University.

Tittle, B. M. (1984) 'Why Montessori for the Gifted?' *B/C/T*, 33, 3–7, May–June.

Torrance, E. P. (1962) *Guiding Creative Talent*. New Jersey: Prentice-Hall.

Torrey, J. W. (1973) 'Learning to read without a teacher: a case study.' In Smith, F. (ed.) *Understanding Reading: Psycholinguistics and Reading*. Newark, DE: Holt, Rinehart and Winston.

Treiman, M. (1993) 'Beginner spellers and letter clusters.' In Clay, M. (1998) *Different Paths to Common Outcomes*. York, Maine: Stenhouse.

Trieze, L. (1974) 'Montessori and South Australian teachers 1907–1930.' Transcript essay. In Turney, C. (ed.) (1983) *Pioneers of Australian Education* 3. Sydney: Sydney University Press.

Turney, C. (ed.) (1969) *Pioneers of Australian Education* 1. Sydney: Sydney University Press.

Turney, C. (ed.) (1972) *Pioneers of Australian Education* 2. Sydney: Sydney University Press.

Turney, C. (ed.) (1983) *Pioneers of Australian Education* 3. Sydney: Sydney University Press.

Van Haeringen, A. (2003) 'Educational resilience: the effects of early childhood risk and protective factors on intellectual ability at five years on adolescent learning.' Queensland Centre for Public Health, an initiative of Griffith University, QUT and University of Queensland.

Van-Kleeck, A. and Schuele, C. M. (1987) 'Precursors to literacy: Normal development.' *Topics in Language Disorders*, 7 (2), 13–31, March.

Vygotsky, L. S. (1934) *Thought and Language*. Cambridge, MA: The MIT Press. Published in English 1986.

Vygotsky, L. S. (1978) *Mind in Society: The Development of Higher Psychological Processes*. Cambridge, MA: Harvard University Press.

Walker, R. and Hamilton, D. (1992) (Speakers) 'Research in the Workplace.' (Cassette recording 1254) Geelong, Victoria: Deakin University Press.

Warger, C. (ed.) (1990) *Technology in Today's Schools*. USA Association for Supervision and Curriculum Development.

Watson, J. B. (1914) *Behaviour, An Introduction to Comparative Psychology*. New York: Holt, Rinehart and Winston.

Weber, E. (1984) *Ideas Influencing Early Childhood Education: A Theoretical Analysis*. New York: Columbia University Press.

Weber, L. (1971) *The English Infant Schol – Informal Education*. Englewood Cliffs, NJ: Prentice-Hall.

Webster, P. E. and Plante, A. S. (1992) 'Effects of phonological impairment on word, syllable, phoneme segmentation and reading.' *Language, Speech and Hearing Services in Schools*, 23 (2), 176–82, April.

Weinberg, C. (1972) *Humanistic Foundations of Education*. New Jersey: Prentice-Hall.

Wells, G. (1981) *Learning Through Interaction: The Study of Language Development*. Cambridge: Cambridge University Press.

Wertsch, J. V. (ed.) (1985) *Vygotsky and The Social Formation of Mind*. Cambridge, MA : Harvard University Press.

Wexler, P. (1992) *Becoming Somebody: Toward a Social Psychology of School*. London: Palmer Press.

Wheatly, H. (1990) 'Erdkinder in Australia.' *Montessori Courier: The International Montessori Journal*, 2 (3), 24, 25, August/September.

Wheeler, O. A. and Earl, I. G. (1939) *Nursery School Education and the Reorganization of the Infant School*. London: University of London Press.

Widmer, E. L. (1970) *The Critical Years: Early Childhood Education at the Crossroads*. Pennsylvania: International Textbook Company.

Willcott, P. (1968) 'The initial American reception of the Montessori method.' *The Education Digest,* 34, October. Condensed from *The School Review*, 76, 147–65, June, University of Amman.

Wing, L. A. (1992) 'The influence of Preschool teachers' beliefs on young children's conceptions of reading and writing.' *Early Childhood Research Quarterly,* 4 (1) 61–74, March.

Wolf, A. (1999) 'Aline Wolf visits London.' *Montessori International: incorporating Montessori Education Magazine*, 9 (2) 5–10, Winter.

Wolf, A. 1996, *Nurturing the Spirit in Non-sectarian Classrooms*. Hollidaysburg, PA: Parent Child Press.

Wood, M. (1994) *Essentials of Classroom Teaching: Elementary Language Arts*. Needham Heights, MA: Allyn and Bacon.

World Health Organization (1986).

Yaden, D. B. and Templeton, S. (1988) *Metalinguistic Awareness and Beginning Literacy*. Portsmouth: Heinemann.

Yopp, H. and Singer, H. (1994) 'Towards an Interactive reading instruction model: explanation of activation of linguistic awareness and metalinguistic ability in learning to read.' In Ruddell, R., Ruddell, M. and Singer, H. (eds) *Theoretical Models and Processes of*

Reading (4th edn). Newark, DE: International Reading Association Incorporated.

Yussen, S. R. (1980) 'Performance of Montessori and traditionally schooled nursery children on social cognitive tasks and memory problems.' *Contemporary Educational Psychology*, 5 (2), 124–37, April.

Zintz, M. V. and Maggrat, Z. R. (1984) *The Reading Process. The Teacher and the Learner*. Iowa: William C. Brown.

Websites

Grazzini, Camillo, Director of Training AMI, International Centre for Montessori Studies Foundation-Bergamo, Italy	www.montessoribergamo.it/ remembering.htm
Kahn, David, Montessori Erdkinder: The Social Evolution of the Little Community, 25th International Congress, Sydney, 2005	www.montessori-ami.org/ congress/2005sydney/ paperdk.htm
Historique de Montessori en Suisse, Association Montessori	www.montessori-ams.ch
History of AMI Teacher Training	www.ami.edu/amtef/amtef/ historyami.htm
Montessori Primary Teacher Training	www.montessoripartnership.com

Montessori associations

Further information about Montessori can be found on websites. Some are listed below.

AMI (Association Montessori Internationale) main website	www.montessori-ami.org./
AMI Head Office	www.montessori-ami.org/ami/ headoffice.htm
AMI Training Centers worldwide	www.montessori-ami.org

Australian Montessori Teacher Education Foundation	http://ami/amtef
AAAA – Australian AMI Alumni Association	www.aaaa.net.au
MANZ – Montessori Association of New Zealand	www.montessori.org.nz
MSA – Montessori Schools Association	www.montessori.org.uk/msa

Teacher-training courses

For a full list of UK Montessori training courses visit	www.montessorimagazine.com training
Montessori St Nicholas Centre	www.montessori.org.uk
MWEI	www.mwei.org.au
MMI Modern Montessori International	www.modernmontessori-intl.com
Maria Montessori Institute, London, UK	www.mariamontessori.org
Montessori Centre International London, UK	www.montessori.uk.com
The Montessori Foundation, USA	www.montessori.org
MWEI Montessori World Educational Institute (Australia) Inc. offers Correspondence Courses	www.mwei.org.au

Newspapers

The Times. (London), January 1914. 'The Montessori Method. A woman's work in Education,' Tuesday 20, Wednesday 21, Friday 23, Monday 26, Wednesday 28.
The Australian, June 1999.

Queensland Parliamentary Papers 1914.

The Montessori System of Education. 38th Report of the Secretary for Public Instruction (1913)

Queensland Parliamentary Papers vol. 1, 24.

Queensland Education Office Gazette 1914.

The Montessori System. October, 445–7, November, 483–6, December, 533–5.

Magazines

Bulletin, 1992. 'A Snapshot of the Early Years of Schooling.' National Board of Employment, Education and Training, 2–3, 10 April.

Communications, AMI, Amsterdam.

Montessori Courier, London.

Montessori International, London. www.montessorimagazine.com

Scribner's Magazine (1916) 'The point of view.' Vol. 60, October.

Other

Montessori Courses: London 1930, 1933, 1946; Laren 1938; India 1942; Paris 1949

Radio interview, London 1950

Conference, 1951, London, Association Montessori Internationale

Conference, 1977, Dublin, Association Montessori Internationale

Lecture, 1933, London, Association Montessori Internationale (1969)

Lecture, 1938, Edinburgh, Association Montessori Internationale (1971)

Lecture, 1942, India, Montessori Training Courses, Hyderabad-1: Canaan Press

Definitions of some Montessori terms

Absorbent mind   The unconscious way in which a young
                    child from birth to about six years learns
                    easily from his environment.

Casa dei Bambini Italian for 'Children's House'.

Cosmic education   Each child is helped to develop his whole
                    personality by being introduced to a wide
                    curriculum.

Deviant child   A child who experiences difficulty
                    concentrating on any 'thing.' He lacks
                    self-control and sometimes escapes into a
                    world of fantasy.

Didactic materials Self-teaching materials which make
                    self-correction possible.

Directress   Dr Montessori's name for a 'new' type of
                    teacher.

Formative years   The important years between birth and six
                    years when a child creates his character
                    from the environment with the help of
                    his absorbent mind.

Horme   A vital inner urge (inner voice) by which a
                    child is able to choose activities which
                    best suit his development at a particular
                    time.

Liberty   Freedom to be active within an educational
                    framework of structure and discipline
                    where each child has rights.

Muscular memory	A child's ability to remember the name of something when he moves his fingers over the object. For example, when a child traces a sandpaper letter he has already been introduced to, he can recall the sound the letter represents immediately through his muscular memory.
Normalized	A child who is calm, happy, self-controlled, adapts easily, and who develops into a well-balanced adolescent and adult.
Order	The meaning given to everything within a child's environment which in turn helps him to organize his own mind and to classify what he finds within the environment.
Phonetic words	Phonetically regular words introduced to English-speaking children in order of length – three-letter words then longer words for composing first then beginning reading.
Phonograms	These appear in non-phonetic words and are made up of two or more letters which combine to make one sound; for example, ay, ea, igh, ough.
Prepared environment	Peaceful and orderly surroundings adapted to children's interests, including the living conditions which enable the child to have the freedom to choose and concentrate on his own tasks and to learn through his own activity, and provide the basis for development of each child's personality.
Psychic embryo	The inborn order through which the child's mental functions are developed over a long period of time.

Sensitive periods	Developmental periods when a child is particularly sensitive to learning specific things. For example, to begin to take a few steps at ten months, to speak single words about the same time, to begin to write and read at four years.
Sensorial exercises	Exercises using didactic materials designed to help development and refine all the senses, providing a foundation for all later learning.
The three-period lesson	The three-period lesson is brief, simple, and objective. The directress uses few words so the child can focus on the object of the lesson.

Index